MANAGEMENT IN BANKING

*To Sarah
remembering LBS
— the course to end all
courses!!*

CIB ASSOCIATESHIP SERIES

MANAGEMENT IN BANKING

Helen V Coult BSc, ACIB, Dip FS

Series Editor: B Julian Beecham

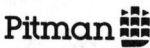

Pitman Publishing
128 Long Acre, London WC2E 9AN

A Division of Longman Group UK Limited

First published in 1990

© Longman Group UK Ltd 1990

A CIP catalogue record for this book is available from the British Library.

ISBN 0 273 03218 6

All rights reserved; no part of this publication may be reproduced, stored in a retrieval system, or transmitted in any form or by any means, electronic, mechanical, photocopying, recording, or otherwise without either the prior written permission of the Publishers or a licence permitting restricted copying in the United Kingdom issued by the Copyright Licensing Agency, 33–34 Alfred Place, London WC1E 7DP. This book may not be lent, resold, hired out or otherwise disposed of by way of trade in any form of binding or cover other than that in which it is published, without the prior consent of the Publishers.

Printed in England by Clays Ltd, St Ives plc

Contents

Series Editor's Foreword   ix
Acknowledgements   x

Introduction   1
   Why study management?   1
   How to use this book   2

1 The bank as part of a political system   4
   The PEST factors   4
   Political and legal factors   5
   Economic factors   6
   Social factors   7
   Technological factors   9
   Competition   10
   Social accountability   11
   Action points   12
   Questions and answers   12

2 The banks' interface with the market place   15
   Competition in the financial services industry   15
   Strengths and weaknesses of the banks   16
   Steps the banks can take to compete successfully   17
   Financial Services Act 1986   17
   Competition between stakeholders   18
   Stakeholders' conflicts of interest   20
   Managing stakeholders' conflicts of interest   21
   Action points   21
   Questions and answers   21

3 Human resource management   26
   Impact of external factors   26
   Recruitment policies   26
   Manpower planning   27
   Training   28
   Employee relations   29
   Trade unions in banking   30
   Factors affecting the industrial relations climate   31
   Action points   33
   Questions and answers   33

4 Organisational design and development   35
   Organisational structure   35
   Organisational culture   41
   Power in organisations   44
   Communication in organisations   47
   Centralisation vs. decentralisation   50
   Cooperation between departments   52
   Action points   53
   Questions and answers   54

5 Information systems   59
   The importance of information   59
   The importance of technology   60
   Information Technology (IT)   63
   Management Information systems (MIS)   65
   Budgetary control systems   66
   Risk assessment and risk management   70
   Action points   72
   Questions and answers   73

6 Personnel systems   78
   Design of work   78
   Job analysis   78
   Job description   79
   Job rotation/enlargement/enrichment   79
   Job evaluation systems   81
   Appraisal systems   83
   Grievance procedures   85
   Disciplinary procedures   86
   Action points   87
   Questions and answers   87

7 The Manager 94
Management theories 94
The Classical school 94
The Human Relations school 96
The Systems approach 98
Contingency theory 99
Management functions or processes 100
Management roles 101
The transition from 'worker' to 'management' 104
Action points 105
Questions and answers 106

8 Managing the system 111
The management job 111
Henri Fayol 111
Forecasting 114
Planning 114
Organising 116
Monitoring 117
Controlling 118
Action points 119
Questions and answers 120

9 Managing the people 125
Choice of management/leadership styles 125
Blake Mouton grid 126
Ashridge model (tells, sells, consults, joins) 128
Action-centred leadership (John Adair) 129
Summary of leadership styles 130
Relationship with internal and external customers, bosses, peers and subordinates 131
Delegation 134
Action points 135
Questions and answers 136

10 People as individuals 142
Differences between individuals 142
Motivation 143
Selection 147
Induction 149
Learning 150
Coaching and development 151
Feedback and appraisal 151
Counselling 152
Action points 153
Questions and answers 153

11 Interviewing 158
General interviewing techniques 158
Customer interviews 162
Selection interviews 162
Appraisal interviews 163
Grievance interviews 164
Disciplinary interviews 164
Counselling interviews 165
Exit interviews 165
Action points 166
Questions and answers 166

12 People in groups 172
Communication — methods and barriers 172
Group dynamics 174
Formal and informal groups 175
Team formation and roles 176
Successful and unsuccessful groups 177
Managing change 178
Meetings 181
Committees 181
Action points 184
Questions and answers 184

13 Organisational staff issues 190
Introduction 190
Recruitment and selection procedures 190
Training and career development systems 193
Equal opportunities 196
Power 198
Action points 200
Questions and answers 200

14 Managing yourself 205
Problem-solving 205
Decision-making 205
Project planning and management 207
Time management 208
Stress management 210
Career management 211
Action points 211
Questions and answers 212

15 How to fail / how to pass! 217
About the examination 217
How the paper is marked 218

How to tackle the examination 218
Answering the questions 224
How to fail / how to pass 225

16 Hints and tips 227
How to revise 227
Approaching the exam itself 227

17 Topical issues 229
Introduction 229
Communication in the European market 229
Business and the community 230
EC Charter 230
The demographic timebomb 231
Women at the top — sex war? 233
Conclusion 233

Index 235

Series Editor's Foreword

This book is one of the Pitman Publishing series of textbooks which are written to cover the post-Wilkinson syllabi of the four core subjects of the Associateship exams of the Chartered Institute of Bankers (CIB).

The author, Helen V. Coult, has examined pre-Wilkinson, Nature of Management exam scripts as a CIB assistant examiner for several years, until becoming the CIB's chief examiner for Business Calculations. The author is young enough to understand students' problems, and yet old enough to have 15 years' experience in a major clearing bank, including management roles in branches, Area Office and Head Office departments, in addition to being a qualified teacher.

The 17 chapters of this book are imaginatively constructed and follow closely the syllabus, especially because the author has had the benefit of discussions with the CIB chief examiner in this subject as the writing of the book progressed. Most books on management are written by academics or lecturers; this book has been written by a practising banker, and therefore gives real-life examples from the banking world.

The Introduction is particularly important; it gives down-to-earth reasons why bank employees need to study management, and how best to study it from this book. You will find the author's style of writing flowing and easy to read, interspersed with humorous and interesting anecdotes—simple but not simplistic—making the subject come alive for the reader.

At the end of each chapter, there are several actual, full exam-length questions, almost all with full-length answers as required in the exams. Reading these questions and answers carefully will give you practice in exam technique, which is vital if you are to do well under the stress of exam conditions. There is a comprehensive index at the end of the book to assist you in locating quickly information you require.

I believe that this CIB 'recommended' book, and the series as a whole, will help you establish a well-grounded understanding of the required knowledge and exam techniques which will help you to do your best in the exam you take.

Good luck!

B. Julian Beecham FCIB
Cardiff

Acknowledgements

My thanks are due to the Chartered Institute of Bankers for permission to reproduce past examination questions and examiner's reports; to Dr Bertie Beecham for encouraging me to write this book in the first place; to Mrs M E Boyce for her help with the proofreading and most of all to my husband, Philip, without whose culinary expertise we would have starved whilst the book was gestating!

The author and Publishers are grateful to Prentice Hall for permission to reproduce the following figures: 4.1, 4.2, 4.3, 4.4, 4.5, 4.6, 4.7. (Henry Mintzberg, *Structure in Fives: Designing Effective Organizations*, © 1983, pp. 11, 154, 159, 170, 198, 225, 262. Adapted by permission of Prentice Hall Inc., Englewood Cliffs, New Jersey.)

Introduction

- Why study management?   ● How to use this book

■ Why study management?

The glib answer might be 'Because I want to pass the exam and get my Diploma'; I think there are other, equally valid reasons.

It is tempting, if you are a fairly junior member of staff in an office or branch, to imagine that 'management' is something with which those more senior than yourself are involved and which has little relevance to your everyday life. But we are all 'managers', even if that word does not feature in our job description or title.

(a) We manage our subordinates.
(b) We manage ourselves (at work and at home).
(c) We manage our bosses (by influencing the way they treat us).

If you are sceptical, the following chapters will demonstrate exactly what I mean.

The Management in Banking syllabus sets out to introduce you to some basic ideas about management; it does not assume that you have any first-hand experience of managing other people although, as I said above, we all 'manage' someone—if only ourselves.

Management is not a dry, theoretical subject: it is about **human relations** in the work-place. It is sometimes argued that subjects such as Practice of Banking are very difficult to pass when candidates have no practical experience of the tasks they are asked to study. I do not believe this criticism can be levelled at Management in Banking. Banking is very much a 'people business', to use some modern jargon. No-one in a bank works in isolation; we are all part of a group, a team, a branch or a department—so how **people interact** with each other, how **groups operate**, and so on is important to us all—and we can all study management at first hand by observing what goes on around us.

Studying management will help you to understand the **motivation** of yourself and others and the ideas you come across in this course can be applied in practice in your everyday work. In the same way, you may well be able to apply real examples from your own experience to the case-study situations which you will find in the exam paper.

From time to time in this book, you will be encouraged to look out for specific examples as part of the 'Action Points' at the end of each chapter. We have all seen examples of 'bad' management at work. Ask yourself why situations were handled badly. How could problems have been better managed? Perhaps you regard one of your managers as particularly good—if so, what does he or she do which is different? What is the measure of his success?

Incidentally, since the English language still has no satisfactory way of expressing 'he or she' or 'his or her' in a single unisex word, and to avoid the clumsy use of s/he or he/she all the time, I have used the convention that the male gender should be taken to include the female throughout the book. I am certainly not suggesting that managers are always male (or for that matter always female) but for simplicity I have tended to use 'he' when referring to a manager.

▎How to use this book

The arrangement of the chapters in this book closely follows the new syllabus published by the Chartered Institute of Bankers (CIB) for Management in Banking. This means that the book is equally useful as a classroom textbook for those attending full-time, day-release, or evening classes and as a source book for those studying at home.

If you are attending classes, you will obviously be guided by your teacher as to the order in which to tackle the topics.

If you are studying at home, I would suggest that you work through the chapters in the order in which they are presented. Once you have covered all the syllabus in this way, you will be able to identify those areas where you are weakest, or where you feel the need for further study, and return to those chapters individually.

In either case, Chapters 15 and 16 of this book give a good deal of down-to-earth advice for tackling both your revision and the examination itself.

Having marked well over a thousand exam papers in Management for the CIB, I have been able to identify many of the common errors made by students—by studying these chapters well you will be able to avoid making the same mistakes!

Each chapter begins with a detailed look at the subject to be covered, broken down into manageable portions. Then a series of Action Points, where appropriate, will suggest other sources of information, or activities which you can undertake to improve your knowledge of the subject. Finally, each chapter contains one or more specimen questions for you to answer to test your understanding of the material in the chapter.

In many cases I have included tips on what **not** to cover, or how to avoid losing marks, as well as a 'model answer' to show you what you **should** have mentioned in your answer.

These questions will either be, or be based on, real questions from past exam papers, or they will be designed to illustrate what future questions may ask. In any case you should have a go at answering them. You may decide to refer to the textbook or to your notes for the first one, and save another for your revision, to be tackled under 'exam conditions'. Don't be surprised if you do not cover **all** the points in the model answer; after all, if you can do that you will get a distinction in every question! Nevertheless, you should feel confident that you would be able to cover at least three-quarters of the suggested points in order to be sure of a satisfactory mark.

Even if you do not attempt to answer the questions under exam conditions, do read the questions and the answers carefully. By expressing ideas in a slightly different way from the text of the chapter, they will give you a valuable revision of the subject matter.

In this examination, it is quite correct (indeed it is encouraged) to use note-form answers. This makes it easy for the examiner to mark your script, and easy for you to marshal your thoughts in a logical way, making sure you have left nothing out and not gone over the same ground twice. Most of the model answers adopt this approach. You will find much more information on how to tackle the questions as you work through this book. In particular, Chapter 15 covers this in detail.

So now, turn to the first chapter, and I hope you will enjoy and profit from your studies.

CHAPTER 1

The bank as part of a political system

- The PEST factors ● Political and legal factors ● Economic factors ● Social factors ● Technological factors ● Competition ● Social accountability

■ The PEST factors

A bank is not an organisation in splendid isolation. It is part of the environment in which it exists. The nature of this environment will have effects on the way the bank operates, the rate at which it has to change, the opportunities it has to make profits and to expand, and so on. The environment is the source of the resources which the bank needs in order to function: staff, customers, buildings, etc.

The external factors which make up this environment can be grouped under four headings: Political, Economic, Social and Technological—which gives an easy to remember mnemonic: the 'PEST' factors (see Fig. 1.1). Legal factors are sometimes separated out as a fifth group, giving the mnemonic: 'LePEST' factors.

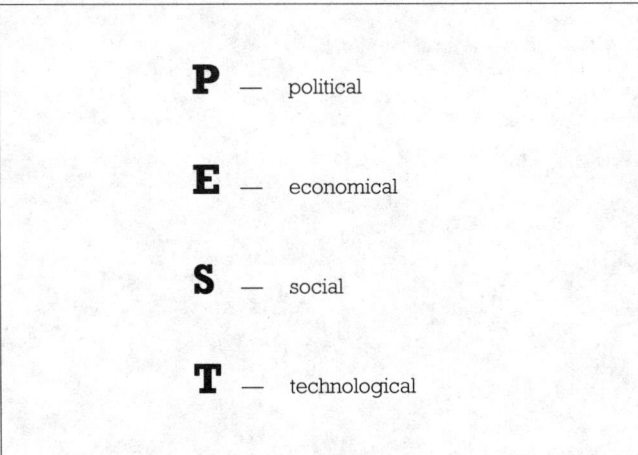

Fig. 1.1 Business environment 'PEST' factors

■ Political and legal factors

Politics does not refer only to the party politics of national government. An organisation such as a bank will be affected by local and international politics too.

National political factors

Changes in national government in the UK may lead to changes in attitude towards the operation of large, highly profitable concerns such as the major clearing banks. The so-called 'windfall taxes' imposed on the banks in the last decade were an example of how a national government can dramatically affect such organisations. The abolition of exchange control in 1979 by the Conservative government, whilst freeing restrictions on the movement of funds overseas and opening up many new opportunities for international business, also resulted in major staffing difficulties as the banks struggled to redeploy specialist staff who had spent years dealing with the detailed exchange control regulations. This is a clear example of the maxim that every threat, if looked at in a different way, is an opportunity (the old proverb that every cloud has a silver lining). This, together with the idea that weaknesses are often strengths in disguise, gives us another easy-to-remember mnemonic—'SWOT' (see Fig. 1.2). These ideas (Threats vs. Opportunities and Strengths vs. Weaknesses) apply in many areas of management, not just when we are considering the business environment, so keep them in mind.

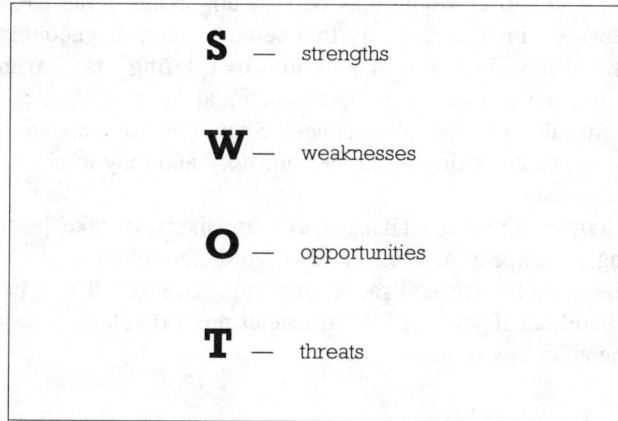

Fig. 1.2 Business environment 'silver lining'

Government policy may also have an impact on regional development—grants to assist new businesses in certain areas of the country may mean new business opportunities for the bank branches which serve them; the changing nature of certain areas, as heavy engineering works (the 'smoke-stack' industries) close down and service industries move in, leads to a requirement for different types of bank services and so on.

Local authority policies will similarly play their part. Planning departments may help or hinder the development of new branch premises; there may be incentives by way of reduced rates for moving into deprived areas, etc.

In general, government policies relating to taxation, inflation, interest rates, credit control, exchange rates and exchange controls will have a particular impact on banks.

Legal factors

Many of the factors mentioned above, such as credit controls, taxation and exchange controls rely on the passing of laws. They can therefore be regarded as legal factors in the business environment of the banks. Other legal factors include employment legislation, consumer legislation and so on. The banks are specifically regulated by the Banking Act 1987 and the Financial Services Act 1986 and are supervised by the Bank of England. Legislation affecting competitors (such as the Building Societies Act 1986 which freed the societies to enter new areas of business) will also have an impact on the banks.

International political factors

Banks with overseas branches or subsidiaries will be particularly vulnerable to changes in international politics. As the relationships between the major nations (sometimes referred to as the global political climate) changes, so the potential for international trade can vary. A few years ago, for example, when the oil-producing countries had money to spare, large sums were lent to the countries of Latin America. Now that oil prices have fallen and the Latin American countries have economic problems of their own, the repayment of these loans is in jeopardy. Further lending to these countries would now be very unpopular in the UK.

Another well-known example is the way that certain countries encourage the setting up of 'off-shore' branches and subsidiaries of major banks by offering a tax haven.

Rules governing the transfer of funds across national borders may restrict the growth of overseas offices, or alter the way they do business. Some governments are highly suspicious of large multinational companies setting up in their territory and may impose stringent controls to protect their local businesses.

Much has been written about the changes that are likely to take place in 1992 with the introduction of a single European market, in other words the removal of some existing barriers to cross-border business by the harmonisation of various controls. There is no space to go into great detail on this here, but if you read the financial press regularly you will be able to keep abreast of developments in this sphere.

Economic factors

UK industrial change

Those areas in the North and the Midlands of Great Britain which were traditionally seen as the industrial heartland have undergone major changes over recent years. Large-scale heavy engineering has closed down, making substantial numbers of employees redundant. Although newer industries have in some cases come in to take the place of the old, the skills required are often not the same and workers may have to be attracted from other areas, leaving a hard core of unemployment. All this means change for the banks in terms of the demand for their corporate and personal services; there is a need for specialist advice for those with redundancy payments to invest as well as for those with a large burden of debt and a much reduced income.

In the South-East of England, on the other hand, increased prosperity has led to increased demand for more sophisticated banking services as the educated consumer has growing expectations of a high quality of life.

International change

Internationally a similar series of changes is taking place. The manufacturing centres of Western Europe are in something of a decline, whereas in Japan, Korea and other parts of Asia manufacturing is booming. Those countries which have traditionally been commodity suppliers have remained underdeveloped as the industrialised countries have forged ahead. These imbalances are key features of the economic environment.

Inflation

In the UK, in modern times, we have come to expect that a positive rate of inflation is inevitable, although there is always pressure on the government to keep the rate down to low single figures. We have not had to suffer the effects of hyper-inflation (say 200 per cent p.a.) as have countries in some parts of Latin America and Eastern Europe, for example.

In most countries there tends to be a cycle between growth and recession. A recession in the economy leads to reduced output, unemployment and poverty whereas a booming economy creates inflation, undermining the value of savings and pensions; this encourages high wage demands which in turn push up inflation still further. Clearing banks in particular have a high cost ratio. That is to say they must make considerable profits to cover the fixed costs of their business—particularly staff costs, which can make up 70 per cent of the total costs in some cases. Banks are therefore considerably affected by an increase in inflation leading to increased wage bills. They are also dependent on interest income for much of their profits—if interest rates are low, the 'turn' which banks can earn (the difference between the rate at which they borrow and the rate at which they lend) becomes smaller, squeezing their profits further. Of course, low rates would encourage borrowing and that would increase the bank profitability.

∎ Social factors

Social changes affect banks both through their customers and their staff. As banking is a very labour-intensive industry (even after the introduction of so much high technology over the past two decades) staffing is a major consideration, especially for the large UK clearing banks, each of which employs tens of thousands of staff around the country.

Education

Higher standards of education, both at schools and colleges and through the media, have led consumers to expect higher standards of service. They are less ready to accept without question what is offered to them. Banks have had to study the market in order to tailor their services to customer demand. Over the last 20 years the traditional bank manager, who sat in his large leather chair in an oak-panelled office waiting for the customers to knock on his door, has changed into a financial salesman (or, increasingly, saleswoman) who is actively 'selling' and marketing the bank's products in a similar way to other retail operations. In the corporate banking market, the large multinational customers have very sophisticated treasury departments, with staff who know just as much about the intricacies of international finance as the bankers whose job it is to deliver the bank's services.

As well as determining the bank's response to its customers, better education has meant higher expectations from staff in terms of job satisfaction, good salaries and working conditions, etc.

Demographic change

A reduction in the number of teenagers due to come into the jobs market over the next few years has changed the way the banks are recruiting staff. More emphasis is being placed on retaining existing staff by improving conditions, attracting back married women by offering crèche facilities, allowing men and women to take career breaks to bring up their families, and so on.

The increasing number of ethnic-minority customers and staff means that attention must be paid to equal-opportunities legislation to ensure that no discrimination, intentional or otherwise, is permitted.

Changing patterns of family life, with many more young people living alone or setting up home together and even starting families without the traditional bonds of matrimony, require fresh attitudes from banks. For example, at one time only married couples or possibly single men would have been considered for mortgages but now even groups of friends, of whichever gender, are considered as candidates.

Social values

Increasingly, the consumer lobby has emphasised the importance of health and safety over the profits of big business. Social accountability is discussed later in this chapter, but the growing acceptance of employee participation in the running of businesses and in the sharing of profits has changed the way many companies view their workforce.

Trade union power has been curbed in the last few years by legislation but unions are still influential in supporting fair treatment for staff. In this they have been helped by other legislation on unfair dismissal, sex discrimination, equal pay for work of equal value, etc.

Even such apparently minor issues as the changing attitude to smoking may have far-reaching consequences for a business: should no-smoking areas be provided for the public? If smoking is not permitted in an office, should breaks be allowed for those who want to smoke to do so elsewhere? Does this amount to discrimination against either the smokers or the non-smokers? Such issues must be resolved at local level unless regulated by law or by the rules of the company, perhaps formulated in response to consumer/staff pressures.

∎ Technological factors

Banks have been dramatically changed by the introduction of new technology of various kinds, particularly over the last 20 years. The major banks have invested hundreds of millions of pounds in introducing and updating computer systems in their branches. These developments affect productivity, the nature of work, the speed of communications and the types of products the banks sell.

Employment changes

The introduction of new technology is often seen as a blessing as it can reduce the mundane, routine aspects of a job. It is certainly true that far less 'paper-shuffling' takes place in computerised offices but, by increasing the rate of productivity, computers mean that much more work can be done by far fewer staff; however, the vision of a three-day working week and more leisure time has not yet materialised!

One major change, though, has been in the type of staff employed. Not all of the former clerical staff were able to adapt to using keyboards rather than pen and paper. New recruits are expected to acquire these skills quickly, and many staff are employed just to keep the technology running. Programmers, computer engineers and mechanics had to be taken on. These staff were required to work shifts to ensure 24-hour computer cover and they demanded high wages to compare with outside organisations. This has led to two- or three-tier recruitment by the banks (clerical, technological and managerial staff). More part-time and consultancy staff are now employed to cope with the peaks of work flow.

Rules regarding the operation of computer equipment, e.g. for VDU (visual display unit) operators, have been introduced to safeguard the wellbeing of staff.

Improved communication

New technology, by making information available more quickly and easily, can reduce the number of management levels required in an organisation and encourage decentralisation.

Head office can keep in closer touch with branches by telephone, facsimile transmission (fax), computer terminals linked to a central mainframe and so on. Likewise branches can send information to the centre more quickly. Ironically this can also lead to greater centralisation, with all decisions being referred to head office, but with speedier responses down the line. It is up to the managers of the organisation to decide how best to structure the company to take greatest advantage of the technology.

In some bank departments it is possible for staff to work from home, or to spend a good deal of time travelling to visit customers, away from their home-base, and still communicate electronically with head office at any time through remote computer terminals, portable phones, automatic paging machines, etc.

New products

Many of the newer banking products could have come into being only with the aid of new technology. For instance, the automatic cash dispenser of the 1970s has grown into a complete range of automatic machines through which a customer can check his balance, order a statement, move money from one account to another, pay bills, deposit money into his account and even print out a statement, all with the use of a plastic card and an identifying code.

The so-called 'smart-card' will be even more sophisticated when it comes into general use as it incorporates a microchip actually built into the card. It can thus store a great deal more information than the present magnetic strip and can interact with the machines in which it is used. It can be 'charged' with electronic credit which is depleted as the card is used. Having its own inbuilt computing power it can function without the need for a counter terminal connected on-line to a central computer (thus avoiding the problems of telecommunications—garbled messages, lines which are 'down', etc.), and can record every transaction for which it is used within its own memory.

Several banks offer their customers home-banking facilities. This means that through a home terminal and a telephone line the customer can communicate directly with the bank's computer to operate his account.

The highly sophisticated international dealing operations of the world's money markets are made possible only by the electronic payment systems and telephonic communications networks which support them.

▎Competition

Banks are only one group of organisations in the financial sector. Students reading this book are most likely to be employed by one of the major clearing banks in the UK (the so-called 'Big Four': Barclays, National Westminster, Midland and Lloyds), but don't forget that there are numerous foreign banks (particularly Japanese and American) in Britain now as well as merchant and investment banks.

These are joined by venture capital institutions, money brokers, other commodities houses, and stockbrokers to compete with the banks in many of their markets. The TSB became a full clearing bank fairly recently, and the Abbey National was floated as the first public limited company building society-turned-bank in 1989.

The building societies in general have long been seen as being in competition with the banks, particularly since the banks took a large slice of the mortgage market in the early 1980s. The building societies fought back by entering the market for current accounts, offering cheque books, standing orders and other traditional bank services.

The ways in which banks may deal with this competition are examined in more detail in Chapter 2. For the moment, remember that the presence of these competitors is an important environmental factor affecting the banks.

■ Social accountability

Social accountability of banks

Like all other limited companies, banks are accountable to their shareholders for the way in which the business is run and the profits which are made. However, companies are becoming more and more aware of their duties to other groups, such as their employees and the local community.

This accountability might include obligations under law (e.g. the Health and Safety at Work Act, equal opportunities legislation, etc.) and a legal or moral obligation not to pollute the environment, not to mislead consumers, and not to disrupt employment patterns in a community unnecessarily.

Changing attitudes towards social accountability

As businesses have become bigger and more anonymous, so consumer groups have become increasingly vocal in lobbying for a more responsible attitude to be taken by the managers of such businesses. There is therefore pressure on companies to behave as good citizens in order to avoid bad publicity.

A classic example in the banking world was the way the major clearers pulled out of their South African involvement in response to public criticism. By monitoring changing pressures such as this, banks may be able to take action in a well thought-out way, rather than being forced into it.

Managers should represent their organisation locally, both to put forward the viewpoint of the company and to monitor changes. Membership of the local Chamber of Commerce and businessmen's associations, involvement in the local council and on various committees, can aid in this representation.

Rather than writing off pressure groups as 'cranks', their point of view should be examined critically to see if an apparent threat can be turned into an opportunity. An example of this approach is evident in the flood of 'green' products which have come onto the market as a result of recent consumer demand. Many of these products are formulated in exactly the same way as before but the companies concerned have taken advantage of current thinking to re-promote a tired product by emphasising an existing but now valuable feature.

You may feel that this does not apply to banks, but consider the number of bank staff who are encouraged to give help and advice to local small businesses, or to assist in local charity work. On a national scale, quite senior staff may be seconded to voluntary, charitable or public service organisations (such as debt advice centres) to provide expert banking knowledge when required. This is a cost to the banks in financial terms but gains valuable prestige and publicity for them.

▌Action points

A great deal of what has been covered in this chapter is just commonsense observation of the world around us. When answering questions on the 'business environment', as we shall see in a moment, much of what you will want to say will be derived from your general knowledge rather than just 'textbook' learning.

To prepare for the examination:

(a) Read the financial section of your daily newspaper to see what is happening in the world of business.

(b) There will very probably be copies of *The Financial Times* available in your branch or office. Take time to read this as often as you can and become familiar with the major issues in the City.

(c) Watch some of the business programmes on the television or listen to *The Financial World Tonight* on Radio 4 in the evenings. Make sure you understand what is being discussed. If you don't, ask your manager to explain.

(d) Consider how your own bank helps in the local community. If you do not know of any such initiatives, ask your personnel department what secondments the bank makes to other organisations. You may well be surprised!

▌Questions and answers

A common mistake in answering questions on this part of the syllabus is to assume that all four of the PEST factors need to be discussed in detail. Make sure that this is really what the question requires. Often it may be confined to one or two, e.g. social factors, or economic and technological factors only. Be sure too that you read **all** the question. Often there is a second part which asks you to describe how managers or organisations should respond to changes in the environment, or asks you to comment on the implications for management. If you omit to answer this part of a question you may be throwing marks away unnecessarily.

Question 1

'Although the political, economic, social and technological environments are important in business success, the key lies within the organisation itself.' Explain this statement and discuss its validity in banking. [Total marks for question — 25]

(*Hint*: In answering this question, you should be sure to tackle the question of what the organisation can **do** as well as what the environmental factors **are**.)

Question 2

In recent years banks and other business organisations have become more sensitive to public opinion, environmental changes and social pressures.

(a) Why has this happened? [15]

(b) What should managers do to respond positively to these pressures? [10]

[Total marks for question — 25]

(*Hint*: The danger here is to jump to the conclusion that all four of the PEST factors are required. Read the question again: the examiner is homing in on the social aspects, so concentrate on these for maximum marks. Also make sure you answer part (b) — it is worth more than one-third of the marks so, if you miss it out, you are very unlikely to gain enough on part (a) to pass!)

Answer 1

The importance of the various environments mentioned is that they offer both threats and opportunities to the organisation. The way that the organisation responds to these threats and opportunities depends upon its own and its managers' strengths and weaknesses — hence the fact that the key lies within the organisation itself.

With particular reference to banking, some of the threats might be as follows:

(a) Competition at home and from abroad may be growing.
(b) Changes are possible to interest rates/exchange rates and controls by government.
(c) Technological advances could leave the bank behind its competitors if it fails to invest.
(d) Changing demographic profiles may lead to shortage of suitable staff.
(e) Pressure groups may demand changes in the way the organisation operates.
(f) Recruitment of specialist staff may cause resentment amongst existing work-force and upset salary planning.
(g) Default of major borrowers due to political changes (e.g. in Latin American countries) may threaten profitability.

Conversely, some of the opportunities presented to banks might be:

(a) Freedom to enter new sectors following deregulation.
(b) Recent economic recovery in the UK and internationally.
(c) Social changes have enlarged the population using bank services.
(d) Uncertainties in the job market have led to more staff stability and higher quality of recruits (though this may be changing).
(e) Trade unions have been reasonably moderate in their demands.
(f) Introduction of advanced technology has led to a reduction in routine work, greater job satisfaction and improved information for speedier decision making.
(g) Technology offers the chance to reduce the cost ratio.

In order to maintain a successful business, its managers must minimise these threats and exploit the opportunities to the full. It is their skill and judgement in doing so which will determine how well the organisation can respond to changes in the environment. They will need to have a definite corporate aim and communicate it to their employees in order to develop plans to achieve it. They must monitor these plans as they are carried out to make sure the organisation stays on course.

If the environment changes they may need to re-evaluate the aims and adjust the strategy accordingly to build on the strengths of the organisation.

Answer 2

(a) There are various reasons why this has happened:

(i) Big businesses are regarded by the public as anonymous faceless organisations. The owners are not recognised as they might have been in the days of local mills, mines or factories where they were visible members of the local community. Consumers feel that they will be passed from person to person and have difficulty in obtaining satisfactory service. The big companies recognise this and try to combat it — for example, by corporate image advertising, or in the case of some banks by allocating personal bankers who will always deal with the same specific customers.

(ii) The increased attention in the media to consumer issues has created public awareness and concern and led to the creation of pressure groups. The new-found power of individuals in a free society has been expressed in environmental groups, consumer protection groups, etc. This has been supported in many cases by government legislation to protect public interests. Companies must therefore ensure that their own interests are voiced and taken into account. Hence groups such as the CBI (Confederation of British Industry) often lobby on behalf of business interests.

(iii) Attitudes within business have also changed. Recognising that employees are likely to be customers too, and that the same people may also these days be shareholders, companies recognise an interdependence of interests. This encourages companies to take these interests into account.

(iv) Competition is so fierce these days, and consumers so well informed on the choices open to them, that any company which does not satisfy public opinion will soon lose customers to its competitors.

(b) To respond positively to these pressures, managers must first be aware of them. This means:

(i) Keeping and developing information systems and monitoring local, national and international opinion. If managers are forewarned of developments, they may be able to take appropriate action—otherwise they will be caught unawares.

(ii) If the pressures do grow, the business must ensure that its views are represented, so that it will have some influence over events. This may mean managers being ready to express the views of the company, to customers and to local people, in local or national newspaper reports or even on television.

(iii) There may be opportunities to be taken if management is sufficiently alert to change. Threats may be modified by reasoned argument or by putting forward viable alternatives.

(iv) If adverse changes cannot be avoided, it may be necessary for the company to re-examine its strategy and possibly to develop a revised one, to suit the new situation.

CHAPTER 2
The banks' interface with the market place

- Competition in the financial services industry
- Strengths and weaknesses of the banks
- Steps the banks can take to compete successfully
- Financial Services Act 1986
- Competition between stakeholders
- Stakeholders' conflicts of interest
- Managing stakeholders' conflicts of interest

■ Competition in the financial services industry

As mentioned in Chapter 1, banks are only one group of organisations in the financial sector. As well as the clearing banks (including TSB, and now Abbey National) there are numerous merchant banks, branches of foreign banks, finance houses, venture capital institutions and insurance companies, to name but a few.

With the de-regulation of the City in 1986, which was popularly known as the 'Big Bang', the barriers between financial institutions were largely removed, allowing many of them to move into new markets. This in turn increased the competition for UK banks as other organisations, both UK and foreign, were able to enter markets traditionally monopolised by the banks. For example, the building societies are now offering not only their own traditionally limited range of services but are also increasingly attacking the mainstream markets of the clearing banks. Retailers are emerging as very real competitors in the financial services industry with almost every major retailer issuing its own plastic cards. For example, Marks & Spencer has nearly three million customers using its chargecard. This not only takes credit/chargecard business away from the banks, but has allowed Marks & Spencer to use the data gathered on these customers, largely at the top end of the socioeconomic scale, to build up an invaluable database for marketing purposes. Marks & Spencer first used this database to market its own range of unit trusts and now provides loans and mortgage schemes to these valued customers. The company is clearly intending to move further into the financial services field, using its reputation for integrity, honesty and expensive but value-for-money pricing as an aid.

The converse effect of 'Big Bang' was that the banks themselves were free to enter markets new to them by setting up or acquiring divisions or subsidiaries in, for example, estate agency, stockbroking and insurance services. This situation was modified in turn by the Financial Services Act 1986 which, among other provisions, required the banks' subsidiaries to choose between acting as independent financial advisers (free to recommend the products of any supplier) and tied units (marketing only the products of the parent group).

The Financial Services Act is examined in greater detail below. Other players in the ever-widening financial services industry include company treasurers (often as sophisticated in their understanding of modern financial instruments as the bank staff they deal with), and the recently introduced 'entirely different kind of bank'—First Direct from the Midland Bank Group—a bank with no branches, where customers conduct all their business over the phone or by post.

One of the dangers in this flourishing market is overcapacity. There is a finite market for financial services, however innovative the suppliers are in devising new products; inevitably some of the competitors will be squeezed out. It is the task of bank management to ensure that their own organisation is best placed to survive.

One good way to examine the effects of competition on the banks is to consider their strengths and weaknesses and what steps they might take to combat increased competition (refer to Fig. 1.2 again).

Strengths of the banks

(a) Reputation—a solid foundation of reliability in the provision of financial services.
(b) The strength and importance of London as a major financial centre.
(c) International experience—many banks have a wide network of overseas branches and subsidiaries.
(d) Innovation—some banks have a very good record of introducing new products and services.
(e) Staff—a pool of high quality, well trained staff.
(f) Technology—most banks have kept at the forefront of technological developments in the financial world.
(g) Branch networks—the major banks have an existing widespread network of domestic branches within easy reach of much of their existing and potential customer base.
(h) Economies of scale are possible for the larger banks.
(i) Asset base—the main banks have substantial capital resources on which to build their business.

Weaknesses of the banks

(a) Over-reliance on past success.
(b) Large bureaucracies—by their nature slow to change and cumbersome to control.
(c) Conservative in their traditions—lacking in radical innovation compared with some of their newer competitors.
(d) Paternalistic—the attitude towards employees is not always in step with the expectations of younger staff.
(e) Resistance by older employees to the idea of 'selling' or 'marketing' of services.
(f) Specialist services require skills outside the scope of some long-term employees.
(g) Growth of other financial centres worldwide, particularly with the ease of communication using modern technology.
(h) Restricted accessibility—being overcome by introduction of longer opening hours, automatic teller machines (ATMs), etc.
(i) Tendency towards inflexibility to customer requirements.

■ Steps the banks can take to compete successfully

The most important step is for the banks to analyse their markets in order to gain a real understanding of what their customers' needs are. Then they are in a position to devise and implement a strategy to satisfy those needs. (If you don't know what your customers want, how can you sell it to them?)

Then the banks must analyse their competitors' strengths and weaknesses—they must exploit their weaknesses and try to 'second-guess' the competitors' strategies.

Banks must promote and market their services effectively, constantly refining them to meet changing customer demands.

It may be necessary for the banks to make changes to the structure of their organisations and the training of their staff in order to get rid of old-fashioned practices which hold the business back. They must develop and reward behaviour which encourages innovation—and discourage behaviour which is overconservative and complacent.

The specific impact of changes in the market place on the banks' staffing policies is considered in greater depth in Chapter 3.

■ Financial Services Act 1986

As such an important recent piece of legislation (as it affects competition in the finance industry), this Act deserves special consideration.

The Act was prompted by Professor Gower's 1981 review of investor protection. Until then, the UK industry was largely self-regulated and a decision was needed as to whether this situation should continue, or whether we should move closer to the United States' example where the Securities and Exchange Commission regulates by statutory controls. The Financial Services Act 1986 is a compromise of self-regulation within a statutory framework.

The principal aim of the Act is to protect the consumer (generally as an investor) from fraudulent dealing. To do so it is very far-ranging, as can be seen from the way the Act itself describes its aims:

> 'The Act is to regulate the carrying on of investment business; to make related provision with respect to insurance business and business carried on by friendly societies; to make new provision with respect to the official listing of securities, offers of unlisted securities, takeover offers and insider dealing; to make provision as to the disclosure of information obtained under enactments relating to fair trading, banking companies and insurance; to make provision for securing reciprocity with other countries in respect of facilities for the provision of financial services; and for connected purposes.'

The power to enforce the regulations of the Act falls on the Secretary of State for Industry, who has largely transferred the power to authorise and regulate to the Securities and Investment Board (SIB). In turn, the SIB recognises five self- regulating organisations (SROs) to regulate the activity of their members:

— IMRO (Investment Managers Regulatory Organisation);
— LAUTRO (Life Assurance and Unit Trust Regulatory Authority);
— FIMBRA (Financial Intermediaries, Managers and Brokers Regulatory Association);

— SA (Securities Association);
— AFBD (Association of Future Brokers and Dealers).

Different subsidiaries of a large banking group may be members of different specialist SROs but the most generally important are IMRO and LAUTRO.

In order to obtain membership of the relevant regulatory body (and therefore the authority to carry out business in that field) the bank must give extensive details of its business, business records, internal arrangements for ensuring compliance with the Act's requirements (e.g. the training of specifically authorised staff) and details of the directors and principal staff (to ensure that they are regarded as proper persons to carry out business in that industry). The bank must then carry out its business in accordance with the SIB and SRO rules. These are detailed and exacting, with severe penalties for both the company and the individual in the event of infringements, the most severe being prosecution and the withdrawal of authorisation.

Perhaps the most well-known principle developed by the SIB which has had a direct impact on the major banks and building societies is that of polarisation. This prescribes that, in selling life assurance, unit trusts, etc., the seller or adviser must act **either** as an independent intermediary **or** as a company representative. It must be clear to the customer in which capacity the seller is acting (previously, banks were able to act in both capacities).

Of the Big Four banks, only National Westminster has opted to act as an independent adviser; the others all act as company representatives, although they may refer customers to their own independent subsidiaries.

▌Competition between stakeholders

A bank's interface with the market place takes place at various levels and with various groups, not just its competitors. When asked to list the stakeholders in a business, most people would first name the shareholders, who have actually invested money in a share of the company, but might have difficulty thinking of others. What is meant by 'stakeholders' is every group of people which has a legitimate interest in the fortunes of the company. This would include:

— shareholders;
— loan stockholders;
— customers;
— employees;
— trade union and other representative bodies;
— suppliers;
— local community;
— the State.

These groups may have differing expectations of the company and one of the problems that the management of the company has to deal with is balancing its sometimes conflicting responsibilities to each group of stakeholders. The following paragraphs list the company's responsibilities to each group and then discuss how potential conflicts of interest may be avoided.

Shareholders

Having bought shares in a company, shareholders are entitled to expect a fair return on their investment in the form of regular and adequate dividends, in line with the profits of the company. They will expect the management of the company to act in a professional and prudent way to maximise these profits and minimise the risk of losses. The company must comply with any relevant legislation regulating the conduct of companies and should provide adequate information to the shareholders on the activities of the company.

Loan stockholders

Loan stockholders of a company provide the long-term borrowing needs of the company, and in return the company must pay them the fixed-interest returns to final maturity of their loans. The company must meet its loan stock interest commitments, in full, even in years when it makes no or insufficient profits. Only after the loan stockholders have been paid their due interest in full, can the company distribute dividends to its shareholders. The company must comply with the trust deed under which the rights of the loan stockholders are protected and must conform to certain restrictions to which it has agreed in the loan trust deed.

Customers

Customers will expect to be given accurate and adequate information on the company's products, on which to base their decision to buy. They are entitled to goods or services which comply with any relevant legislation and which are reasonable value for money. Where appropriate, adequate after-sales service will also be expected (e.g. repair or replacement of faulty goods; maintenance facilities; correction of any mistakes in the case of services, etc.)

Employees

The treatment of employees by company management is now well covered by legislation (Sex Discrimination Act 1975; Health and Safety at Work Act 1974; unfair dismissal laws, etc.), but employees will expect that the company will comply with the spirit as well as the letter of good employment practice—for example, that all employees will be treated fairly with no discrimination, that fair reward will be given for good work, that a responsible attitude will be taken to continuity of employment (e.g. not taking on staff knowing that they will shortly be laid off), and that adequate opportunities for training and career development will be provided for suitable staff.

Trade unions etc.

Staff associations, trade unions and other representative bodies will expect the company to provide adequate information on its intentions as they affect the staff, to negotiate fairly and openly, and to set up agreed procedures for the handling of grievances.

Suppliers

If a company is to build up a good relationship with its suppliers, it should ensure that negotiations between the two parties are carried out openly and fairly. The company should make payment for supplies of goods or services within the time agreed and should keep the supplier informed of any changes in company policy or strategy which will have an impact on the supplier's business.

Local community

As explained in Chapter 1, the importance of a good relationship between a company and the local community within which it operates has become increasingly important over the past five to ten years, as the consumer lobby, environmental consciousness and other pressure groups have gained in influence. The company should respect the local environment in its plans for expansion of premises, disposal of waste, etc. It should be aware of the effects of changes in its employment policies on the local economy and set high standards as a good employer wherever possible.

The State

The company owes an obligation to the State to abide by laws and regulations affecting its operations, for example to file accounts at Companies' House each year and to abide by all the other regulations of the various Companies Acts, to follow employment legislation and Health and Safety provisions, and in all other respects to act as a good and responsible 'citizen'.

Stakeholders' conflicts of interest

It will be clear from the above that the needs of one group of stakeholders may conflict in some cases with those of another. For example:

(a) Shareholders will expect profits to be used to increase dividends—employees will want those profits used to raise wages—customers will expect lower prices—whereas the management themselves may prefer to invest in the development of the company.
(b) Customers will be in favour of longer opening hours, high levels of service and quick delivery times—staff will want shorter working hours, and better conditions of work generally.
(c) Employees will prefer standardised products and services—customers will demand a flexible range of products or services to suit their needs.
(d) Shareholders expect profit maximisation—the State requires a reasonable level of taxation income which will of course reduce profits.
(e) The company may wish to expand its premises in a way which conflicts with local environmental considerations.

For each pair of stakeholders you will be able to think of a series of possible conflicts of interest; these are just a few but the list is almost endless—anything which benefits one group can almost certainly be seen as detrimental to another group.

The skill of management then is to manage these conflicts to ensure maximum satisfaction all round. Note that we are talking of conflicts of interest rather than physical ones. It may not be possible, as the old saying goes, to 'please all of the people all of the time' but the art of management here is to achieve a satisfactory compromise.

∎ Managing stakeholders' conflicts of interest

The main way to avoid or manage conflicts of interest between stakeholders is to keep all sides well informed of developments in company policy and strategy. When both sides can see things from the other's point of view, understanding may replace antagonism. In the past such conflicts have often been ignored until it was too late for an amicable solution to be reached without considerable bitterness. Good forward planning by management can help to reduce unexpected crises and allow the company to respond flexibly to the changing requirements of its customers, employees, etc.

The specimen question 2 at the end of this chapter is taken from a recent examination paper; the model answer gives a fuller list of methods of managing conflicts of interest.

∎ Action points

(a) Consider how many groups of people you deal with in your work: do you have dealings with customers, suppliers (for example, insurance companies, surveyors, solicitors), other employees (almost certainly), unions or staff associations, the local community (perhaps you are involved in the local Chamber of Commerce, Round Table, or school banking projects), or the State (perhaps you send off forms to government departments relating to tax)?

(b) List any ways in which your dealings with these groups may give rise to a conflict of interests. Remember that a single person may belong to more than one group—an employee may also be a shareholder, a supplier may also be a customer, and so on.

(c) To which regulatory organisations does your bank belong? If you don't know, have a look on your headed notepaper or compliment slips. Think about what this means in your daily work (e.g. duty of care).

∎ Questions and answers

The point to watch in answering a question on stakeholders is whether the examiner asks for information on **all** stakeholders or just **some**. Then be sure to read **all** the question as it may ask for more than just a straightforward description.

Question 1

What are the strengths and weaknesses of the banks in relation to increasing competition?

[16]

What steps do they need to take to compete effectively? [9]

[Total marks for question—25]

(*Hint*: Make sure you spend just as much time on the weaknesses as on the strengths, and do not forget to tackle the last part of the question on what the banks can do— it carries one-third of the marks!)

Question 2

Among the 'stakeholders' in a large bank are:
  (i) the shareholders;
  (ii) the employees (both as individuals and as members of representative bodies);
  (iii) the customers; and
  (iv) the State.

(a) List the bank's main responsibilities to each of the stakeholders mentioned above. [9]

(b) Choose **two** of the following pairs of stakeholders. For each pair, identify conflicts between the interests of the two stakeholders **and** specify steps which can be taken by the bank, its directors and staff to manage these conflicts:
  (i) shareholders and employees;
  (ii) employees and customers;
  (iii) the State and shareholders. [16]

[Total marks for question—25]

(*Hint*: Note the split of marks—the examiner has indicated that the second part of the question is more important, yet many candidates when tackling this question spent a long time on part (a) and wrote only a few lines on part (b). In particular, note that as well as identifying possible conflicts of interest you are required to specify steps which could be taken to manage them. If you omit to do this you will lose marks. Note that in the specimen answer given, all three pairs of stakeholders are considered, to cover all possible answers, but you are asked to consider only **two** pairs. If you were to write on all three in the examination, the third pair would be ignored and you would have wasted your time.)

Answer 1

Strengths of the banks in the face of competition include:

  (a) Solid record of achievement in provision of financial services.
  (b) The importance of London as a major financial centre.
  (c) Useful international experience through a worldwide network of major subsidiaries.
  (d) Some banks have a very good record of innovation in new products and services.
  (e) High quality, well trained staff.
  (f) Technological innovation.
  (g) Branch network.
  (h) Economies of scale.
  (i) Financial strength.

Weaknesses of the banks in the face of competition include:

(a) Over-reliance on past success.
(b) Large bureaucracies—slow to change.
(c) Conservative traditions, lack of radical innovation compared with some competitors.
(d) Paternalistic employer attitudes out of tune with the expectations of younger employees.
(e) Only fairly recent realisation of the importance of marketing services.
(f) Inexperience in managing some of the newer services in some cases.
(g) Growth of other financial centres worldwide.
(h) Restricted accessibility (opening hours).

Not all of these will apply to all banks, of course.

The steps which the banks can take to compete effectively begin with gaining a real understanding of market needs, and then designing and implementing a strategy to satisfy those needs.

The banks must understand their competitors' strategies, strengths and weaknesses: they must anticipate their strategy and exploit their weaknesses.

Management must assess the organisation, the staff skills and behaviour and their own management style against current customer needs. They must then make appropriate changes to these factors to encourage innovation and change. Practices which are rooted in the past must be searched out and tested against current realities. Behaviour which will encourage more competitive attitudes should be rewarded; behaviour which encourages complacency and conservatism should be discouraged or even punished.

Answer 2

(a) Bank's main responsibilities

To shareholders:
— to provide a fair return on investment;
— to comply with legislation relating to the regulation of companies;
— to provide information on the activities of the organisation.

To employees:
— to provide fair reward for effort;
— in the regulation of relations between organisation and staff, to comply with appropriate legislation or received ideas as to best practice, e.g. discrimination, disciplinary and grievance procedures, Health and Safety at Work Act 1974, etc.;
— to provide an opportunity for career development;
— to provide relevant information;
— to negotiate openly and in good faith.

To customers:
— to provide value for money;
— to comply with the Health and Safety at Work Act, etc. ,in customer contact areas;
— to provide information as to products and services available.

To the State:
— to account for all taxes due to the State;
— to comply with laws regulating the operation of companies;
— to comply with or at least take account of other regulatory mechanisms (e.g. Bank of England);
— to show a responsibility to the community.

(b) Conflicts

(i) *Shareholders and Employees*

- Distribution of revenue

Shareholders' interests served by:
— higher dividends;
— conversion to investment capital;
— retention as asset base.

Employees' interests served by:
— higher remuneration;
— investment in improving the working environment;
— investment in increased human resources.

- Maximising investment

Shareholders' interests served by:
— drive for efficiency;
— concentration on the 'bottom line'.

Employees' interests served by:
— stable working conditions;
— slack use of human resources;
— commitment to long-term deployment.

Conflicts managed by:
— keeping both sides informed of developments and strategies;
— encouraging employee representation;
— establishing an open and fair negotiating system;
— encouraging employee participation as shareholders;
— establishing a reward system including 'payment by results';
— use of sophisticated manpower planning techniques to plan the future use of human resources;
— establishing a sound management accounting system to ensure that the use of all resources is maximised.

(ii) *Employees and customers*

Customers' interests best served by:
— concentration on qualitative aspects of service;
— flexibility of products and services to meet customer needs;
— enhancement of customer contact areas of premises;
— allocation of more time to contact with customers and potential customers (e.g. longer opening hours, more work during unsocial hours).

Employees' interests best served by:
— standardised procedure and products;
— improved working areas of premises;
— shorter working hours;
— regular working hours;
— concentration on 'controllable' aspects of service (more likely to be quantitative).

Conflicts managed by:
- specific training for customer care and product/service knowledge;
- enhancing both staff and customer areas;
- flexibility with regard to working hours and reward system;
- clear targets set as to quality of service given;
- sufficient resources available to achieve qualitative targets;
- clear guidelines with regard to product/service flexibility applying consistently at all levels throughout the organisation;
- integrated promotional/advertising campaigns.

(iii) *State and shareholders*

Shareholders' interests served by:
- profit maximisation;
- lack of constraining legislation and regulation;
- low levels of taxation (if any);
- free market economy;
- restriction of foreign competition at home but competitive freedom abroad;
- stable monetary policy.

State interests served by:
- fair taxation levels;
- legal and ethical standards maintained by legislation or self-regulating bodies;
- a (variable) balance between free market and controlled economy;
- a (variable) balance between competition and restriction at home and abroad;
- ability to regulate the economy.

Conflicts managed by:
- dialogue between State and industry/commerce;
- commitment and contribution to representative or regulatory bodies;
- compliance with fiscal and other regulatory laws/rules;
- public education as to the organisation's commercial and strategic aims;
- awareness of public opinion.

CHAPTER 3
Human resource management

- Impact of external factors • Recruitment policies • Manpower planning •
Training • Employee relations • Trade unions in banking • Factors affecting the industrial relations climate

∎ Impact of external factors

In Chapters 1 and 2 we have examined the factors in the external business environment which affect the way a company, particularly a bank, is managed and we have looked at the various influences which groups with an interest in the future of a company may have on its operations. One of the main areas of operation which is affected is that of the company's personnel policies, often referred to as 'human resource management'. Labour costs form the largest slice of a bank's expenditure—rather than regarding staff as a necessary evil, there has been a move in recent years to take a more positive view and see staff as the bank's most valuable asset, as they are the interface between the company and its customers.

Changes in the strategy of the company must be reflected in the way it plans its recruitment, training and retention of staff.

∎ Recruitment policies

The traditional stereotype

For many years, most people would have had a definite stereotype in mind if asked to describe the typical bank clerk or bank manager. He would be male, smartly but conservatively dressed, quiet and well spoken, probably with a grammar school education and certainly with 'O'-levels or their equivalent in Maths and English. He would join the bank from school or university, intending to remain with the same company for the whole of his working life, probably retiring as manager of his own branch.

This stereotype is no longer valid. Around 60 per cent of staff employed by the major banks are women, with increasing numbers reaching managerial level. The job of a bank clerk is no longer concerned just with 'paper-shuffling' but is much more sales-orientated. Several of the banks have introduced uniforms or 'career-wear' for their frontline staff to make them readily identifiable in open-plan sales areas. Most financial organisations now expect their staff to go out of the office into the customer's place of work (factory, farm, shop, etc.) to sell their financial services rather than waiting for the customer to come to the bank. There is no longer a stigma attached to leaving one organisation and joining another in order to further one's career; indeed, some of the key posts in several of the major banks are currently held by people who have joined from outside the organisation rather than working their way up from the 'shop-floor'.

All of these changes mean that, when looking for new recruits, bank personnel departments must be clear as to the type of people they are seeking.

The new image

The skills of a salesperson are not necessarily the same as those sought in the past. It may be more important that the candidate has an outgoing personality with the ability to lead and inspire a team of young enthusiastic people, than that the candidate has traditional paper qualifications.

Demographic studies show that the fastest growing groups in the UK adult population are the 25–34-year-olds and the 45–50-year-olds. Meanwhile the age groups in fastest decline are the 15–19 and 20–24-year-olds, the very groups from which banks would traditionally look to recruit new staff. As the pool of school leavers dwindles, banks must look to other means to maintain staff levels: recruitment of older people, either to be trained or with existing skills in other organisations; attracting married women back into the job market; re-training existing staff to suit them for new jobs within the organisation, and so on.

As the type of jobs carried out by bank staff has changed (e.g. with the introduction of more and more technology into the workplace) so the type of staff needed has also changed. Bank personnel departments have had to develop skills in selection and recruitment of a variety of specialist staff—computer programmers and operators; project managers to oversee the major new developments; specialists in, for example, insurance, estate agency, pensions, and whatever other functions the group has become involved in.

▌Manpower planning

Recruitment may take place at a local level, with each manager recruiting his own staff as required, or it may take place under the control of a regional or central personnel function. However, each company should have a centrally monitored manpower plan, developed in line with the organisation's overall strategic plan, and taking into account both the demand for labour as a result of the strategic plan and the current and potential availability of labour supply to meet that demand.

Every element of the strategic plan (marketing, operations, organisational structure, systems, etc.) has manpower implications. For example, if the bank decides to group branches together under area offices there will be a need for senior managers to run those offices, but there may be a reduced requirement for middle managers in the branches themselves; if the bank sets up a series of divisional computer centres to decentralise account maintenance operations, specialist staff will be needed to run those centres; if the strategic plan calls for a particular emphasis on marketing services to small businesses, it will be necessary to ensure that staff are recruited or trained to have the necessary expertise in that market segment, and so on. Changes in strategy may be so great that the existing branch network is no longer suitable as a delivery mechanism; this could have a tremendous impact in terms of possible redundancy, redeployment, retraining and recruitment of staff. Each part of the strategic plan must therefore be carefully thought through as it impacts on manpower planning.

Although the idea of a manpower plan may be simple, its application is far from straightforward. Any forecast of the future is doomed to be inaccurate in one way or another. If we could predict the future with absolute accuracy there would be no need for the skilled and expensive planning departments which large organisations employ in an effort to get somewhere near the truth. Thus in manpower planning people may leave the organisation in larger or smaller numbers than predicted, or the strategic plan may not develop as foreseen—cash flow problems may delay implementation, technology may not become available when expected, key personnel may leave for a rival company, the anticipated graduate recruits may choose to join another company, and so on. Nevertheless, the existence of a plan is important to ensure a sense of direction and to give a benchmark against which deviations can be measured.

With the acknowledged shortage of school leavers over the next decade, one option for the banks is to retain their existing staff longer by providing incentives to remain with the company.

For example, the Midland Bank has commenced a programme to open up to 300 crèches around the country over the next few years. Staff will be offered the chance to place their preschool children in the crèche on their way to work in the morning; the child will be looked after by trained staff during the day, and can be collected by the parent on the way home in the evening. This is likely to appeal particularly to female staff but is also open to male staff. By providing this facility, the bank is hoping to encourage mothers (in particular) to return to work after the birth of a child, thus making the most of the bank's investment in training that member of staff, and retaining a pool of skilled staff. Such provisions may also help to build up a sense of loyalty to the organisation by demonstrating that the management has a paternalistic interest in its staff.

▎Training

Impact of environmental changes

The problems of training and retraining in a changing environment have already been touched on above. All large organisations, such as banks, have well-established training departments co-ordinating the provision of internal and external training courses for their staff. With changes in the business environment or in the strategic plan of the organisation, it is essential that corresponding changes take place in the range and type of training carried out.

Ideally the changes in training will take place prior to changes in the organisational structure, marketing plans, etc., of the company, so that the staff are prepared in advance for new products, marketing ideas, etc., and can present them to customers in a professional and confident manner.

The introduction of new ways of working, particularly (though not exclusively) new technology, makes particular demands on the training department. In recent years the main high–street clearers have taken a radical look, not only at the products they offer, but also at the way those products are processed and delivered, and at the levels and quality of service required. As a result there has been considerable segmentation of the market (into personal, small business, large corporate, multinational, etc.) with a corresponding division in the staff who are specifically trained to deal with each group of customers.

High technology

In order to cope with the ever-increasing use of high technology equipment, not only for money transmission and account maintenance but also in the office, training must be given frequently to staff at all levels to keep them abreast of what is going on around them. This technology includes electronic mail systems (allowing staff in different departments, offices or even towns to communicate and transmit messages or documents almost instantaneously), word processors (which have revolutionised the work of secretaries and typists, often allowing managers to create their own documents to professional standards), facsimile transmission machines (fax) (which can send a copy of any document between offices or even between countries as easily as making a phone call), conference phone systems (which allow executives in remote locations to see and speak to each other as though holding a meeting in the same room), desk-top publishing systems (which allow word-processed documents to be printed like a professionally published document), as well as the computer-based facilities such as spreadsheet packages (to aid accounting, budgeting, forecasting, etc.), and databases (which effectively act as an automated card index system—allowing data to be sorted, selected and organised as required); the list is virtually endless.

∎ Employee relations

Background to unionism

Controlling the human resources of a company means keeping a balance between the inflow of staff (by recruitment and transfer between departments or group companies), the outflow of staff (by retirement, resignation, transfer out, maternity leave, redundancy, sacking, etc.), and the level of staff required for the optimal running of the business.

Back in the last century, company owners or bosses simply hired workers when required and laid them off when work was slack. Thus many workers had no security of employment from one week to the next and, since there was no proper welfare system, destitution was a real fear.

Various pieces of legislation in this century have ensured that the situation in the UK is very different today. Provided a worker does his job satisfactorily, after a probationary period he cannot be sacked without notice or be dismissed unfairly. This has implications for the employer, who cannot necessarily control the level of the workforce as closely as would be ideal from a cost point of view.

The growth of trade unions in the UK was one of the main factors which led to the development of employment legislation to protect the rights of employees. However, when the power of the unions was seen as becoming too great in the 1970s, this in turn led to the passing of legislation to limit union power.

Collective bargaining

The system which controls the relationship between employers (or employer federations) and employees (usually through their representative groups) in British industry in general is collective bargaining. Under this system, governed by a legal framework, levels of pay and conditions of work are settled by negotiation between employer and employee representatives (often trade unions). The disadvantage of this type of bargaining is that it inevitably leads to a 'them and us' attitude, which can result in divisiveness and conflict unless both sides are prepared to take the other's point of view fully into account.

Trade unions in banking

Traditionally, white-collar workers such as bankers did not join trade unions. For the first half of this century they preferred to make individual arrangements with their employers. However, during the 1960s and 1970s this began to change as the settled nature of a bank career came under threat.

(a) Bank workers began to see their levels of pay eroded in comparison with those workers who were represented by strong unions.
(b) The introduction of new technology was seen as a possible threat to banking jobs.
(c) Traditionally, most bankers had been recruited from the middle classes, who had a cultural resistance to joining a union; increasingly, bank clerks were being drawn from working-class backgrounds where no such attitude prevailed.
(d) Unions began actively to seek white–collar members to strengthen their numbers as some of the more traditionally unionised industries declined (e.g. shipbuilding and other heavy engineering).
(e) Government legislation in the 1970s prevented employers from discriminating against employees who joined a union and this too encouraged membership.
(f) The concentration of large numbers of clerical workers on single sites (perhaps doing boring repetitive jobs and feeling remote from effective management) is an ideal situation for union recruitment.
(g) As blue-collar workers gained many of the benefits usually associated with white-collar jobs (pensions, longer holidays, notice periods, and sickness pay) the latter saw differentials being eroded and moved towards union membership for support.

The truth behind (g) above is illustrated by a survey published in the magazine *Personnel Management*, in late 1989. Of the 83 companies surveyed, more than 80 per cent had holidays, pensions and redundancy pay harmonised between manual and office workers. As many as 85 per cent of the firms had harmonised eating and parking facilities, loans and product discounts. Wages, grading structures and hours worked are lagging behind, but these demarcations are also being eroded between the two groups of workers.

Advantages and disadvantages of union membership

For the employee, union membership offers the benefit of the support of others in negotiating improvements in pay and conditions, or in dealing with disciplinary or grievance procedures. The union has the resources to offer professional advice and support and to research the business of the employer more thoroughly than an individual employee could hope to do. Possible disadvantages include the loss of individual freedom if the employee abides by union instructions. Some still fear discrimination from an employer for joining a union, but this should be an unfounded fear nowadays.

From the employer's point of view, negotiating with a single well-informed union (or a small number of unions) rather than a multitude of individual employees is usually seen as an advantage, as defined procedures can be laid down and followed. However, this does limit the employer's ability to reward individuals outside the agreed framework. Now that the bank employers' federation has broken down, the advantage of a standard set of pay and conditions across the industry, restricting competition for staff between employers, has been lost.

Factors affecting the industrial relations climate

There is a whole range of factors, both inside and outside a business, which affect the climate of industrial relations between workers and management at any one time. Not all of these are necessarily applicable to banks but a general list is as follows:

Environmental:

(a) Levels of profitability—if the products or services of the company are in high demand, employees will expect to share in this success and management may be willing and able to make higher settlements (and vice versa).
(b) Degree of competition—if high, this will influence the ability and willingness of the company to make high salary awards, as the company must not price itself out of the market.
(c) Levels of unemployment—will influence employee attitudes and their ability to seek alternative employment.
(d) Competition between unions—may complicate the bargaining procedure.
(e) Legal constraints—may affect either party.

Technological:

(a) Labour-intensiveness or capital-intensiveness of the business—will determine the significance of salaries as a cost factor.
(b) Perishability of the product—workers handling highly perishable goods or time-critical services have a stronger hand in negotiations as the firm may stand to lose a great deal of money if production/supply of services is delayed due to industrial action.
(c) Key personnel—if the personnel involved in the negotiations are vital to the operation of the business (e.g. computer staff in the banks) this will have an impact on the seriousness of any dispute.
(d) Rate of technological change—has implications for future employment.

History:

(a) The history of staff–management relationships in the company or industry.
(b) The management style.
(c) The style of negotiation of the union or staff association (militant or moderate).

(d) The personalities involved and their interaction.
(e) The local culture.

The bargain itself:

(a) Degree of understanding of the real issues by all parties.
(b) Degree to which a 'win–win' solution is possible.
(c) Degree of solidarity within each side.

In banking, the most important issues currently are the effects of strong competition; the pressure on profits due (particularly) to high levels of bad debt provisions for problem country debt; continuing technological change; rationalisation of staffing to contain costs; and the changing attitudes of younger management coming to prominence in the major banks, with more modern ideas.

The current position of unions in banking

At the time of writing, there are two unions representing the staff of the clearing banks, with several staff associations which are not affiliated to the Trades Union Congress (TUC).

The Banking, Insurance and Finance Union (BIFU), formerly the National Union of Bank Employees, developed after World War I. It was exclusively concerned with banking until 1979 when the name was changed to reflect a wider potential membership in the financial sector. BIFU had 170,481 members at the end of 1989, ranking as the twelfth largest of the TUC-affiliated unions.

The Management, Scientific and Finance Union (MSF) developed from the merger in February 1988 of TASS (Transport Salaried Staffs Association) and ASTMS (Association of Scientific, Technical and Managerial Staff). Although MSF has a total membership of around 653,000, within the banks it has a much smaller membership than BIFU, and correspondingly more limited bargaining rights. MSF had its largest membership in Midland Bank (derived from the old Midland Bank Staff Association), but in 1989 Midland ceased to recognise the union, which has thus lost most of its power in representing bank staff.

In 1980 an amalgam of staff associations became the Clearing Banks' Union (CBU). There was always a good deal of rivalry between the CBU and BIFU as the latter regarded the CBU as far too 'soft' in negotiations. In 1988 the CBU finally dissolved back into its component staff associations in NatWest and Barclays Banks.

During the late 1980s, the Federation of London Clearing Bankers, which previously represented the employers in negotiations with the unions, began to break down, as first Midland and then the other banks pulled out. Negotiations are now carried out purely between individual banks and the unions/staff associations concerned. This in turn has led to the possibility of differing settlements in different banks.

Negotiations generally cover such things as basic salary ranges for clerical grades 1–4, age-related salary ranges for clerical grades 1–2 and the length of the working day/week, and may (depending on the organisation) include overtime conditions, territorial allowances, holiday entitlement for junior grades, allowances, minimum managerial salary, and the clerical job grading system.

Action points

(a) Think of your own office—what outside factors have affected recruitment of staff to your branch/department over the last year?

(b) Of the last two or three people who moved from your office, what were their reasons? Did this cause any problems for your manager in staffing the team?

(c) What training have you received in the last three to five years? How much of this was related to changes in the bank's strategy or in the range of products you were asked to sell?

(d) Which union/staff association represents staff in your bank or office? Find out from your local union representative just what benefits are to be gained from joining the union.

(e) Which elements of your pay and conditions package are negotiated by the union and which are set by the bank? (For example, the terms of the staff mortgage scheme are often not negotiable.)

Questions and answers

Question 1

What are the probable implications of technological change for

(a) the organisational structure of banks; [13]

(b) staffing in the banks? [12]

[Total marks for question—25]

(N.B. Only the second part of the question is answered below—the first part is covered in Chapter 4 under the heading 'Organisational structure'.)

Question 2

(a) Describe briefly the major trade unions in UK banking. [4]
(b) What are their bargaining rights at the national level? [4]
(c) Trace the growth of trade unionism in the UK banking industry and explain why it happened. [10]
(d) What are the advantages and disadvantages of trade unions from an employee's point of view? [7]

[Total marks for question—25]

Answer 1

For part (a) see Chapter 4.

(b) Implications for staffing:

— Numbers: staff reductions might result from the automation of routine processing. However the

rapid growth of new services might create a demand for additional staff.
- New skills will be required: some traditional skills will become obsolete and some redundancy/unemployment may result if the imbalance cannot be corrected simply by retraining (e.g. if existing staff are unsuitable or refuse to retrain).
- Management skill changes: as technology becomes more sophisticated, managers whose jobs were concerned simply with processing information may be displaced.
- Job structures will change: this will raise new issues for staff motivation.
- Specialist staff: banks may need to look outside the financial sector to recruit staff, as the technological skills needed might not be available from within.
- Career patterns: the traditional 'cradle to grave' banking career pattern will broaden as the new skills can easily be transferred to another business.
- Competition for key staff: shortage of skilled specialist staff will have implications for salary structures.
- Retraining of those with outdated or obsolete skills to enable them to adapt to new jobs will become increasingly important.
- Training of existing staff to keep them up-to-date with rapid change will be important.
- Management styles will need to change as more professional staff are employed.

Answers 2

For (a) and (b) please refer to text in this chapter.
(c) The major growth took place in the 1960s and 1970s for the following reasons:
- employee relations legislation made union membership 'respectable';
- changes in attitudes and values: white-collar workers felt they were losing out against manual workers who were organised;
- security was threatened as a result of mergers, etc, in banking industry;
- trade unions moved to attract a share of the increasing numbers of white-collar workers;
- more white-collar workers were from working-class families, sympathetic to trade unions;
- companies wanted a means of demonstrating equal treatment between all employers and to all employees;
- companies find it easier to deal with representatives rather than individuals.

(d) The advantages of trade union membership, from an employee's point of view, include:
- mutual support;
- protection in disciplinary/grievance matters;
- professional advice and representation;
- professional research and intelligence services available.

The disadvantages include:
- possible loss of individual freedom;
- more impersonal relationship with employer;
- less reward for initiative;
- possible danger of collusion between employer and trade union.

CHAPTER 4
Organisational design and development

● Organisational structure ● Organisational culture ● Power in organisations ● Communication in organisations ● Centralisation vs. decentralisation ● Cooperation between departments

▌ Organisational structure

The structure of an organisation does not refer to the bricks and mortar of its buildings, but to the way the various parts of the organisation are linked together to carry out its aims—in other words, how work is divided into tasks and how it flows through the organisation; how departments are set up and linked to each other; whether there are many branches and whether these are grouped under the control of area or regional offices or report directly to the head office; how many staff each manager is responsible for and what are the lines of communication: all these factors contribute to the organisation's structure.

To some degree, every organisation can be said to be different from every other, and in some ways at least this would be true. However, to be able to consider organisational structure in a more general sense it is helpful if we can distinguish broad groupings of structural types and see how these differ from each other.

Mintzberg's 'Structure in 5's'

Henry Mintzberg suggested that all organisations are essentially made up of five elements (see Fig. 4.1): the strategic apex, the middle line, the technostructure, the support staff and the operating core.

(a) The strategic apex. This is composed of the senior managers of the organisation who are responsible for its direction (i.e. the board of directors and the senior executive management).
(b) The middle line. This comprises the middle management of the organisation at both regional and branch level.
(c) Technostructure. This is made up of the control activities of the organisation, e.g. personnel, training, strategic planning, Organisation and Methods (O&M), etc.
(d) Support staff. These include lawyers, staff concerned with public relations and

industrial relations, the payroll department, canteen, post room, etc. Whilst essential for the operation of the organisation, they could be contracted out without destroying the nature of the organisation.

(e) Operating core. This is the heart of the workforce of the organisation. It consists of the clerks, salesforce, machine operators, etc.

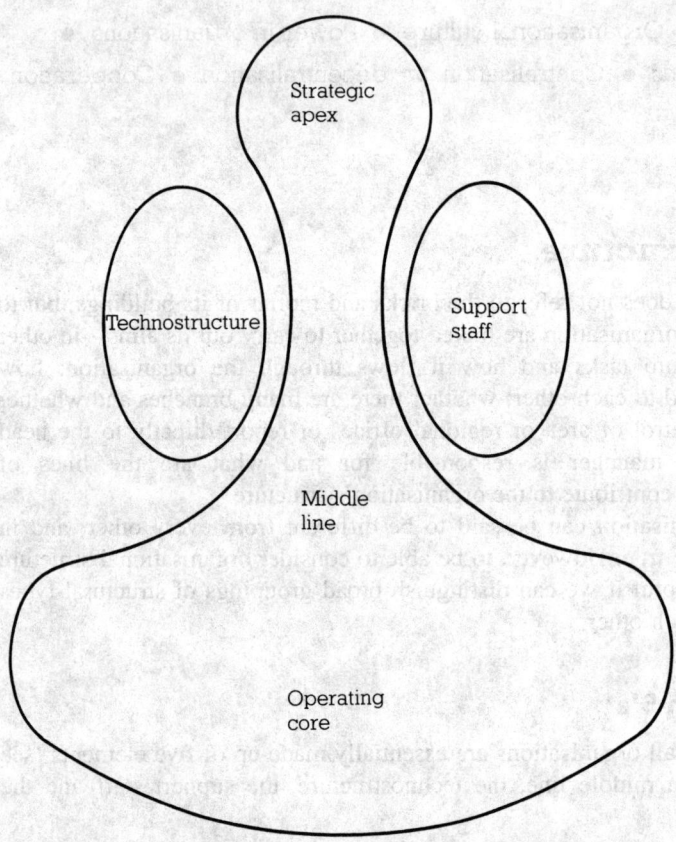

Fig. 4.1 The five elements of organisational structure

Mintzberg described a series of organisational types in which these elements are variously more or less important, but suggested that there is always a tension in the organisation as the five elements pull in different directions (see Fig. 4.2).

Organisational design and development

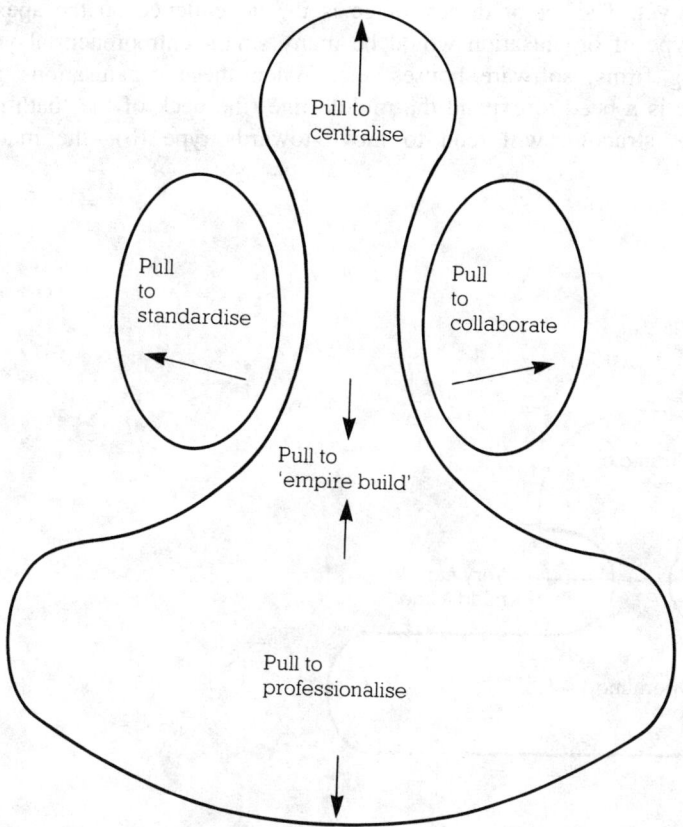

Fig. 4.2 The five pulls on the organisation

(a) The strategic apex will tend to pull towards centralisation of control.
(b) The middle line will tend to try to 'empire build' around themselves.
(c) The technostructure will pull towards standardisation of procedures.
(d) The support staff will tend to congregate towards other members of their own specialty in other organisations (e.g. lawyers working in the various banks may pull towards collaboration with each other—seeing themselves as lawyers who happen to work in banks, rather than bankers who happen to be lawyers).
(e) Finally, Mintzberg considers that the operating core of the organisation will tend to pull towards autonomy, or professional status for themselves.

These pulls may have negative effects on the organisation but they are always there, so the challenge for the organisation is to manage them.

The main types of structure which Mintzberg identified are, briefly, as follows:

(a) **Simple structure**. Here only the strategic apex and the operating core are fully developed (see Fig. 4.3). Control is by direct supervision from the top; it is capable of rapid, flexible response; the structure is informal and centralised with no development of standards, procedures and planning as yet. The major disadvantage is the dependence on the apex for control. Examples of this type of organisation would be many small, entrepreneurial young businesses such as building firms, software houses, etc. When these organisations grow beyond a certain point there is a need to expand the middle line (the neck of the 'bath-plug' shape in Fig. 4.3) and the structure will tend to move towards type (b)—the machine bureaucracy.

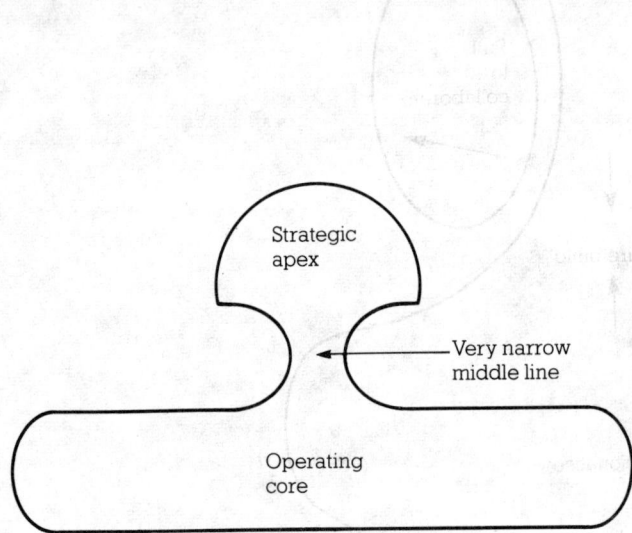

Fig. 4.3 Simple structure

(b) **Machine bureaucracy**. Here the middle line has become fat and bloated by numerous layers of middle management, with a considerable volume of technical and support staff (see Fig. 4.4). The strategic apex is rather remote, with coordination and control being by means of standardisation of work. This structure can lead to many management problems: coping with interdepartmental conflict; motivating the demotivated core (e.g. British Rail or the large retail stores); coping with the strength of the technocrats; and perhaps most vital, trying to shift the unwieldy monster in the face of environmental changes. On the positive side however, the large size can be a benefit in ensuring relative stability, a security-orientated labour force, the economies of scale of mass production technology and a measure of control over the environment due to the influence of sheer size. Examples of this structure are the major car manufacturers, the Post Office, and many of the major banks. As this structure becomes too unwieldy, it will tend to move towards (c)—the divisionalised form.

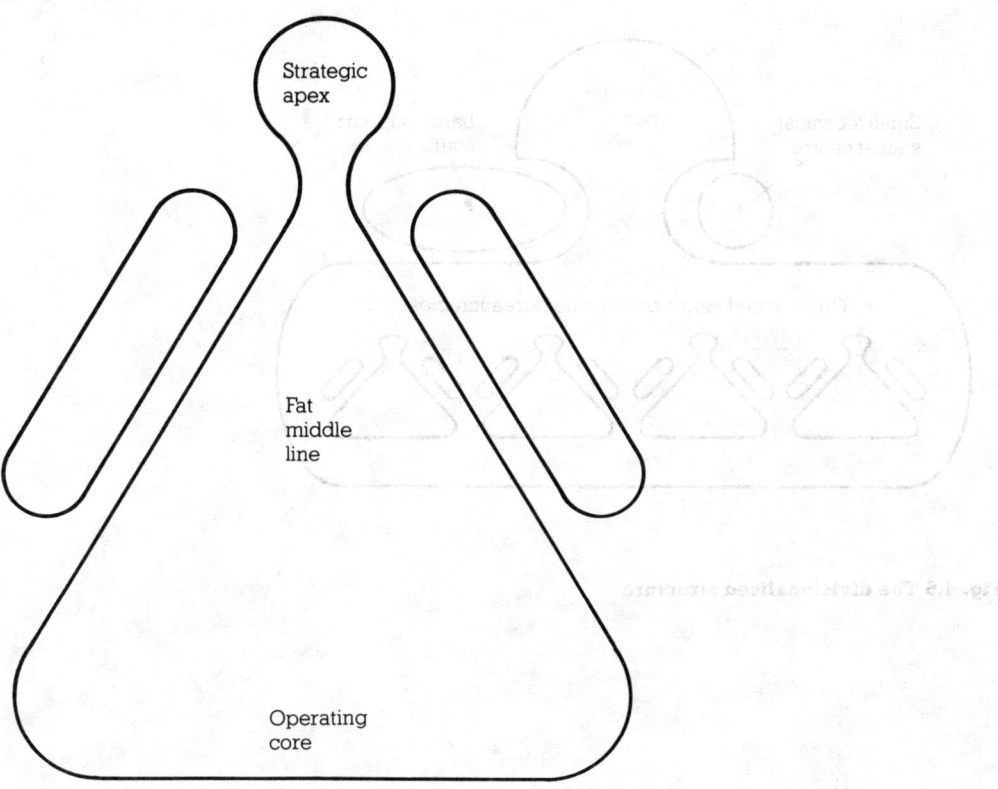

Fig. 4.4 Machine bureaucracy

(c) **Divisional structure**. This is effectively a series of coordinated machine bureaucracies (see Fig. 4.5). Examples are many of the large multinational groups such as Hanson or Grand Metropolitan. The strengths are that each division can manage its business in the best way to suit local needs and the requirements of its particular industry. The weakness is the difficulty of retaining central control over these autonomous units—divisions may conflict over the use of resources and the nature of their goals and may tend to compete with each other rather than the opposition.

(d) **Professional bureaucracy**. As the name suggests, this structure is typical of a group of professionals (lawyers, consultants, etc.) drawn together by their skills. There will tend to be a well-developed support staff, but little technostructure or strategic apex (see Fig 4.6). The management problems are those of coordinating a team of independent professionals—serving rather than directing them—and protecting them from their environment. Other examples are hospitals and universities.

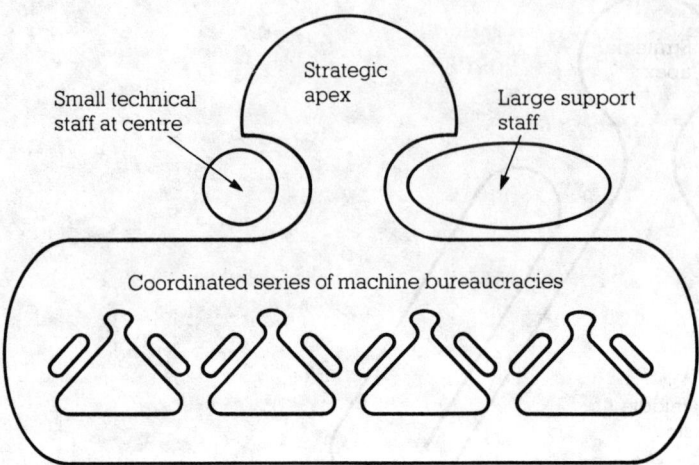

Fig. 4.5 The divisionalised structure

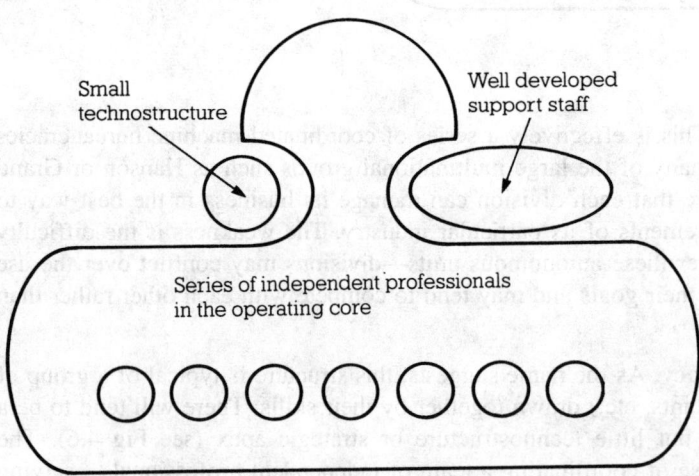

Fig. 4.6 Professional bureaucracy

(e) **Adhocracy.** This is the structure which tends to develop when a group of disparate people are brought together for a specific project—for example, a film production team, an aerospace project, or some IT (Information Technology) projects. There is no permanent operating core; operators will be hired as needed on a task-by-task basis (see Fig. 4.7). This structure allows complete flexibility to react to change, with power resting with expertise, wherever that happens to be. The main management problem is to cope with high levels of uncertainty and to ensure that in the pursuit of the extraordinary, the team does not lose sight of the more mundane essentials. There is a tendency to slip back into a bureaucracy structure.

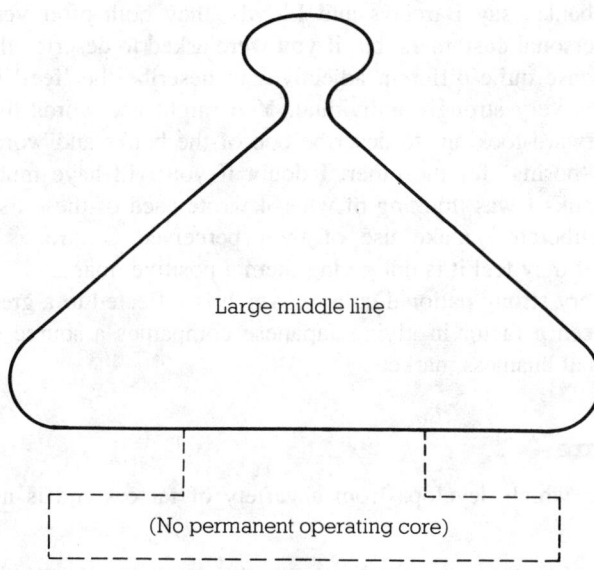

Fig. 4.7 The adhocracy

Organisational culture

What is 'culture'?

Organisational culture (sometimes called organisational or corporate style or climate) refers to the 'feel' of the organisation, the way things are done, what the norms of behaviour in the organisation are—the unwritten rules. For example, companies differ in their approach to the basis on which staff are promoted or rewarded; the extent to which planning is important; the extent to which risk-taking is acceptable; the degree of security of employment in the firm; the importance of smart dress and impressive offices, etc.

A newcomer to an organisation needs to pick up clues to the culture—the expected behaviour—if he is to fit in easily.

For example, in some organisations, even though the working day is officially 9 a.m. to 5 p.m., it is expected that everyone will be in his office and at his desk well before 9 a.m. and stay until after 5 p.m. If the newcomer arrives at exactly 9 a.m. and leaves on the dot of 5 p.m., he will probably experience hostility from the rest of the staff. Similarly there are often 'acceptable' excuses in an organisation: in some it will be considered 'OK' to apologise for lateness by saying you had a heavy night the night before, laughing it off and putting in an hour or two extra in the evening; in another organisation it would be unacceptable to admit to having overindulged and the latecomer would be better off saying that the train was late, or that the alarm failed to go off.

That is a fairly trivial example but it makes the point that different standards of behaviour are 'acceptable' in different cultures.

If you think of two of the major banks, say Barclays and Lloyds, they both offer very similar products and services to their personal customers, but if you were asked to describe the **way** in which they operate you might use quite different adjectives to describe the 'feel' of each bank. This is the culture and it is very strongly individual. You might use words like 'brash', 'bright', 'young', 'pushy', 'forward-looking' to describe one of the banks and words like 'conservative', 'solid', 'reliable', 'boring' for the other. I doubt if you will have much difficulty guessing which of the two banks I was thinking of when I wrote each of these lists of adjectives. Some organisations deliberately make use of their perceived culture as a marketing ploy; others try to change it if they feel it is not giving them a positive image.

It has been suggested that Japan's very strong national culture, which is reflected to a great degree in its corporate cultures, has been a factor in giving Japanese companies a source of competitive advantage in the international business market.

Factors which influence culture

An organisation's culture is something which develops from a variety of factors and is not easy to 'manage'. The main factors are:

(a) Values demonstrated by management, e.g. attitudes to quality and service to the customer.
(b) Leadership style of management, e.g. whether cautious or open.
(c) History and origins of the business, e.g. an organisation which began as a family business will often retain elements of that culture.
(d) Nature of the business, e.g. the culture in investment banks will differ from that of retail banks as their type of business and their clients will be very different.
(e) Workforce: the age, level of education, proportion of men to women and of long-serving to new staff will all alter the culture.
(f) Life cycle stage of the organisation: younger organisations tend to be less formal, older ones tend to be governed more by rules and regulations, whereas staff in an organisation in decline will exhibit apathy and lack of initiative.

How to identify the culture

A variety of characteristics of an organisation gives clues as to its culture:

(a) **Attitude to customers.** We have all been irritated by shops in which the assistants seem more concerned with chatting to each other than with serving the customers—whereas in other retail outlets the staff are very pleasant and helpful. Banks have tried to influence their public image in recent years by deliberately moving towards a less formal culture, with open-plan customer areas, reception desks, staff on the same side of the counter as the customer, etc.

(b) **Visible structure.** An extension of (a) is the physical architecture, layout and furnishings of the company's offices. In the Civil Service and still in many other organisations, there is a very well defined hierarchy of status—the size of your desk, the type of chair you may have, the amount and depth of carpet on your office floor are all predefined. This suggests a very rigid and formal culture, whereas an office where everyone from the boss downwards has a similar desk and amount of floor space suggests a much more democratic way of working and an informal culture.

(c) **Brochures/letterheads, etc**. The corporate literature may say a lot about a company. An annual report which consists of glossy photographs of the plant and machinery, the interior of the elegant and expensively furnished boardroom and the exterior of the head office building might suggest a company which is more interested in output and status; a report which centres on the newest retail outlets, with photographs of customers being served, managers meeting customers in their own premises, etc., suggests a company which may be more concerned with customer service and satisfaction.

(d) **Behaviour rewarded**. Is the successful member of staff regarded as the person who achieves the highest level of sales, regardless of the cut-throat methods used to achieve them, or is it the person who receives the most praise from customers? Do management reward those who 'fit in'—the 'yes-men'—or do they encourage discussion and contributions from the staff?

(e) **Stability**. Does the corporate attitude encourage young high fliers, or are people promoted only for long service, regardless of merit? Are the rules and regulations regarded as sacrosanct or is some element of initiative encouraged?

Schein, in 1985, identified three levels of culture: the artifacts and creations of the organisation (the physical environment, products and visible behaviour); the values of the organisation (rationalisations of behaviour, e.g. the 'acceptable excuse', standards and principles, e.g. whether staff trust each other or whether they have to watch their own backs); and the assumptions of the organisation (what can be taken for granted about people, e.g. trust, extent of risk-taking).

An amusing anecdote is that of the company described by a disillusioned ex-employee as having a *Watership Down* culture. If you have read the book or seen the film, you will know that a part of Watership Down was populated by dark, gloomy, well-fed rabbits. In this company there were big open-plan offices, with no privacy; staff were well paid, but when occasionally someone left, nothing was said, work continued as though nothing had happened and it was as though that person had never existed. In the case of the Watership Down rabbits, this was because they were being farmed for the butcher's slab, but in the company it was a curious reaction to anyone who 'dared' to leave and break away from the accepted behaviour patterns.

Strong cultures

The success of a company may depend less on the nature of the culture than on whether that culture is a strong one. Strong cultures facilitate communication and decision-making because there is shared understanding, and they facilitate cooperation on the basis of trust. They are characterised by high levels of trust; they tend to run throughout a company, rather than being a series of separate cultures in different divisions or at different levels in the organisation; they tend to exist by consensus rather than enforcement and they tend to result in high levels of involvement rather than apathy.

Fred Luthans, writing in 1985, listed six attributes of strong cultures. They are:

(a) Learned, not picked up outside the organisation.
(b) Shared by at least a significant proportion of the staff. (In Marks & Spencer, for example, the corporate culture is strongly shared by all the staff whereas in Ford Motors it is only the management who share a common culture.)
(c) Transgenerational; in other words, a culture established by the founder of a company will be passed on down the generations.
(d) Symbolic: the symbol is often the founder or the image of the company itself, so that staff will say 'this is the way so-and-so would have done it' or 'that is the IBM way'.
(e) Patterned; in other words, the culture fits in with the whole of the business in all its aspects.
(f) Adaptive: although the culture is continuous, it is possible for it to adapt to change, and even to internationalisation in some cases.

However, cultures don't adapt well to mergers and takeovers. This has been a problem where, for example, a retail bank has taken over a stockbroker, or a travel company, where totally different cultures exist. Also in the banking world, if the possible merger between Midland Bank and the Hong Kong and Shanghai Banking Corporation takes place, it will be interesting to see to what extent there is a cultural mismatch between the two organisations. Statements by both managements have indicated that they consider there are in fact close similarities.

■ Power in organisations

Another way to classify organisations is by the way power is exercised. Charles Handy identified four types of organisation in this way:

- Power-based organisations.
- Role-based organisations (or bureaucracies).
- Project-based (or task-based) organisations.
- People-based organisations.

While you are reading through the descriptions of these four types, remember that they are not mutually exclusive—a large organisation may contain elements of several of the types—and think how they relate to your own organisation or parts of it (see Fig. 4.8).

Organisational design and development

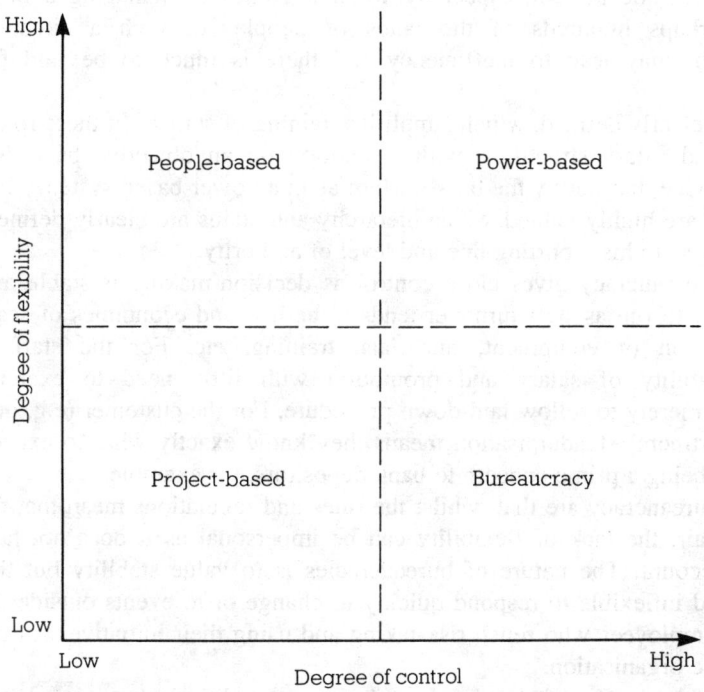

Fig. 4.8 Power in organisation

Power-based organisations

These are usually small, entrepreneurial businesses, controlled by one key individual. There are few rules and regulations since all decisions are channelled through to 'the boss', who thereby keeps control of the organisation in his own hands.

There is often a very exciting atmosphere in such organisations as there is a strong will to win. However, the boss usually has favourites and only those who support and agree with him will get on.

Individuals are judged by results, but since communication is all through the centre, some parts of the organisation may be unaware of what is going on elsewhere.

Examples of this type of organisation would be Richard Branson's Virgin empire (certainly in its early days), Alan Sugar's Amstrad, Sir Freddie Laker's Laker Airways in the 1970s, and many small businesses run by one charismatic leader.

Bureaucracies (role-based organisations)

A bureaucracy is an organisation where almost all activities are governed by laid-down rules and procedures. Nowadays the word is often used in a pejorative way, but there are in fact many advantages to a bureaucratic system, especially when it comes to managing a huge organisation employing perhaps hundreds of thousands of people. In such a situation innovation and individualism may lead to inefficiency and there is much to be said for standardisation.

In a bureaucracy jobs are clearly defined, which simplifies training of staff to fit these roles. There are defined career and salary structures, with promotion on an objective basis (on performance or length of service, but not by the boss's whim as in a power-based system). Job security and a good pension are highly valued. Since hierarchy and status are clearly defined, each member of staff is clear as to his reporting line and level of authority.

For the management, a bureaucracy gives close control as decision-making is stable and consistent. It may be cheaper to run as staff turnover tends to be low and economies of scale operate due to standardisation of equipment, materials, training, etc. For the staff, a bureaucracy offers predictability of salary and promotion with little need to exercise judgement or take risks, but merely to follow laid-down procedure. For the customer (e.g. of a bank or a government department) standardisation means they know exactly what to expect, with the safety and stability being a prime concern to bank depositors, for example.

The disadvantages of a bureaucracy are that, whilst the rules and regulations mean that the system can be seen to be fair, the lack of flexibility can be impersonal as it does not take individual situations into account. The nature of bureaucracies is to value stability but this means they are too large and inflexible to respond quickly to change or to events outside the confines of the rule-book. Employees who relish risk-taking and using their initiative will not feel at home in a bureaucratic organisation.

The 'unacceptable face of bureaucracy', to paraphrase a famous political quote, is what is now termed 'red tape'. In other words, a preoccupation with rules and regulations to such an extent that the reason for their existence, in the first place (to serve customers, for example), is overlooked and they become an end in themselves. This was seen to be happening in many government departments and nationalised industries, which is one of the rationales behind the current spate of privatisations. However red tape is a threat not only in the public sector, but many large companies have also had to examine their procedures, to cut down on unnecessary form-filling, and duplication of effort, in the current economic climate where cost-cutting is the name of the game.

Most of the banks have tackled this by sweeping away many of the checks and double-checks which used to be required on every clerical activity. It has been calculated that the potential losses which may be incurred by clerical error do not justify the enormous expense of such close supervision.

Project-based organisations

This has similarities with the adhocracy (see Fig. 4.7) described above. Such organisations are usually involved in a series of separate projects (e.g. a film production company, or a civil engineering firm) at any one time, so staff will be taken on as required and relocated to different sites as necessary.

The organisation will typically have a small core of permanent staff with very little hierarchy or status consciousness. Communication travels easily both horizontally and vertically through the organisation and all staff are encouraged to be flexible and show initiative. Creativity and achievement of group goals are rewarded and individuals have a good deal of freedom.

Problems may arise where a member of the staff has more than one boss—a functional boss and a project manager—and their authority may conflict.

An example in a bank might be where individuals from different departments within the bank are co-opted into a project team to set up a new computer system. There will be representatives of the user departments, the control functions, perhaps the finance function plus the computer specialist, project management team, etc. Many of these will have bosses in their 'home' departments, as well as reporting to the project manager for the lifetime of the project itself.

People-based organisations

These organisations often exist as a partnership or other grouping of professionals (see Fig. 4.6, above). An example is a group medical practice, where a central administrative and nursing function serves the needs of a group of doctors. There will be little interaction between the professionals and a low level of control from the centre. This type of structure is sometimes seen in consultancy groups, law firms, etc.

Communication in organisations

Here we are concerned with communication between different parts of an organisation. Communication between individuals is considered in detail in Chapter 12 and all the factors mentioned there apply equally here.

The need for good communication

There is an after-dinner joke which perhaps sums up the essential need for good communication:

> 'Three managers were discussing communication in their own organisations. The first manager said: "We work on the pyramid principle; executive management at the top of the pyramid take decisions, they pass the information down to senior management, who cascade it down to middle management, who tell junior management and so on, down to the bottom." The second manager replied: "Oh no, we work on the wheel principle. Central management at the hub of the wheel pass information out along the spokes to middle managers, who communicate with junior managers and so on, out to the workers on the rim of the wheel." "Ah!", said the third manager, "Our organisation works on the mushroom principle. We are kept totally in the dark for weeks at a time, then occasionally someone opens the lid and dumps a load of manure on us!"'

No doubt we all work for organisations which profess to follow one of the first two principles, but equally certainly, in practice we may feel we are treated in the third way from time to time—kept in the dark until the last minute, then expected to cope with all the problems which are heaped upon us!

To avoid this problem, management at all levels in the organisation should be aware of the importance of good communication, both inside and outside the organisation.

What is communication?

Communication is all about the passing of information. It is either a request for information: 'What are the sales figures for credit card this month?' or the supply of information: 'These are the figures for credit-card sale this month'. Information is needed for all aspects of management in an organisation: for better planning, to aid decision-making and problem-solving, to create understanding between people, and for effective control.

Most of the communication effort in an organisation is directed within the organisation and is never seen outside; the remainder concerns groups external to the organisation (e.g. customers, suppliers, etc.). Here we are concerned with internal communications.

The manager needs to communicate with his boss, colleagues, subordinates, other departments, perhaps staff representative bodies, and so on. There are dangers both in communicating too little, so that people are not kept fully informed of what they need to know to perform their jobs properly, and in communicating so much that people are swamped with information and cannot easily pick out what is important.

Need to know

The American phrase used to sum up this dilemma is 'Need to Know' vs. 'Nice to Know'. In other words, there are some pieces of information which a person **must** know to do his job; there are other bits of information which may be interesting but which, if that person is busy, will only distract him from the essentials. The skill of management is to be able to separate the two.

Some managers tend to withhold information to enhance their own power or status; others divulge information too widely, when it should be kept to a particular level of management or to a particular part of the organisation. However, within organisations there can be a tendency to withhold information unnecessarily. This can be the cause of friction between management and workers, since the workers will continue to speculate on matters on which management is being secretive—leading to rumour and gossip which can be more damaging than if the truth had been told in the first place.

Means of communication in an organisation

The manager must first decide with whom he needs to communicate. This will help determine the best method—oral or written.

Oral communication may be by telephone, face-to-face with one individual or a small group, in a presentation to a larger group, or by making use of the organisational structure to cascade information down to the right people.

Within the organisation, formal communication will often be written to ensure that a record is kept. Written communications can take a variety of forms:

Reports

These are often prepared by a subordinate for the boss or for a more senior group of people.

Letters

These would normally be used for communication downwards, e.g. to advise a member of staff of a change in his employment conditions (salary or grading change, promotion, etc.).

Memoranda

A memorandum (a note, usually in a standard format, for communication within an organisation) is often used when one person needs to communicate with several others, either colleagues or subordinates. A copy is sent to each person who needs to read it.

Noticeboards

Where many people need to receive information, but do not need their own copy, a noticeboard may be used. The disadvantage is that it is difficult to force people to read items on a board, which often becomes cluttered with out-of-date material unless someone is specifically charged with looking after it.

Company newspaper/house magazine

Most large organisations have such a publication, which is circulated to all staff on a regular basis. It is a good platform for management to communicate in a fairly informal way with their staff and for the sections of a large group to keep others informed of what they do. In modern companies, written communications of this sort are often supplemented by videos in which the senior management can communicate their message to the staff in a more friendly and direct way. This may be the only time that staff in distant branches ever see the faces of their ultimate bosses.

Circulars

These are a familiar means of communication in most banks. They are used when management must advise the staff formally of changes in rules or procedures and for other information which must be distributed widely and quickly. The danger is that people will be swamped with too many circulars and be unable to keep up-to-date with all the changes.

Manuals and workaids

These are also very familiar to bankers. The 'book-of-words' or 'bible' sets out the approved method of dealing with a variety of work situations, avoiding inconsistencies and mistakes which might result if there were no standardisation.

Annual Report and Accounts

As well as being a statutory requirement for all limited companies, the production of an Annual Report gives the company the opportunity to tell shareholders, customers and city analysts more about the company, and in particular about its successes during the year. It is becoming more and more common for a company to produce a special edition of this report for its staff, explaining the company's performance during the year and outlining the role the staff have played in achieving this.

Emphasising the dangers of swamping staff with information was a survey of accountancy and personnel managers carried out recently and reported in the *Sunday Telegraph* in October 1989. Two-thirds of the managers surveyed stated that memos 'ruled their lives' and reported that they received an average of between 10 and 20 memos each week, most of which were useless. A clinical psychologist, commenting on these results, suggested that certain types of managers use memos as a vehicle for orders and commands, as a reminder of who is in charge. He felt such managers were probably insecure in their status, had little faith in their ability and had possibly been overpromoted. Can you recognise any of your managers in that description?

■ Centralisation vs. decentralisation

How an organisation can be divided

As soon as an organisation grows larger than a single office or a few staff, the question of how it is to be divided arises.

The most common ways, with examples from banking, are:

- by geography (e.g. country, region);
- by division (e.g. retail banking, merchant banking, treasury);
- by function (e.g. sales, marketing operations, administration);
- by product (e.g. mortgages, deposits, loans, credit cards);
- by customer (e.g. personal, small business, large corporate);
- by process (less common in banking—used for example in production line manufacturing);
- by letter (e.g. one person deals with customers whose surnames begin with A, B, and C; another with D, E, and F, etc.).

If you consider these options, you will see that the same company could choose to divide its operations in several ways. For example, a bank could group its personnel functions for all its divisions, or it could have separate personnel departments in each division, grouping all the functions in its merchant banking division together.

The decision concerning which way to divide the organisation is a strategic one which will be taken by the executive management, usually based on what they see as the most logical or most cost–effective solution, or the way which most closely matches the goals and aspirations of the organisation.

Centralise or decentralise?

An essential element in the design of a corporate structure is the extent to which authority should be kept at the top of the organisation or passed down the line to management in the divisions or branches. If all decisions are taken by the owner of a small business, or by a very small group of senior managers in the head office of a large organisation, then this is described as a centralised structure. Conversely, if the power to take decisions is passed down the line, then this is a relatively decentralised structure.

We are referring here to nonroutine decisions, since routine decisions (once made at the centre) can be repeated by lower-level management, when the same set of circumstances arises, without the need for discretionary authority.

The traditional view was that, by reserving these discretionary nonroutine decisions for top management, they were made more effectively, with better use of management time. The problem in large organisations is that there are only a limited number of people in this decision-making core and beyond a certain point they will become overloaded and inefficient—it will take too long for decisions to be transmitted back to 'the sharp end'.

One practical solution is to decentralise decision making to appropriate divisions, functions, etc. (as described above). These semi-autonomous units then have a free hand, within clearly defined limits, and the main board confines itself to really important policy decisions. This also has the benefit that the divisions are more closely in touch with market conditions, changes in the business environment and so on, and can therefore respond more quickly and more effectively to changes than if all decisions have to be referred upwards, with supporting information and recommendations.

In the banks, many have taken this route by decentralising decisions on lending propositions to regional or divisional management centres, with only the very largest propositions (perhaps £10m, £50m or £100m and above, depending on the size of the bank) being referred upwards to the top management or the board.

Benefits of decentralisation

Decentralisation is a useful means of encouraging participation and commitment from the groups and individuals lower down in the organisation. It may help solve some of the problems of 'worker participation' which stem from the difficulty of incorporating the views of large and diverse groups of workers at the policy-making levels of large organisations. Arguably, uniformity has been stressed too much and we should look for a diversity of approach reflecting the various skills and attributes of the different units of a large organisation and the people who work in them.

Other advantages are the freeing of valuable senior executive time and the positive training benefits of allowing more junior staff to take the responsibility for decisions.

Disadvantages of decentralisation

These include the potential loss of control, and a possible lack of unified direction in the organisation.

Factors affecting the decision to decentralise

When a large company is formed from the merger of smaller units, some degree of centralisation may be necessary in the early stages until a sense of cohesion is achieved, then decentralisation may take over to get the best from each unit.

If customers demand quick decisions, this will indicate a need for decision-making at a local level, particularly if competitors can gain an advantage in this respect.

A major factor to be considered is the extent to which senior management trust their more junior colleagues; clearly such trust is a prerequisite for decentralisation.

Sir Adrian Cadbury, a past Chairman of Cadbury Schweppes, is quoted as saying:

> 'When faced with more intense competition, British companies typically found themselves overmanned, overcentralised and trying to control too many activities. To survive they had to take action on two fronts. The first was to cut their costs, the second was to speed up their ability to respond to more rapidly changing markets. They cut costs by reducing the number of employees and by reducing the burden of central services. They speeded up decision-making by eliminating as many levels of authority as they could and by pushing the point of decision as near to the marketplace as possible.'

∎ Cooperation between departments

As soon as an organisation is divided up into departments, there arises a possibility of conflict between those departments. This is particularly true if there is perceived to be competition for scarce resources (staff, machinery, computer time, etc.) or where the goals of the departments are different.

To avoid such conflicts requires management to exercise a coordinating function (see Chapter 8, Managing the system).

Importance of shared goals

As mentioned above, one reason for noncooperation may be a difference of perspective or goals. For example, a production department may be aiming to produce a perfect product, however long that takes, whereas the sales department may be anxious to have products available quickly to satisfy customer orders, even if those products are not always of the highest quality. To overcome this, the senior management of the company must ensure that the overall goals of the organisation are clearly defined and well explained to the next level of management, who in turn must ensure that each department is well aware of these goals, and of the way that the aims of the department fit into the overall plan.

The internal customer

Each department in the organisation will be dependent on others, or will have others depending on it. For example, the sales department depends on production to supply the goods, but conversely production relies on sales to find the customers to take the goods and generate the profits. Each will depend on the accounting function to keep the paperwork running smoothly and to pay their wages on time, and so on.

In other words, these departments are customers and suppliers to each other, just as much as the external customers and suppliers, and must equally be treated with courtesy and respect if the relationship is to be a mutually beneficial one.

To improve understanding of each other's roles, it is helpful if staff from each department can visit one another from time to time. It is much easier to deal with someone you have met, rather than just speaking on the telephone or perhaps only receiving a curt memo from time to time. This can be extended to social visits—inviting contacts from another department out to the pub one lunchtime, or to join in a sports event, can help enormously in breaking down barriers of suspicion or mistrust.

Appropriate reward systems

The company should also ensure that the reward system (pay scales, bonuses, etc.) encourages cooperation between departments towards shared goals, rather than competition between departments towards individual and conflicting goals at the expense of the overall organisational benefit.

See also the answer to Question 4 at the end of this chapter for more ideas.

▊ Action points

(a) What type of organisational structure do you think your company has? Is the structure of your local office any different from other local offices?

(b) How does your management try to cope with the problems this structure brings? Do they succeed?

(c) How would you define the culture in your own organisation?

(d) What clues would a newcomer to your office pick up about the culture?

(e) Where would you place your organisation on the matrix in Fig. 4.8?

(f) What steps has your bank or office taken recently to cut down on 'red tape'?

(g) Count up how many types of communication you have received or been exposed to in your organisation in a week.

(h) How effective was each method—do you think it was the right medium in each case for the type of message being delivered?

(i) Is your organisation moving towards more centralisation or more decentralisation? Why?

(j) Think which other departments in your organisation are your internal customers. Is your department the customer of another department? How could relationships between the departments be improved in each case?

Questions and answers

Question 1
What are the probable implications of technological change for

(a) the organisational structure of banks; [13]

(b) staffing in the banks? [12]

[Total marks for question—25]

(N.B. Only the first part of the question is answered below. The second part is addressed in Chapter 3, under the heading Human resource management.)

Question 2
As an organisation grows in size and complexity, one of the problems which it needs to address is to what extent decision-making authority should remain centralised.

(a) Describe the factors which influence the extent to which an organisation is decentralised [18]

(b) What developments have led to the current trend towards greater decentralisation? [7]

[Total marks for question—25]

(*Hint*: Note the split of marks between the two parts, and be aware of the use of the words 'decision-making authority' in the first sentence—this question does not ask about decentralisation in general.)

Question 3
Although many banks offer similar services, they often adopt contrasting styles in their approach to business operations, organisation, staff and customers.

(a) How do you explain these differences of style? [15]

(b) How can a bank change its style? What should it do and what methods should it use? [10]

[Total marks for question—25]

(*Hint*: Remember that the word 'style' in this context is another way of describing 'culture' or 'climate.')

Question 4
A recently appointed senior manager of a large city branch is concerned that the work of the branch does not flow smoothly.

His departmental heads are capable managers. The objectives which they set their departments are clear, challenging and generally achieved.

Nevertheless:

— A worrying number of customers have complained of delays when the work of more than one department is involved.

— Reports which require input from different departments are generally submitted close to deadlines and are sometimes late.
— There is an atmosphere of competitive rivalry (or even hostility) between departments.
— There is evidence of a number of breakdowns in communication between departments.

(a) What are the possible causes of this lack of interdepartmental coordination? [12]

(b) What steps could be taken to deal with this problem? [13]

[Total marks for question—25]

Answer 1

For part (b) see Chapter 3.

(a) *Decision making:* The possibility of speedy access to a wider range and depth of information has important implications. It might encourage centralisation because headquarters can assemble information and despatch it very rapidly. On the other hand, it could encourage decentralisation because local managers would be able to get key information which was not accessible before, or took too long to obtain.

Management status: It is likely that operational managers will become more dependent on support services and specialists who supply the information and may suffer a reduction in status as a consequence.

Computers: As computers become more sophisticated, the integrated and systems nature of the organisation may become more apparent.

Traditional hierarchical values: These might be challenged if power is pushed down the organisation, and the power of specialists and support groups becomes more obvious.

Work design: Technology encourages the creation of very interesting work for some, but it is also possible that some jobs (e.g. data input) might become extremely boring and those responsible for establishing work patterns might have to balance the theoretical advantages against the need of staff for job satisfaction.

Move from mechanistic to organic structures: This may result as the emphasis will be on systems, integration and cooperative decision-making as opposed to individual, fragmented hierarchical structures.

Branch structure: There could be dramatic modifications to the branch and regional structure as routine business is increasingly automated.

Answer 2

(a) Factors influencing the decision to decentralise include:

(i) The organisational culture – does it have a background of tight central control, or one of subordinate independence?

(ii) The organisation's size—as it grows, communication becomes more complex and thus there is a tendency towards decentralisation.

(iii) The rate of growth—an organisation which is growing quickly is unlikely to be able to set up rigorous central controls.

(iv) The demands of the marketplace—does the organisation provide the quality of service demanded by its customers (e.g. the turnaround time for a decision)? Does the service provided measure up to that of the competition (e.g. can the customer get it more cheaply next door)?

(v) The capacity of the management—are the senior managers capable of relinquishing their authority? Are the junior managers capable of accepting it?

(vi) The impact of the decision—what will be the effect on the performance of the organisation as a whole of relatively important decisions being taken by relatively junior management?

(vii) The need for consistency—to what extent will the organisation be 'embarrassed' if two local managers make conflicting decisions?

(viii) The nature of the decision—is special expertise needed (e.g. legal)? Are line managers likely to possess the relevant expertise, or even sufficient knowledge to know that they must take advice?

(b) The developments which are leading to decentralisation are:

(i) Technology—information systems have enhanced the ability of local management to make appropriate decisions. Communication systems have also made it possible for speedier decisions to be made and for central management to be able to monitor the activity of local management more readily.

(ii) Social and educational developments have led to a more sophisticated workforce better able to make appropriate decisions and less likely to appreciate strong central control.

(iii) The pressure for change has led to the need for organisations to develop their people more rapidly than in the past. This is often accomplished through a process of decentralisation.

(iv) The trend towards entrepreneurial activity within society at large has led to entrepreneurial activity within organisations being accorded a higher value than hitherto.

Answer 3

(This answer is given in abbreviated note form. Slightly more detail would be advisable in a real examination so that the examiner is sure you know what you mean.)

(a) Banks differ because of:
— origins and history,
— economic circumstances,
— leadership style,
— organisational policies and practice,
— organisational values, e.g. attitude to risk and customers,
— organisational structure, e.g. degree of decentralisation, extent of hierarchy, etc.,
— nature of business, e.g. merchant banking vs. retail banking,
— the life stage of the organisation.

(b) Bringing about change in the approach requires:
— a vision of a new way of doing things,
— leadership which can communicate the vision,
— a series of action steps which can bring about the new approach,

- setting of standards to ensure that the vision is realised publicly and praise for changes in the direction of the new approach to encourage the belief that change is possible and realisable,
- reward for those who change their approach,
- punishment for those who resist,
- handling problems at the earliest moment.

Answer 4

(a) The question implies that the lack of departmental coordination arises from:
   (i) Lack of clarity about the goals of the branch.
   (ii) Lack of direction as to how the branch goals are to be achieved.
   (iii) Interdepartmental rivalry encouraging a spirit of competition rather than cooperation.
   Further possible causes are:
   (iv) Different time horizons applying to the work of the various departments.
   (v) Inappropriate organisational structure which does not foster interdepartmental communication, coordination or control.
   (vi) Differences in departmental culture and language which make it difficult for departments to appreciate each other's point of view.
   (vii) A reward system which discourages or fails to encourage the achievement of interdepartmental goals.
   (viii) Interpersonal conflict between departmental heads.
   (ix) A history of interdepartmental competition which may have been beneficial in the past but which is no longer appropriate.
   (x) A lack of training or education designed to establish where the work of each department fits into the work of the branch.

(b) The branch manager could deal with the problem by:
   (i) Setting clear goals covering not only the individual objectives of each department but also the branch objectives which depend upon departmental cooperation.
   (ii) Setting each departmental head the goal of improving coordination and cooperation between his department and others affected by his work.
   (iii) Setting guidelines which indicate how branch goals, as opposed to departmental goals, are to be achieved.
   (iv) Monitoring progress towards the achievement of these goals.

In addition he could:
   (v) Examine the organisational structure to ensure that (a) it is appropriate to the branch; and (b) at key points where the work of two departments needs integrating, a coordinating mechanism exists.
   (vi) Set up or encourage interdepartmental coordinating mechanisms by means of committees, working parties, liaison officials, networks or project groups. He should ensure that these operate at the lowest level at which cooperation is required.
   (vii) Reward behaviour which encourages solutions to interdepartmental problems at the lowest possible level.

(viii) Encourage awareness of the work of other departments by job rotation or specific training initiatives.
(ix) Promote social activities which establish informal lines of communication across departments.
(x) Establish a concept of loyalty in which loyalty to the organisation and the branch is seen as being at least as important as loyalty to the department.

CHAPTER 5
Information Systems

● The importance of information ● The importance of technology ● Information Technology (IT) ● Management Information Systems (MIS) ● Budgetary control systems ● Risk assessment and risk management

■ The importance of information

The major importance of information can be summed up in the phrase: 'information is power'. Some people see that the possession of information will give them power; they suck it in, store it and use it in, say, a committee to wrong-foot an opponent or to suppress an inadequately prepared proposal.

The opposite style is to spread information very widely, so nothing is hidden and everyone has access to all that is available.

Both approaches have disadvantages. The manager who hides information may feel he is benefiting himself, but the efficiency and effective running of his organisation will suffer. The manager who floods his staff, colleagues and superiors with a mass of information is in danger of swamping them with unnecessary facts. They will spend so long sifting the important from the irrelevant that they will have less time to do their real work.

Information is a crucial element in every one of the management functions. Without information, plans would bear no relation to reality, decisions would be made in ignorance, there would be no way to measure success or failure and nothing to communicate to others. Information which is used by managers to make decisions and run a business is often referred to as 'Management Information' or MI, and the computerised systems which help provide it are called 'Management Information Systems' or MIS (see below).

Management information is of value only if it is accurate, timely, appropriate and correctly interpreted:

(a) Accurate, because incorrect information can lead to wrong decisions being made.

(b) Timely, because out-of-date information may be too old to be of use and may be misleading.

(c) Appropriate, because a mass of irrelevant information will just obscure that which is useful.

(d) Correctly interpreted, because unless the person receiving the information understands what it means and how to make use of it, it will be of little value.

The Americans coined a phrase which is becoming common in UK organisations—'Need to Know' vs. 'Nice to Know'. In other words, there is a distinction to be drawn between information which is important for someone's day-to-day work (that which they **need** to know) and information which they will find interesting but which is not essential (that which is **nice** to know).

This division is sometimes extended to three categories:

(a) Must know—essential information.
(b) Should know—important information.
(c) Could know—interesting but relatively unimportant information.

▌The importance of technology

Bank managers have always collected information about their customers to help them control lending, obtain new business, etc. With the aid of computers, the same information can be found much more quickly, sorted and selected in a chosen order, reported only when something goes wrong, and so on. In this way the manager can make the most of his time by avoiding the need to search manually through files full of paper for the information he needs.

There is no need here to go into the highly technical details of the way computers manipulate and produce information—any computer textbook will give you technical details if the subject interests you. What is important for the Management in Banking syllabus is that you should appreciate the ways in which technology can assist the manager in the speedier, more efficient provision of information.

Computers cannot generate information out of thin air, but what they can do is to take in raw data and, by means of programs written by intelligent human beings, sort, analyse and interpret the data so that it becomes meaningful information.

Computerised information for businesses

Well programmed computers can easily produce information for the managers of any business, sometimes in almost too great a profusion. For example, statistics about sales, purchases, capital expenditure, value-added tax, payrolls, etc., can give excellent control of cash flow, credit allowed to customers, departmental expenditure in relation to budgets, etc.

There is a danger in some industries that the statistics on the amount of work done by, for example, check-out operators or typists using word-processors linked to a computer, may be used by managers to discipline members of staff, or decide rates of pay, without looking into the different circumstances in which the members of staff may be operating. For example, a typist dealing with complex legal documents will almost certainly have a slower rate of output than a typist dealing with straightforward letters. The moral is that computer information, like all statistics, must be treated with care and one should not make important decisions based on a single piece of information in isolation.

Computerised information for banks

Computerised management information may be delivered in the form of a display on a VDU (visual display unit) for instantly required items, or printed out, either immediately by a printer in the branch or department, or by a central printer and despatched to reach the branch the next morning.

The types of reports which can be produced to give management information are virtually limitless. They may be designed by the head office or regional office to be standard for all branches, or they may be specified by the particular manager concerned.

The simplest example perhaps is the response to a balance enquiry. Each bank will have its own particular format, but most will have a system by which a member of staff in a branch can tap in a simple enquiry over their terminal keyboard and obtain a picture or printout of the balance of a customer's account, perhaps showing whether the balance is cleared, whether any overdraft limit has been agreed, whether any debits or credits have been presented in that day's clearing which will affect the balance, and whether there are any other associated accounts held by that customer.

Other examples are:

(a) Warning list of accounts which will go overdrawn or over-limit if cheques presented in the morning clearing are paid.
(b) Notice of items in the clearing which cannot be automatically applied to the relevant account (perhaps an item drawn on a closed account, or one which has been transferred to another branch).
(c) List of accounts with limits which are due for review.
(d) Accounts which are dormant, or which have not received any credits within a certain period (this is a possible early warning sign of default and needs investigation).
(e) Printouts for regional management comparing one branch's performance with another: number of accounts, volume of lending, level of bad debts, achievement of targets, profit generated and so on.
(f) Analyses of the various accounts, plastic cards and other services used by a customer—these are used in marketing campaigns to help identify possible sales targets (they can be adapted to corporate as well as personal accounts).
(g) A printout of the charges to be levied on each account can be prepared prior to the passing of the charges, to give the manager an opportunity to adjust them in the light of his personal knowledge of the account. This is an example of a situation in which what the computer has calculated may be strictly accurate, but the human touch is needed to make it also appropriate.

All the various printouts which your branch or department receives are forms of management information. The examples above relate particularly to branch banking, but if you work in a merchant bank, an investment bank or some other financial institution, I am sure you can draw up your own list of the useful computer-produced printouts you or your manager receive.

The use of computers in banks

The introduction of computers to the operation of the major clearing banks' branches, which started around 1970, revolutionised the way the branches operate.

Tasks which had previously been carried out laboriously by hand or using cumbersome ledger posting machines could be processed much faster and in greater numbers by computer. At first it was assumed, as in many industries, that this would result in a significant reduction in the numbers of staff required to carry out the basic clerical tasks. In fact it soon became clear that the development of computerisation was taking place at the same time as a huge rise in the numbers of people wanting to open bank accounts. As a result staff were redeployed to tasks involving more direct customer contact, whilst the computer dealt with the basic bookkeeping tasks.

At first sight, the uses of the computer listed below may not seem to have much to do with management information but in every case, as well as performing some function (often account maintenance or money transmission), the computer is also providing management information. Whether the managers make full use of this information is another matter. This will depend on various factors as discussed under 'Management Information Systems' below.

Cashiering

In the last few years, many banks have adopted a system of counter terminals, where the cashier can enter details of items cashed or paid in over the counter directly, via a keyboard, to the central computer. Depending on the individual bank's practice, the cashier may also make balance enquiries before cashing a cheque, or carry out transfers between accounts at a customer's request, etc.

Standing orders

Before the advent of the computer, a series of index cards had to be maintained: one for every standing order, for every customer, filed in date order. The standing-order clerk had to create a Bank Giro credit or internal voucher for every payment to be made, with a corresponding debit to the customer's account (often the card itself), then refile the card carefully at the date of the next payment due. Nowadays the clerk fills out a standing order input form, on first receipt of the customer's instructions or on any future amendment. This programs the computer to make the necessary payments, on the due dates, either until the final payment or until further notice, as appropriate. The Bankers' Automated Clearing System (BACS or Bureau) sheet showing the debit to the customer's account is received by the branch a few days before the debit is made, giving the manager time to return or 'bounce' the payment if the customer does not have enough money in his account to cover it. The credit to the beneficiary is also made through the BACS system.

Direct debits

The introduction of computers made possible the system of direct debits, which is now a widespread method of settling bills, particularly annual or monthly amounts which may vary. Effectively, a direct debit is a standing order initiated by the recipient rather than the customer. The customer signs a Variable Amount Direct Debit mandate authorising the beneficiary to request payment, through the BACS system again, from the customer's account on the due date. This is ideal, for example, for water rates payments which occur 10 times a year and may vary slightly from month to month, or for an annual subscription which tends to increase each year. It is even possible now to pay your telephone bill by direct debit. Once again, the manager has advance information to allow a decision on payment to be made.

Securities department

Full details of the security held against a loan may be maintained on the computer, allowing checks to be made that security has been completed, that insurance payments on a property are up-to-date, etc. This also means central management may analyse the security held throughout the bank—the percentage cover on mortgage loans, for example. The calculation of interest on mortgages, particularly with the complications of MIRAS (Mortgage Interest Relief At Source), is made much simpler by the use of a computer, which can take in its stride the numerous changes in interest rate and consequent changes in monthly repayment that are inevitable at a time of rapidly fluctuating rates.

There is no need to run through all the departments which use the computer—this will have given you a flavour for what a difference it has made. Try to make a list of all the times you make use of a computer in your day's work and imagine what your job would be like without it!

▌ Information Technology (IT)

What IT means

Over the last few years the initials IT for Information Technology have been springing up all over the place. Every newspaper article relating to management, education or office practice seems to refer to the 'IT Revolution', but what does IT really mean?

In essence, IT refers to the integrated use of high technology linking a whole variety of activities in the office. Advancing computer technology brings more power at lower prices. Telecommunications and electronic office machines are becoming ever more flexible, more sophisticated, yet easier to use. Computers are linked together within organisations and between organisations by telecommunications networks. British Telecom's exchanges are being computerised and can be linked with data transfer systems.

Traditional office machines are being replaced by high-tech alternatives: the facsimile transmission machine (fax) can send a copy of any document down a telephone wire to be printed out by a similar machine anywhere in the world within a few seconds or minutes.

The word processor is replacing the typewriter and, when extended to an office automation system, allows documents and messages to be sent across a network to any linked terminal elsewhere. This is one step towards the 'paperless office' which was much heralded a few years ago. It is unlikely that paper will ever disappear completely, but as people learn to rely on the performance of automated data storage and retrieval systems, the quantity of paper files will at least be reduced.

Many managers now have a terminal on their desk which gives them access to electronic mail, simple word processing to allow them to create their own notes and memos, a database on which they can look up financial information or statistics on their company or departmental performance, a spreadsheet package to allow them to set up accounting information for themselves, and so on.

Calendars, diaries, filing cabinets and wallcharts can all be made obsolete by office automation systems now available.

It is vital that managers understand IT and how it may affect their firms and their jobs, so that they recognise the opportunities which IT offers. It is likely that IT will change the management environment. In the process some managerial jobs may be eliminated but others will be created. Younger managers may adapt to the changes relatively easily and learn the necessary new skills, though they may find that there are fewer management jobs for which to compete. Older managers may find the changes more difficult, but if they are too resistant to the challenge of IT, they may find that their organisation is not prepared to retain their services.

You may know managers yourself who will always ask a junior member of staff to get the manager's balance out of the terminal, or perform other simple tasks. This may be an attempt by the manager to assert his status by not deigning to operate 'the machine', but it may also indicate that the manager is frightened by the new technology which he does not understand. Gradually these managers are being forced out of the banks, as newer managers with more flexible ideas come through.

IT means more than just computers, it is the bringing together of all aspects of information handling. In particular IT denotes the marriage of conventional computing with telecommunications.

Computer productivity and centralisation

The first computers, in the 1950s, cost a million pounds or more, needed air-conditioned rooms the size of a tennis court, broke down often and had a limited capacity.

Now, for a few thousand pounds one can buy a more powerful, much speedier computer to fit on a desktop, with a far greater storage capacity. The cost of power and capacity is reducing all the time.

In the early days of computing, hardware was expensive and software relatively cheap. Now the position is reversed, with hardware costs falling by around 90 per cent every seven years whilst the labour-intensive software (programs) costs are still rising rapidly.

There is an increasing trend towards buying 'off the shelf' software rather than having it tailormade for the specific organisation. The proliferation of software houses has meant that there is a very wide choice of ready-made packages, e.g. for the hotel industry, travel firms, airlines, the estate agent, the solicitor, the farmer, even the publican. Very large organisations such as the clearing banks may still have software written specially, but even they tend to buy a package and customise it rather than start from scratch.

Another change has been the extent to which computers are fully utilised. When a computer might cost £100,000 it had to be kept fully utilised to justify the investment. Programmers commonly had to wait days for computer time to test their programs. Now it is the labour costs which are high and the programmer will have immediate access to a powerful computer from the terminal on his desk. Similarly, managers and other users who need instant information have immediate access through a desktop terminal even if, like the telephone, it is used for only a few minutes a day.

The high cost of early computer equipment inevitably led to centralisation. However, the need for the information the computer can provide is largely at the periphery of the organisation, not at the centre. The use of networks of terminals, linked electronically to a central computer, has overcome this difficulty. Users now expect to wait only a matter of seconds for the information they require to appear on their terminal.

Management Information Systems (MIS)

What is MIS?

The term Management Information System (MIS) is usually employed to mean a computerised system which marshals information from a variety of sources, and presents it in a form most useful to the manager and in a way which will assist in the decision-making process. MIS systems attempt to overcome the tendency of many data-processing techniques to swamp the manager with data. The cynic has long recognised that an effective way to hide an important item of information is to surround it with a vast amount of other information which may be correct, but is irrelevant. The answer is to use 'exception reporting', where only information which falls outside given parameters or normal values is reported.

In designing an MIS, the most important step is the establishment of an effective database, geared to the requirements of managers throughout the organisation, in which an item of information is stored only once, but account is taken of its different aspects so that it can be kept up-to-date and made available in different contexts to managers of different levels in different functional areas.

Questions of access to information, security, classification and indexing, information input and updating, the length of time data is to be stored, arrangements for storing old data and information in archives, contingency arrangements in the event of a system fault, etc., all need attention before the MIS is set up.

MIS as an aid to decision-making

Both decision-making and control are essential functions of management that depend on information, which may be regarded as data to which some meaning has been attached.

Exception reporting can help management both in controlling and in decision-making, since only departures from the plan which are sufficiently great to merit the attention of the particular grade of manager concerned are reported to him for control purposes and in decision-making, only those factors thought to have a significant bearing on the decision at that level are taken into account.

There is a danger with exception reporting, though: the manager may become out of touch with the reality of what is happening at the lower levels of the organisation.

The vast improvement in dataprocessing which has been made possible with the common use of computers has allowed managers to think in terms of some decision-making being reduced to routine, whilst other decisions can be made more effectively. The computer can rapidly perform such calculations as are required in programmable decision-making, whilst other decisions may be improved by information being available much more quickly.

In branch banking, an obvious example of programmed decision-making is the automation of credit scoring. A series of scores are given to an application for an account, a loan, a credit card or some other product, depending on a scale of values designed to reflect the reliability of the customer. These scores are fed into a computer terminal and analysed by a program which gives a decision (or recommendation, if preferred) on a purely statistical basis. This allows the granting of a facility to be delegated to a much more junior level of staff than if personal experience were to be a factor in the decision.

An extension of this type of program is the 'expert system'. This is a computer program which is designed to take the accumulated wisdom of a person (or persons) expert in his field and make it available to anyone accessing the program. This concept has been used to devise diagnostic programs for use in the medical profession—by answering a series of questions on symptoms, etc., the program will suggest clinical tests which should be carried out, give possible diagnoses and so on. It has also been used to enable a customer in a travel agency to choose a holiday by answering a series of questions on a computer screen so that the program can recommend a suitable destination, hotel, etc. There are possible applications for expert systems in almost any business or profession—the scope of the idea is only just beginning to be tested.

Future developments in MIS

Management Information Systems are designed to be used by the non-systems professional manager, so they are as 'user-friendly' as possible. They may be menu-driven, leading the user step-by-step through the facilities available, or they may allow access by means other than the keyboard, e.g. by use of light pens, a 'mouse' (a handheld gadget which can be moved around on the desktop to move the cursor on the screen—a click on the mouse will select the item being pointed to on screen), or a touch-sensitive screen. Computers which will respond to the spoken word are still being developed.

A major development still on the horizon are the so-called fifth-generation (5G) computer languages which claim to be interactive with the user. The idea is that the computer will learn the habits of the user in order to respond more quickly the next time. For example, if a manager wants to call up the sales figures for a particular region for the last month, he might type in 'What were the sales for Essex in March?'. The computer holds data for 'Units Sold', but it has been programmed to accept a variety of substitutes for some words. It might respond 'By Sales do you mean Units Sold?'. The manager replies in the affirmative, and the computer stores the information that Mr Smith uses the word Sales to mean Units Sold. Next time Mr Smith logs on, the computer already knows some of his idiosyncrasies and will not need to ask the same question again. This is a simplistic example, but illustrates the way a computer can be programmed to learn from the user.

▌Budgetary control systems

Budgets

A budget is a statement expressing plans for a future period, usually in monetary terms. A bank may decide that, next year, there will be an increase in the number of university branches to bring in more student accounts. That is a plan, but to put it in monetary terms requires a budget. This will detail the amount to be spent on the new premises, the number and cost of additional staff involved, the anticipated income to be generated, and so on.

Each department will prepare its own budget; these are sent up the line to be amalgamated into higher level budgets, and finally the overall budget for the organisation itself. By moving upwards in this way, it is possible for higher-level management to ensure that lower-level budgets are in line with overall corporate strategy. The central finance function will be able to plan how much money needs to be raised from external sources or how much can be invested at different times of the year.

You probably do some kind of budgeting yourself, so that you know how much you can afford to put aside in savings, whether you will be able to save enough in time for your holiday this year, or whether you can afford to buy that luxury item next month. If you run a household, your budgeting will be more complex—allowing for all the bills, food, the mortgage, etc., as well as deciding how much you can spend on clothes and entertainment and still have enough left to buy your season ticket. The principle is exactly the same for a company—it must budget to make sure it can afford to pay its staff their wages, settle suppliers' bills, etc., and have enough left from the income generated by sales to cover capital investment. Otherwise the company must either prune its expenditure plans, or plan to raise money in other ways (from a bank, by making rights issues, or issuing debentures etc.).

Budgetary control

A budgetary control system compares actual costs and achievements with planned achievements and allocations of financial and other resources, and is probably the most widely used of all methods of financial control.

Upper spending limits (or minimum performance standards—sales or production levels, for example) are set for a variety of activities or functions, e.g. salaries, overtime, purchase of supplies, expenditure on training, replacement of office equipment. The budget is usually set for 12 months, and actual expenditure or performance is reviewed against the budget periodically, often monthly. There are five main steps in achieving budgetary control:

- **Prepare Budget**—preparation of a budget for each section of the organisation and the aggregation of the sectional budgets into a full organisational budget. This can be expressed in the form of a forecast Profit and Loss Account and Balance Sheet.
- **Record Actuals**—recording of the actual expenditure and income in the same framework as the budgets.
- **Compare Budget/Actuals**—comparison of budgeted and actual expenditure.
- **Reasons for Variances**—ascertaining reasons for any variances from budgeted amounts.
- **Take Corrective Action**—taking action to bring the results of the current period into line with the original budget or any agreed revision of it.

A good budgetary control system should:

(a) have the support of top management;
(b) be in line with long-term aims and strategies of the organisation;
(c) be prepared in good time;
(d) involve managers at every level of responsibility;
(e) be flexible enough to allow revisions;
(f) be understood by all who use it.

It is much better if the budget is drawn up by the managers who will be responsible for controlling the expenditure mentioned in it, rather than being drawn up centrally and imposed on management lower down the organisation.

Reasons for variances

When the actual expenditure in a certain category is compared with the budgeted expenditure there will almost always be a variance, since budgets are estimates of the future and, without the help of a crystal ball, are unlikely to be precisely accurate.

If the variance is small it may well be ignored, but if the percentage variance is more than (say) 10 per cent, the cause must be examined.

To take a banking example, suppose the central statement despatch department budgets £12,000 for envelopes for the year. The budget expenditure for one month is therefore £1,000. If in a certain month the actual expenditure on envelopes is £1,300 (a variance of +30 per cent against the budget), we must ask why.

There are a variety of possible reasons for the variance:

(a) The cost per envelope has gone up because:
    (i) The supplier has raised prices, or
    (ii) more expensive envelopes are being used.
(b) The number of envelopes used has gone up because:
    (i) more accounts are being opened so more statements are being despatched, or
    (ii) a new machine has been installed which damages more envelopes than before, or
    (iii) there has been a loss of stock due to pilfering.

The management must examine all these possibilities to determine whether it is possible to reverse the variance by taking action (e.g. having the machine serviced to reduce damage, or changing the supplier to cut costs), or whether the cause is outside the control of the department (e.g. more accounts leading to more statements), in which case the budget needs to be revised to take account of this external factor.

The latter is an example of a case where an apparent adverse variance is in fact a desirable result, as it reflects increased sales.

The best type of budgetary control system will produce a report which highlights this fact by showing exactly what has happened and why. Indeed, the budget report is a vital element in the budgeting process. It should be produced regularly (often monthly) and show directly comparable figures for actual and budget amounts so that like is compared with like. The report should be simple and straightforward, avoiding overloading the recipient with excess information.

Taking corrective action

The most important and perhaps the most difficult part of budgetary control is ensuring that the fifth step is actually taken, i.e. that those responsible for the company's success **do** take the appropriate action to remedy problems revealed.

Since a budget is usually drawn up some time before the period to which it refers, which itself may be 12 months long, it is almost inevitable that events in the environment or inside the company will change during the life of the budget and may require corresponding amendments to be made to the budget.

For example, in banking, an unexpected and dramatic change in interest rates will have far-reaching implications for the income stream of the bank. Similarly, government legislation may alter the way the bank has to do business (e.g. the introduction of MIRAS—mortgage interest relief at source—caused extra work for the banks, whereas the abolition of exchange controls in 1979 had substantially reduced staffing requirements in some departments). Such changes must be reflected in revised budgets, or comparison of actual and budgeted figures will be nonsensical. Budgets are often reviewed and revised quarterly.

Methods (good and bad) of creating budgets

When a manager is asked to prepare a budget for his department, he could start with a blank sheet of paper and calculate what he needs to be able to do his job satisfactorily. This is sometimes known as 'zero-based budgeting'. The zero-based approach attempts to solve the problem of managers deliberately overspending in order to increase future allocations. There is no presumption that the amount allocated for the period will be repeated; instead, each budget is initially set at zero, so that heads of department must argue for new allocations at the start of every period. The benefit is that managers are forced periodically to review their plans and working methods and are thus encouraged to identify high-cost activities. The disadvantage is that an enormous amount of managerial time and effort must be devoted to the budgetary process.

An alternative is for the manager to take the previous year's figures, adding a percentage to cover inflation, and adjusting to allow for any known external factors (e.g. suppliers' price rises due) and for changes in the volume of work expected. When incorporating inflation into budgets, it is important to remember that its effects are not evenly spread. Not all costs go up by the same amount: for example, the cost of computer hardware may actually fall from one period to the next, whereas the cost of oil for heating may go up or down depending on the movements in the oil market. Any element of the budget which is dependent on payment to or receipts from an overseas country must also take account of likely exchange rate fluctuations (very important for banks), and so on.

Unfortunately, since many organisations have a tendency to prune departmental budgets when they are passed up the line for approval, many managers will automatically add a safety margin to all the items on their budget so that, when reduced, the values will be in line with what they really wanted in the first place.

This is not uncommon, particularly in large organisations, and gives budgetary control a bad name. It is most common when the committee vetting the budgets is more concerned that the overall number looks good than with examining the individual budgets to see that they represent a realistic appraisal of likely business conditions over the following period.

Another false method of creating the budget is to pad the figures in the first place, so that actual results will show a favourable variance and reflect credit on the apparent skill of the manager in controlling spending (and will cover up any minor slippages!). This should be spotted by the central control function, particularly if a certain manager consistently produces large favourable variances year after year. Clearly it is undesirable for these practices to be permitted as they bring the system into disrepute and make a mockery of what should be a serious and useful exercise to aid control of the business.

Depending on the nature of the business, separate budgets may be drawn up for different functions, such as Sales budget, Capital budget, Cash budget, etc. It is not necessary to study these in detail for the Management in Banking examination, but if you go on to take the Financial Studies Diploma you will study business planning and control in much greater depth.

Some problems of budgetary control

Some of the devices which poor managers may use to distort the budgeting process have been described above. There may also be a problem if managers become so cost-conscious that they regard cutting costs as more important than implementation of the measures needed to improve performance.

If budgets are too detailed, not only will they inevitably be inaccurate (since the more specific the predictions of the future, the greater the likelihood they will be wrong), but also the time spent preparing such detailed budgets will be inordinately long and costly.

Once a budget has been allocated, some managers will seek to spend the entire amount, even though realistically not all the funds are needed, out of a misguided fear that to underspend will mean a reduction in budget allocation for the following period.

It is difficult to distinguish between a budget which has been exceeded through incompetence and one exceeded through genuine additional spending needs. This is where the identification of the reasons for variances, discussed above, becomes so important.

▌ Risk assessment and risk management

Risks and management

Taking risks is part of the essence of management: not taking unnecessary or foolish risks, but taking calculated risks—balancing risk against reward.

A manager who never took a risk would never achieve anything, he would simply maintain the *status quo* and not progress. His staff would perhaps feel very safe and secure, but they might also be very bored and would always be left behind in any change or innovation going on in the organisation.

Everyone makes mistakes sometimes, and one can never eliminate risk altogether, but by:

(a) identifying the areas where risk can arise,
(b) measuring the degree of risk,
(c) agreeing on an acceptable level of risk, and
(d) managing the business to the agreed level of risk, by instituting the appropriate controls and monitoring procedures,

the manager can **manage** the risk effectively.

Here we are talking of:

— the risk that a decision will be wrong,
— the risk that a job entrusted to a subordinate will be done badly,
— the risk that the wrong person will be chosen,
— the risk that a forecast will be inaccurate,
— the risk that a product will not sell well,

- the risk that the boss will be displeased,
- the risk that a suggestion will be rejected, etc.,

in fact the sort of risk which accompanies almost every decision or action a manager takes.

The skill of the manager is in balancing these risks with the benefits which will accrue if the decision is correct, if the subordinate does well, if the person chosen turns out to be exactly right for the job, and so on.

This balancing act is the management of risks. The successful manager will weigh up the pros and cons of a decision or an action and calculate the consequences before deciding if the risk is an acceptable one, or if it is too high in comparison with the possible benefits.

One of the keys is to be in possession of sufficient information on which to base decisions. If one can examine the likely consequences of an action, and follow these through to see the possible ramifications of a good or a bad outcome, one can make an informed decision and minimise the risks to the organisation.

Risks in banking

In the world of banking, risk has a more precise meaning, although there is still a whole variety of types of risk, including:

- credit risk (the risk that a borrower will be unable to repay),
- portfolio risk (the risk of a category of lending as a whole, e.g. mortgages, being adversely affected),
- industry risk (that a particular industry, e.g. property and construction, shipbuilding, will hit problems and put lending at risk),
- product risk (e.g. the risk associated with off Balance Sheet products such as swaps and options),
- settlement and delivery risk (the risk that a dealing counterparty will fail to pay over funds due to the bank),
- country risk (risk associated with lending to countries in political or economic difficulties (e.g. Latin America or Nigeria).

The principle of balancing risk against reward still applies. A lending banker will want to charge a higher rate of return by way of interest rates or fees for lending which is seen as inherently more risky. He may ask for security for a loan, both as an indication of the commitment of the borrower and as a safeguard if things go wrong. However, he will probably reject an application for a loan if the risk is too high, whatever the security or rate of return offered, as banks are naturally fairly conservative and tend to avoid what they see as 'pawnbroking'—deliberately placing themselves in a position where they are likely to have to call on the security to repay a loan.

However, other financial institutions may take a different view. For instance, a customer who might not qualify for a personal loan from a bank to buy a car may be able to borrow the money from a finance company, who will repossess the car if he fails to keep up the payments.

Managing the risk

One method which banks are increasingly adopting to manage the risk of lending is credit scoring. The customer fills in an application form which asks a series of questions about his job and marital status, whether he has children and owns his home, how long he has lived at the same address and banked at the same branch, and so on. The answers are scored by means of a template which allocates predetermined values to each reply. The values are totted up and if the total exceeds a set level, the facility is granted.

This system works on a system of averages. It has been found by experience, after examining many thousands of applications in the past, that certain characteristics tend to indicate that one person will be, on average, a better risk than another. These are usually related to stability—a married man with three children who has lived for four years in the same house, and who is buying the house on a mortgage, is much less likely to disappear without repaying his debts than, say, a young, single, unemployed person, who has no ties and lives in a rented room. Obviously this is not always the case, and such systems can be criticised on the basis that they pigeonhole people without regard to individual circumstances. There may be an allowance for managerial discretion in some cases, but overall it has been proved time and again that, of those loans which go bad, many will be the result of a manager overriding the credit score.

Senior management of the bank will decide the proportion of bad debts which is acceptable and the pass mark for the credit score will be set at an appropriate level to match this.

Credit scoring is mainly used for smaller loans and personal borrowing at present, but systems for the automatic sanctioning of business lending are being developed. For larger loans, a local manager may be required to pass his recommendation to a more senior colleague at a regional or divisional office; again this minimises the risk by calling on a more experienced person to take a second look.

For very large loan applications, banks minimise the risk by requiring a committee of senior managers to review the application (on the basis that two, or more, heads are better than one).

Most banks employ departments to study the economic conditions in the UK (and abroad if they do business overseas) and make recommendations as to the likely changes, factors influencing different industries and regions, demographic influences on markets, and so on. This information, if accurate and heeded, can help minimise risk by forewarning of problems ahead.

There are numerous other examples within banking but the common thread is that by obtaining additional information or making use of past experience one can manage risk.

▌ Action points

(a) How many types of management information have you received or made use of in a single day?

(b) List the occasions on which a computer has helped you or provided information to you (directly or indirectly) in your day's work.

(c) Plan your own budget for the month or the year. This will give you an idea of the stages a company must go through.

(d) At the end of the month, draw up a chart to show any variances of your actual spending against your plan. What were the reasons? Could you take any steps to correct them next month, or were they outside your control?

(e) What risk management activities are you involved in (credit reference searches, taking security, credit scoring)?

(f) Borrow a copy of the Chartered Institute of Bankers Cambridge Seminar 1988 booklet, *The Banks and Risk Management*, for a more detailed look at this topic.

(g) Have a look at your bank's organisational structure chart, or the internal telephone directory. How many departments have 'Risk' in their title? Do you know what they all do? If not, find out.

(h) Sir John Quinton's presidential address to the Chartered Institute of Bankers at the end of 1989 was entitled 'IT is here to stay'. Read a transcript of his speech in *Banking World* (January/February 1990) pp.23–6.

(i) In the same issue of *Banking World*, pp.69–70, is an article entitled 'Banks and risk', reporting on the Eighth Annual Banking Law Seminar, which will help you further.

▌Questions and answers

Question 1

In which areas of personnel management will the introduction of information technology have most impact over the next five years? Give reasons for your choice and outline the major changes which you expect. [Total marks for question—25]

(*Hint*: When this question was set, some candidates simply discussed how the personnel office could computerise staff records. There is a great deal more to the answer than that, so think very broadly before you begin to answer.)

Question 2

(a) Define what is meant by a Management Information System. [4]

(b) Briefly define Information Technology. [5]

(c) Give four examples of management information which is used in your branch or department. In each case explain how the information is used and how technology has been (or could be) used to improve the effectiveness of the supply of the information. [16]

[Total for question—25]

Question 3

(a) What is meant by a budgetary control system? [3]

(b) 'I don't see why I have to spend so much time working on these budgets', complained a colleague. 'They're just a way of making sure the head office accountants run the business. They're of no importance to me. It takes ages before I get agreement from my boss and then head office change all my figures. After that it's as if the figures are set in concrete but by that time the situation has changed. I don't know why they don't just let us get on and manage!'

It seems strange to you that your colleague—who regularly expects customers to produce budgets—dislikes the process of budgeting so much.

(i) What arguments would you put forward to convince your colleague of the importance of budgets? [10]
(ii) What could be done to overcome the objections which have been specified? [12]

[Total marks for question—25]

Question 4

You are an assistant manager in the management accounting department of your bank. Your manager is annoyed and disappointed at the lack of cooperation from other departmental managers in establishing and maintaining a useful budgetary control system. He has asked you to accompany him on his visits to each manager to talk over the purpose of budgets and their importance in running the business effectively.

Prepare a draft of what you will say to the managers. This should include a definition of budgeting and an explanation of its importance. It should also anticipate the main objections that managers might have to budgets and set out your counter-arguments.

[Total marks for question—25]

(*Hint:* At first glance, you may think that the answer to this question and question 3 will be the same. This is not quite true, as the emphasis is slightly different—read them again!)

Answer 1

The term 'personnel management' is normally used to cover the following aspects of policy and practice:

(a) recruitment, selection, training and development
(b) reward systems and benefits,
(c) conditions of work and welfare,
(d) industrial relations, and, in some instances,
(e) organisational development.

Information technology is enabling very significant changes to take place within banks. It will also affect external relationships as methods are developed to link the banks with their clients in novel ways. Each of the developments will have impact to some degree on personnel management. The interactions are complex but since personnel management is involved in the core activities of staffing and training it will be affected in virtually every case.

IT will affect the organisation in the following ways:

(a) The introduction of new systems and channels of communication.
(b) A quicker and more accurate processing of information.
(c) The need to change structures to make effective use of (a) and (b).
(d) Providing new opportunities for business development as well as posing threats. How these are handled will affect organisational structure and the number and quality of staff required.
(e) The leadership style most appropriate to the new organisation and the expectations of its staff will have to be considered.

How the bank deals with these issues will be influenced by its traditional values and by social attitudes to radical technological change. If potential change is very significant, it may involve a redefinition of the aims and objectives of the business. The impact on personnel management in particular will therefore include:

(a) Recruitment, selection, training and development will be affected by the need to:
  (i) draw up a manpower plan to avoid unnecessary redundancies but also to ensure that the organisation is staffed with people with the right skills for the new era;
  (ii) choose selection methods which will attract the appropriate people;
  (iii) devise training programmes to allow staff to acquire the appropriate skills, knowledge and behaviour; and
  (iv) offer developmental opportunities to provide the motive for hard work and commitment.
(b) Reward systems which attract the appropriate people, keep them and encourage them to give their energy to the task: these might be quite different from existing systems of reward.
(c) Concern for conditions and welfare to ensure that staff are given work which does not impose unreasonable physical or mental stress and is sufficiently interesting to absorb attention and provide a spur to learning.
(d) Foster good industrial relations. In a period of intense change, to obtain staff cooperation it is vital that they understand clearly what is happening, are fully consulted about issues which might affect them (e.g. redundancy, redeployment, retraining, etc.), and that they have strong institutions to represent their interests and to help resolve conflict through fair negotiation or agreed grievance procedures.
(e) Organisational development. Careful thought will need to be given, from both a business and an employee relations points of view, to such matters as:
  (i) the degree of centralisation or decentralisation of decision-making;
  (ii) the channels of communication;
  (iii) the appropriate leadership style; and
  (iv) the design of jobs.

Answer 2

Refer to the text of the chapter. Since each reader will work in a different department or type of office, it is not possible to give a full suggested answer to this question, but the examples in the chapter should help you to think of examples from your own work.

Answer 3

(a) Budgets are forecasts which indicate the resources allocated to an organisation's activities or to the achievement of its objectives within a specified time.

They are generally used as a standard against which performance during the period is measured.

(b) Budgets are important because:

(i) They are usually stated in terms which are common throughout the organisation (generally financial) and thus provide a means of comparing, coordinating and controlling a wide variety of organisational activities.
(ii) They concentrate on an important area for control, namely costs.
(iii) Variances between performance and budget are susceptible to analysis.
(iv) They establish a clear standard of performance.
(v) They have a high apparent validity because they are directly comparable with end-of-period statistics.
(vi) They provide basic information for rapid feedback and adjustment of performance.
(vii) As they are often compatible with the accounting system, they simplify the production of end-of-period accounts.

The objections expressed by the colleague and possible means of overcoming them are:

(i) *Length of time they take*: Point out that if used properly they will save time overall by enabling the manager more readily to control and allocate his resources.
(ii) *Allow accountants to run the business*: Explain that the departmental budget is a useful tool for the departmental manager. The organisational budget is a necessary planning, coordinating and controlling tool.
(iii) *Of no importance*: Point out how they can be used as a management tool to check on progress towards predetermined targets.
(iv) *Figures have been changed*: Explain that building a budget is a complex organisational process which enables there to be an agreed allocation of scarce resources between competing departments.
(v) *Figures are set in concrete*: Suggest that the organisation should examine its budgetary policy. Budgets are for guidance and should be adjustable.

Answer 4 (outline only)

Definition

Budgets are statements which identify the resources allocated to certain activities or to the achievement of specific goals within defined time periods. Any planning and control system must incorporate budgets because the figures normally become the standard against which future performance is measured.

Importance of budgets

— Usually stated in monetary terms and therefore provide a common denominator for a wide variety of organisational activities.
— Can be used by the existing accounting system and focus on a key resource (capital) and a key goal (profit).
— Usually easy to identify the responsibility for the budget.
— Help to establish clear and unambiguous standards of performance.
— Deviations can quickly be detected.

- Provide the basic information for rapid feedback and action.
- Provide a major means of coordination as well as control.

Managerial objections and answers to them

- *Time-consuming to provide figures*: Overcome by explaining the considerable benefits which enable the manager to control his resources better.
- *Figures take too long to process and therefore provide evidence too late for effective action*: Check on the time scale and attempt to meet required deadlines.
- *Figures not readily helpful to managers because they seem irrelevant or obscure*: Check how they can be improved; suggest training in interpretation.
- *Fear that budgets lead to rigidity*: Explain that budgets are for guidance and can be changed.
- *Suspicion that managerial control will pass from managers to accountants*: Explain that budgets are produced as tools for managerial planning and control.

CHAPTER 6
Personnel systems

- Design of work • Job analysis • Job description • Job rotation/enlargement/enrichment • Job evaluation system • Appraisal systems • Grievance procedures • Disciplinary procedures

▍Design of work

In the last century, very few people worked with their minds. The vast majority were labourers, hired for their physical strength and endurance. A few were skilled craftsmen, but very few were clerical or office workers compared with the huge numbers today. Automation, the introduction of computers, and the increase in service rather than manufacturing industries have reduced the number of routine jobs requiring little or no thinking. Increasingly, workers are more willing to change their jobs, or even their professions.

The result is that people are no longer willing to do something merely because they are told to; they no longer expect to work without thought. Since motivation (see Chapter 10) depends on factors such as responsibility, self-fulfilment and achievement, it is not likely therefore that a boring, repetitive job will increase the motivation of the worker.

This means that managers must consider carefully the design of work and of jobs to build in motivating factors.

▍Job analysis

Job analysis can be defined as determining **what** is done in a particular job, as distinct (for example) from skills analysis, which is concerned with **how** a job is done by a skilled worker.

Both techniques are associated with 'work study', or 'work measurement'—methods of studying a job to record exactly what tasks are undertaken, often broken down into simple activities (find file in filing cabinet, fill in a certain form, input details to the computer terminal, etc.) so that the optimum way of carrying out a job can be designed.

Job analysis can be thought of in two stages: the job description and the personnel specification. The latter defines the characteristics, qualities and experience of the ideal person required to do the job. This is considered in more detail in Chapter 10 in connection with recruitment and selection.

In a large organisation, standard job descriptions and personnel specifications may be drawn up for certain jobs (e.g. in a bank: for cashier, manager's clerk, loans officer, sales officer, etc.) to ensure consistency across the organisation.

▌Job description

A job description is a written statement of the tasks and responsibilities associated with a particular job.

Listing the special features of an individual job in this way provides a useful guide to the job holder as to the extent and limits of his responsibilities and authority. It also provides a guide in the selection of a suitable candidate when the job is to be filled, and acts as a guide to the training of the successful applicant.

In general, a job description should contain:

(a) the job title;
(b) purpose (what should be achieved, the reason for the job and its significance to the organisation);
(c) place in the structure (to whom the job-holder reports, for whose work he is responsible, with whom he should coordinate, etc.);
(d) primary duties, accountabilities and authority, and subsidiary activities;
(e) skills and knowledge required.

The job description should ideally be drawn up by a combination of observation and consultation with the present job-holder. To give their best performance, people need to know what is required of them and what is expected. A list of tasks to be performed may be sufficient for those who are simply employed, as described above, for their physical labour; it is not enough where they are expected to use initiative and intelligence. They need to understand the aims of the department and how their job fits into that overall purpose.

All too often, an employee has no written job description but is expected to understand what is expected, almost by second sight! It is assumed that, because the job has been done before, a newcomer will automatically realise what is wanted. This is clearly a recipe for misunderstanding and dissatisfaction. If the manager reprimands a member of staff for not doing something, when the staff member had no way of knowing it was required, neither party will be happy and resentment may build up on both sides. Far better to discuss the purpose of the job in detail, make sure that both sides have the same understanding of what is meant, and then ask the job-holder to prepare the first draft of the written job description himself. This can then be refined in further discussions between the worker and manager, resulting in an agreed document which can be 'signed-off' by both parties and used as a reference point in future.

A job description should not be regarded as immutable. It should be reviewed at least annually as there will undoubtedly be changes in the organisational structure, goals, etc., which may have an impact on the tasks and responsibilities appropriate to the job.

The aim of the job description should not be to be so rigid as to define every action, but to allow the job-holder as much discretion and freedom as possible to carry out tasks in his own way within the confines of his authority.

▌Job rotation/enlargement/enrichment

One aim of management should be to make work interesting and stimulating for the staff, thus increasing motivation and consequently the quality and even quantity of output. One approach to making work more interesting is to change the job structure in one of three basic ways:

- Job rotation.. swap jobs
- Job enlargement .... widen jobs
- Job enrichment............................. heighten jobs

Job rotation

This simply means that employees swap jobs at regular intervals with other employees of a similar grade.

In branch banking this might mean that the cashiers, enquiries clerks, standing-order clerks and safe-custody clerks take turns to undertake each of these four roles. This provides variety to avoid employees becoming stale in one particular job.

Job enlargement

Job enlargement means that an employee carries out a wider range of related tasks of a similar grade—the job is extended horizontally. This has been used in production line manufacture, for example in car works, so that a single worker will carry out many different tasks on the car, rather than repeatedly carrying out a very short simple task, then doing the same on a second car, and so on.

As a banking example, suppose that, at present, one clerk checks the details on a standing order request form received, passing it to a second clerk to prepare the computer input form, who in turn passes it to a third clerk to input the details to the computer terminal. With job enlargement, each clerk takes a batch of forms and processes them through the whole cycle.

Job enrichment

Job enrichment differs in that the scope of the job is extended vertically, to incorporate tasks which might normally be seen as requiring more highly graded staff to carry them out. This gives greater responsibility, skill training and the freedom for the employee to use his initiative.

Writing on this topic, Frederick Hertzberg stressed that the principles of job enrichment require that the job be developed to include new aspects which provide an opportunity for the employee's psychological growth. Merely adding one undemanding job to another (as may be the case in job enlargement) or switching from one boring job to another (as is the danger with job rotation) is not enough—these are merely horizontal job loading. Hertzberg suggests that job enrichment should look for ways to load the job vertically so that opportunities for achievement, responsibility, recognition, growth and learning are built in. This could involve looking for ways of removing controls while retaining or increasing the individual's accountability for his own work, granting additional authority, giving the person responsibility for a natural complete unit of work, making reports available directly to the worker rather than just to the supervisor, and introducing new, more difficult tasks, etc.

In branch banking, a cashier in conversation with a customer might well discover that the customer is thinking of buying a car. The normal outcome would be simply to refer the customer to the enquiries desk for a leaflet. With job enrichment, the cashier will offer the appropriate personal loan application form, asking the customer to return the form to the same cashier in due course. When the form is returned, the cashier will credit score the application, advise the customer if the loan is to be granted, and ensure that the funds are placed on the customer's account ready to be drawn.

This gives the cashier a much more responsible and interesting role by following the transaction right through from beginning to end, a process which might otherwise require four or five people to become involved.

Obviously this process cannot be applied to just one employee; the whole branch or department must have its tasks allocated and jobs designed with the aim of achieving maximum motivation for the staff. The system also relies on having staff of the right quality and with appropriate attitudes.

The Volvo experiment

A classic example of using job enlargement and job enrichment to improve motivation and output, which is often quoted in management textbooks, is the Volvo experience in Sweden.

During the 1970s, in a bold experiment inspired and supported by the company's chief executive, Volvo built a new assembly plant at Kalma in Sweden so that the work could be restructured in a revolutionary way. Instead of each worker doing a highly specialised task, all members of a team were encouraged to learn each other's jobs (sometimes called 'multiskilling'). Groups of 25 workers, each in their own bay, complete a whole subassembly of the car, rather than each person repeating the same task on a series of vehicles passing down a moving assembly line. The workers in the team decide for themselves who will carry out which job, and can regulate their own speed.

After initial teething troubles, productivity was as good as in Volvo's traditional plants; personnel turnover and absenteeism were 5 per cent lower; the vast majority of workers preferred the new system and wanted to take responsibility for the quality of their output.

∎ Job evaluation systems

Job evaluation is carried out by most large companies, including banks, in an attempt to rank jobs on a rational basis and thus produce a hierarchy of salaries which is seen as fair within the organisation and which enables the bank to compete for staff in the market place.

It is concerned solely with the nature of the job itself and not with the person doing the job. Thus an employee who is required to cover for a colleague by carrying out a more highly graded job will not necessarily acquire the grade of that job, but will often be described as 'deputising' for the absent colleague in the more highly graded post. Conversely, a worker who is temporarily, for whatever reason, filling a role regarded as being below his normal grade, is often described as retaining his 'personal grade' while undertaking the role, rather than taking on the lower grade of the job. Thus job and person must be seen as two separate entities.

The need for a job evaluation system is made clear if we consider the job titles used in different organisations. An 'executive' in one organisation may mean a very senior manager with a seat on the board; in another organisation the title may be given to a junior sales manager, in order to give him apparent status when dealing with customers. Similarly words such as 'director', 'administrator', and indeed 'manager', may mean quite different things in different organisations or even in different parts of the same organisation. A way of defining the jobs more scientifically is therefore needed if they are to be compared throughout the organisation and between organisations.

There are basically two types of job evaluation system:

(a) Nonquantitative systems rely on a committee to rank jobs based on the job descriptions.
(b) Quantitative systems aim to be more objective by giving points for various elements of a job such as knowledge and skills, extent of the job, importance of the job, and responsibility. The points are totalled to give a score on which jobs are ranked.

Nonquantitative systems

In this approach, jobs or groups of jobs are ranked in order of the responsibility, etc., associated with the job. This was once very popular for office jobs, where the higher levels are seen to call for greater degrees of responsibility. Having ranked the jobs it is straightforward to establish appropriate salary differentials. The drawback is that the system is not very objective, since it relies on the subjective views of the ranking committee or panel.

Generally, job evaluation is applied separately to three categories of workers (manual, clerical, management) as it has proved very difficult to apply one system across the whole spectrum of jobs.

Quantitative systems

Job evaluation on a points basis attempts to isolate the various essential elements of a job (such as skill, knowledge, training, responsibility, and physical and mental needs), which are then scored on the basis of the percentage of each attribute estimated to make up the whole.

Examples of ratings would be:

(a) Skill and knowledge—a branch manager's job requires a wide range of skills and will be scored higher than a junior clerical job which requires few skills.
(b) Training—a job which requires someone who has undertaken a lengthy training (such as a lawyer) will be scored higher than a job which requires minimal training.
(c) Importance of the job—a job which has an impact on many others will rank above a job which does not.
(d) Responsibility—a job with a great deal of freedom to take decisions (and therefore make mistakes!) will score more highly than one which operates within strict guidelines and close supervision.

There are many other ratings used, depending on the type of jobs and the nature of the organisation's work.

The total points score for a job is usually related to the wage or salary to be paid. Thus salary scales can be seen to be fair throughout the grades to which the evaluation is applied, which implies that they should be acceptable to the workforce, provided that the scoring system is seen to be objective in the first place. For this reason it is not unusual for organisations to employ firms of specialists to carry out the initial grading.

To allow for the fact that different workers may perform better or worse than each other in jobs of the same grade, a system of merit awards, or payment by results, is usually incorporated into the salary system. Thus the better worker will obtain a higher salary rate, through increments, than one who merely achieves the minimum required of a worker in a certain grade of job.

■ Appraisal systems

Job evaluation can provide a framework for determining salary rates, but these should also be related to how well the incumbent carries out the job. To determine this element, a system of staff performance appraisal is necessary. If people are to be encouraged to accept responsibility and perform well, they should be rewarded for their performance. They should know that their performance is being assessed in a systematic and reasonably objective manner.

The appraisal system usually consists of a performance review form, completed either by the appraiser (who should be the line manager with direct responsibility for the member of staff concerned, so he is fully familiar with the employee's performance) or by the person being appraised. This form will then provide the basis for discussion in an appraisal interview. Interviewing is discussed in detail in Chapter 11; here we will concentrate on the overall system.

The aims of the review form and the associated appraisal interview should be:

(a) to compare performance with objectives set for the period (usually one year);
(b) to let the person know how the manager views his performance;
(c) to allow the person to give his own views on his performance and career ambitions;
(d) to identify the employee's strengths, on which he can build, and any weaknesses which can be worked on with help and counselling from the manager;
(e) to identify future training and development needs;
(f) to provide a basis for determining the employee's reward package.

The employee should be given at least a week's warning of the appraisal interview and a copy of the review form, so that he can add his own comments on how well or badly he has performed, if there are external factors which have affected his performance, and any other matters he wishes to mention. He should be asked to identify any notable successes during the year, what he regards as his strengths and weaknesses, how he feels he can improve his performance, and what help or guidance he would like from his manager (e.g. opportunities for training).

Appraisal should be an on-going process between manager and subordinate, not confined to the annual interview, so nothing on the form or in the interview should come as a surprise to the employee (or to the manager, for that matter: if the employee has problems or grievances, the good manager should have been aware of these without having them come out unexpectedly in the appraisal interview).

Effective work should have been noted and commented on at the time; poor performance should have been discussed with the employee and suitable corrective action agreed to bring performance back up to standard.

Reward policy

There is a variety of ways of rewarding employees whose appraisal shows that they are performing up to or above the required standard:

(a) *Promotion to a higher grade*: in a pyramidal organisation only a few people will rise all the way up the ladder, so this can demotivate those who do not achieve promotion. It can also lead to good technical people being pushed into administrative and management posts for which they are poorly suited.

(b) *Salary increments:* these should not be automatic, linked only to time served, but they should be related to how well the employee has performed. Thus it is possible for a highly skilled specialist to achieve a high salary without having to leave the type of work at which he excels. The top rate for one grade may overlap the starting salary of the next, or even the next-but-one grade. The calculation of how well someone has performed is relatively easy with, say, a sales officer who has well defined targets and achievements, but it is much more difficult when an employee's objectives are expressed in qualitative rather than quantitative terms. For example, an officer who is concerned with avoiding bad debts can never quantify how much the losses would have been if he had **not** performed well.

(c) *One-off bonuses:* special effort to achieve a specific objective can be rewarded in this way.

(d) *Profit sharing:* more and more organisations now offer their employees the chance to share in the company's success by cash payments or by taking shares in the company under preferential terms (the Inland Revenue allows tax concessions for such schemes to encourage staff to participate). The disadvantage is that such a system can never really be fair. Individual employees cannot be rewarded in proportion to their own contribution, so there is usually a flat rate across the company—whether this is given as a percentage (say, 6 per cent of basic pay) or as a flat sum (say, £600 each), there are bound to be complaints from one group of employees or another, particularly if one division of the company is known to have made greater profits than another.

(e) *Perquisites (commonly known as perks):* there is a huge variety of possible fringe benefits, ranging from interest-free season ticket loans, to health insurance, company cars, subsidised canteens, uniforms (or 'career wear' as the banks like to call it) and preferential mortgage rates.

(f) *Working conditions:* in some cases it may be possible to offer shorter hours, longer holidays, flexitime, improved pension provisions, etc., as a reward for good work.

(g) *Thanks:* last but not least, a word of praise or genuine thanks from managers can mean a great deal. For example, a letter to a colleague in another department who has been particularly helpful (perhaps copied to his manager) will help give a feeling of satisfaction, and a willingness to help again next time. A visiting dignitary from head office could be asked to speak particularly to star performers, or a mention could be made in the house journal.

In general, over the last few years, the banks have begun to offer much more flexible and imaginative reward packages as they have had to cut costs and concentrate their pay policies on rewarding the better performers and retaining high flyers, rather than giving flat-rate increases across the board as had tended to be the case in the past.

Grievance procedures

In an ideal world, grievances would all be settled at an early stage by discussions between staff and managers, before frustration or resentment has a chance to build up. Unhappily we do not live in such a Utopia, and it may be that the grievance itself results from personal friction between manager and subordinate. It is therefore necessary, particularly in large organisations like banks, for a set grievance procedure to be laid down, usually after discussions and agreement with the staff representative bodies, so that staff know to whom to go if they are aggrieved at the way they have been treated, and what the stages of the process will be.

It is important for managers to realise that people see things in different ways. The important fact is that the member of staff feels that there is a problem, whether the manager interprets it in the same way or not. It is the feeling of grievance which must be handled, just as much as any real underlying cause.

The details of the process will vary from company to company, but there are several characteristics which will be common to all good grievance procedures:

(a) They will be in writing.
(b) They will be agreed with staff representative bodies, e.g. unions.
(c) They will be known (or details will be easily available) to all staff.
(d) They will state whom to approach first.
(e) They will allow for a friend or union representative to accompany the complainant.
(f) They will list the stages to be gone through (i.e. appeals procedures) if the grievance cannot be settled at the first meeting.
(g) They will state the timing between the various stages.
(h) They will specify that written records of all meetings should be kept and sent to all participants.

The usual pattern would be for the personnel department to be involved as a first stage, if informal discussions with the immediate boss have failed. They will either act as mediators from the start, or be kept informed as meetings with the boss, then the boss's boss, take place. If all these fail to satisfy the complainant, there will probably be a meeting with a senior manager (in each case, with a friend or representative allowed to be present). This may be the end of the process, or there may be a facility to involve an outside agency as arbitrator.

The method of conducting a grievance interview is covered in Chapter 11, but the pattern should be: identify the issues; meet and discuss the issues; consider the issues; respond with a suggested solution.

A time scale will have been set by the procedures to ensure that each stage follows fairly rapidly on the previous one (say, a maximum of a week between each) so that the issue does not drag on for too long.

External agencies

When the grievance concerns claims of unfair dismissal, or discrimination on the grounds of sex, race, disability, etc., then the complainant has an alternative—to take the case to an industrial tribunal set up under government legislation to decide disputes between employees and employers.

Although such a step may involve a long and stressful ordeal, similar to taking a case to court, the majority of people who have done so are glad they pursued their claims (81 per cent according to an Equal Opportunities Commission survey), even if they finally lost.

▌Disciplinary procedures

In a sense, this is the converse of grievance procedures. In disciplinary cases it is the employer who is unhappy with the conduct of an employee. This may relate to standards of behaviour (courtesy to customers, for example, or absenteeism) or to more serious matters such as dishonesty.

As with grievance procedures, the exact form will vary from company to company but usually:

(a) It will be in writing.
(b) It will be agreed with staff representative bodies, e.g. unions.
(c) It will be known (or details will be easily available) to all staff.
(d) It will specify those offences covered by the procedures.
(e) It will specify the penalties appropriate to each offence, and state which penalties may be imposed by managers of certain levels.
(f) It will allow for the member of staff to state his case before decisions are taken, and for a friend or union representative to accompany the member of staff.
(g) It will list the stages to be gone through (including appeals procedures).
(h) It will state the timing between the various stages.
(i) It will specify that written records of all meetings should be kept and sent to all participants (and for how long a note of the disciplinary action is to be retained on the staff file).

The stages are usually:

(a) Informal verbal warning (by immediate supervisor or manager). This is often all that is necessary with a minor offence. Provided that improvement in behaviour or performance is seen within a stipulated time, there is no need to go further.
(b) Formal verbal warning (by immediate supervisor or manager). In this case a note is made on the staff file.
(c) Formal written warning (by a senior manager), after a disciplinary interview has taken place—see Chapter 11.
(d) Final written warning (by a senior manager) after a second disciplinary interview, if no improvement has been seen.
(e) Dismissal (not usual for a first offence, except in the case of gross misconduct).

Examples of misconduct in the case of a bank employee might be: persistent lateness; persistent and unexplained absence; neglect of duties; contravention of the bank's rules or of, for example, Health and Safety Regulations; unsatisfactory performance or inefficiency.

More serious offences classified as gross misconduct would include: serious disobedience or insubordination; incapacity at work due to drink or drugs; serious contravention of bank rules or legal regulations; dishonesty, e.g. misappropriating bank funds, or giving confidential information to a third party.

Examples of penalties would be loss of pay, downgrading (with or without loss of pay and possibly including transfer to another job), suspension from duty (with or without pay), and ultimately, dismissal. In the case of serious dishonesty, criminal proceedings could also follow, although banks tend to be reluctant to bring action as they do not relish the resultant publicity.

The Financial Services Act 1986 lists certain events which the bank is obliged to report to the appropriate regulatory body. These particularly relate to employees involved with investment business and include conviction for dishonesty, bankruptcy, dismissal for certain offences or breach of the bank's rules and procedures for investment business.

▌Action points

(a) Do you have a written job description? If not, try to draw one up for yourself. If you have, then see if it can be made more accurate or relevant and then discuss your suggestions with your manager.

(b) What method of work measurement is used in your organisation? Are you required to submit completed timesheets for such a system? Do you think it is effective?

(c) How are jobs evaluated in your organisation? Try to get a copy of the guidelines and see if you can work out how the grade of your job was calculated or determined.

(d) Does your manager give you regular appraisals? If not, consider asking for more regular feedback so that you know how well you are performing.

(e) Do you know what the procedure is if you have a grievance? Get hold of a copy of your bank's procedures. Do you think they are clear and fair?

(f) Get a copy of your bank's disciplinary procedures and see how they fit with the notes above. Do you think they are satisfactory?

▌Questions and answers

Question 1

What are the advantages and disadvantages of work specialisation? How is it possible to combine job satisfaction and work specialisation? Identify a job with which you are familiar and explain how it might be changed to improve both efficiency and job satisfaction.

[Total marks for question—25]

Question 2

(a) What is job evaluation and what are the advantages and disadvantages of a job evaluation system? [18]

(b) Describe briefly the quantitative and nonquantitative approaches to job evaluation systems.

[4]

(c) Outline the steps an organisation should take in order to implement a job evaluation system. [3]

[Total marks for question—25]

Question 3

Geoff Randall does not believe in appraisal systems. In his experience the bank's system contains a high degree of bias; interviewing is badly done and no action has ever resulted from staff appraisals. He concludes that the whole process is not only useless, but damaging. In order to convince Geoff that his objections can be overcome, set out in detail the key features of an appraisal system that would work effectively. [Total marks for question—25]

Question 4

What factors would you take into account when assessing the strengths and weaknesses of a bank's staff appraisal system? [Total marks for question—25]

Question 5

(a) One of your subordinates has a grievance. He feels he has been passed over for promotion. He insists on making an official complaint. How would you handle the matter? [15]

(b) Explain either the grievance procedure used in your own bank, or the usual grievance procedure used in a UK bank. Comment briefly on the merits and demerits of the procedure you describe. [10]

[Total marks for question—25]

Question 6

You are an assistant in the personnel department and you have been asked to review the bank's disciplinary rules and procedures which have not been changed for several years. Against what criteria would you assess them? [Total marks for question—25]

Answer 1 (outline only)

Advantages
— No one person can master all skills required in a complex job. Specialisation enables the various parts of a large job to be shared among many people.
— People can master the skills required more easily.
— A greater proportion of the population is able to cope with jobs.
— A greater variety of jobs is available.
— People can more easily be matched to a suitable job.
— Results in greater efficiency and productivity.

Disadvantages
- Jobs are so divided as to become boring and monotonous.
- Causes alienation from job and demoralisation.
- Gives an individual opportunity to exercise only a very limited range of skills.
- Presents little challenge to the individual.
- Can result in lower productivity and efficiency.

Opportunities to combine benefits
- Increase the scope of the job to include a wider range of skills.
- Introduce rotation of workers through a number of jobs.
- Give employees greater responsibility to organise their own jobs.
- Give them more opportunity to set their own pace of work.
- Get employees involved in identification of potential performance improvements.

Personal example
Your example should show how either the scope or the depth of the job could be changed to provide greater interest and commitment.

Answer 2

(a) *Definition*
Job evaluation is a system which aims to produce an ostensibly fair payment structure by a formalised comparison of jobs or job components to determine the appropriate relationship of one job to another.

Advantages
- Can be fair and equitable and be seen to be so.
- Provides a coherent basis for the salary structure.
- Can be explained to employees.
- Can be understood by the employees.
- Can be used to reward factors which are seen as important to the organisation.
- Concentration on job components can be used across a variety of different jobs.
- Is capable of taking account of changes in job content.
- Gives a clearer understanding of job design.
- Enables grievances in respect of salary to be explained on a rational basis.
- Can facilitate job rotation.

Disadvantages
- Assessments are inevitably subjective.
- Systems are generally expensive to install and thus tend to become rigid.
- There is a need for continual monitoring as changes occur, both in the jobs and in the relative value of the factors involved.
- It can be difficult to incorporate all jobs in an organisation into the same system.
- The systems are not responsive to changes in market forces—thus, if one category of staff becomes more marketable, the system has to be altered or weighted to take account of this.
- Although the system establishes the relative value of each job to the organisation, it does not indicate what level of pay is appropriate.

(b) *Quantitative* (e.g. Hay MSL)

Jobs are ranked by point scoring each job on the basis of a number of predetermined factors such as knowledge and skills, responsibility, and importance of the job.

This type is particularly useful where a wide variety of jobs have to be evaluated.

Non-quantitative (e.g. benchmark system)

All jobs are ranked—generally by a committee—on the basis of job description.

This type of system is normally used in small organisations to determine a vertical hierarchy of jobs which in general are functionally comparable. It is relatively cheap and easy to install in a suitable environment.

(c) *Implementation*
— Choose most appropriate method of evaluation.
— Discuss reasons for the choice, the design of the system and the operation of the system with the staff.
— The system should include the right of appeal against an evaluation.
— The system should include the right to apply for a re-evaluation when the content of the job has changed.
— Administration of the system should be carried out by a committee or committees, representative of all staff levels.
— The system should be continuously monitored.

Answer 3

An appraisal system can work under the following conditions:

(a) *Objectives*: Its objectives should be clear, specific and focused. Problems arise when systems are designed with complex and incompatible aims.

(b) *Measures:* Once it has been decided what the appraisal system should appraise, an appropriate form of measurement should be chosen. Nowadays the emphasis is usually on behaviour or performance. Under either heading the appropriate standards must be agreed. They should be specific, quantifiable, concerned with quantity as well as quality and have a time scale. The measures should be tailored to meet the needs of the company, not borrowed from elsewhere.

(c) *The appraiser*: Who does the appraisal, and why, must be clear. Opportunity must be created for the appraisee to review his own performance. Training must be given in understanding the system and also, crucially, in interviewing skills.

(d) *Action:* The appraisal must be followed up so that action results. Paperwork should be kept to a minimum. Managers must 'own' the system.

Answer 4 (outline only)

The factors to be taken into account are:
— What are the purposes of the system? Are they clear to the appraiser? Are they clear to the appraisee?
— Are the criteria used to appraise appropriate to the purpose, i.e. if the appraiser is concerned with performance, do the criteria focus on performance rather than personality issues?

— Are there reasonably uniform standards of appraisal across the organisation?
— How far is the appraisal a joint process between appraiser and appraisee?
— Are there checks and balances to assure reasonable objectives, e.g. a father/grandfather system?
— What training is given in appraisal skills?
— How long do interviews last?
— Is the appraisee given time to prepare for the interview?
— Is there a written summary of the action? Is it agreed jointly?
— Who 'owns' the process—the managers or the personnel department?
— How easy is the administration of the system?
— How time-consuming is it?
— How frequent are the appraisals?

Briefly, an effective system will spell out the aims clearly and these will be widely understood by the organisation. The criteria used as a basis for measurement will be appropriate to the purpose. They will be reasonably objective to ensure standardisation and objectivity across the organisation. This will be reinforced by an appraisal of the appraiser and the right of appeal against alleged unfairness.

The interviews will be treated seriously both in terms of the time devoted to them and training for those who do them. Appraisees will be encouraged to prepare for the appraisal and the total process will be regarded as a joint problem-solving exercise. The managers will feel that they 'own' the process.

Answer 5

(a) Handling a grievance involves an exploration phase, a consideration phase and a reply phase.

Exploration phase
At this stage the manager must aim to find out the nature of the grievance and get as much information as possible. The manager should:
 (i) listen and be seen to listen,
 (ii) dig as deeply as possible to get at and understand all the facts,
 (iii) summarise the facts, and
 (iv) consider the possible cause of the grievance.

The manager should not pre-empt the issue at this stage by suggesting solutions. Nor should he give the impression that, whatever the employee says, there will be a negative outcome. The issue must remain open.

It is important that the manager dealing with the grievance has a full picture concerning its cause, bearing in mind that the 'cause' presented to him may mask the true facts. Thus he should try to get at the underlying or latent issue(s) surrounding the grievance; otherwise there is a danger that symptoms rather than causes are dealt with.

Having satisfied himself that the facts are clear, the manager might want to adjourn to consider what has been said.

Consideration phase
The manager should:
 (i) check the facts raised by the employee,
 (ii) consider the options open to him in terms of responding to the issue, and
 (iii) examine the implications for himself and others of any offer or response which might subsequently be made.

If he is able to resolve the issue by the provision of certain information or by clearing up misunderstandings, the problem might be solved at that stage.

Assuming, however, that the manager wants to adjourn the meeting to get further information, for example, then the employee must be told when the meeting can be resumed. It is not uncommon for grievance procedure to specify a 48-hour reply period for this purpose.

Reply phase

Having considered the facts and the options open to him, the manager should reconvene a meeting to reply. Prior to this, the manager should review the previous discussion in order to ensure that nothing has been forgotten or omitted to which he should reply. He must support his decision with appropriate arguments and reasons. Otherwise the possibilities of greater disaffection increase.

As far as possible, the manager should aim to achieve a 'win–win' solution so that both he and the employee can feel that honour has been satisfied. Obviously this will not be possible for all issues, bearing in mind that:
  (i)   The manager may not have the authority to resolve the case.
  (ii) The employee may wish to pursue the matter further (in procedural terms).
  (iii) The manager may be unable to concede to the requests made by the employee—in which case appropriate reasons should be given.

Having replied and listened to counter-arguments, the manager should formally conclude the meeting and the outcome (agreement or otherwise) should be recorded in writing.

(b) Most grievance procedures include the following steps:
  (i)   A meeting with the immediate boss accompanied by a friend or representative. If this fails—
  (ii) A meeting with the boss's boss, again accompanied.
  (iii) A meeting with a senior manager—also accompanied, if so desired.
  (iv) In some companies the procedure ends at this stage. In others it might be referred to a mediator or joint consultative body.
  (v)   It is normal for the personnel department to be kept informed of the stages through which the grievance is processed to ensure that equitable treatment is preserved between one case and another.
  (vi) Normally strict time limits are specified between stages—five working days is typical. This ensures that the matter is dealt with as speedily as possible.

Answer 6 (outline only)

Disciplinary rules and procedures should conform to the following criteria:
  — All disciplinary rules should be written down.
  — A procedure should exist through which disciplinary matters can be resolved; this should also be in writing.
  — All employees should be aware of the rules and procedures.
  — All managers should be aware of their rights and obligations under the procedures.
  — The rules and procedures should operate speedily.
  — The range of disciplinary actions should be specified together with who is authorised to take disciplinary action.
  — The rules and procedures should allow for a fair hearing and right of representation.

- No one should be dismissed for a first offence (unless gross misconduct: offences under this heading should be specified and made known to all employees).
- All employees should have the right of appeal, and immediate superiors should not have the right to dismiss without reference to senior management.
- Managers and workers' representatives should be trained in knowledge of the procedures and the skills of applying them.

CHAPTER 7
The Manager

- Management theories • The Classical school • The Human Relations school •
The Systems approach • Contingency theory • Management functions or
processes • Management roles • Transition from worker to management

▍Management theories

Management, as a subject for academic study, is relatively new when compared, for example, with mathematics or medicine. Prior to the beginning of the 20th century most companies would be run by the family which created the business, or by managers appointed by that family. It was taken for granted that such managers had absolute authority over the workers. Indeed, this was demonstrated by the ease with which workers could be dismissed if they failed to obey the instructions of the 'boss'. There was no security of employment, no possibility of compensation for unfair dismissal and generally no form of unemployment benefit or welfare support except from charities. Workers were therefore conditioned to obey the rule of the owner or manager without question or risk losing their livelihood.

From the late 19th century and early 20th century onwards this situation began slowly to change and the study of management methods and practices became an acknowledged discipline.

Although there is unlikely to be a question in the examination purely about management theory, you may well be asked to apply theory to real life situations. It is important to be aware of how thinking has changed and developed over the years. Theories of how people behave and therefore how they should be managed have changed radically since the beginning of the century.

There are four main schools of thought which describe how organisations and the people in them function, and how those people and organisations should be managed:

— the Classical school;
— the Human Relations school;
— the Systems approach;
— Contingency theory.

▍The Classical school

In the early part of the 20th century, a number of writers on management developed similar ideas which can be grouped together as the 'Classical school'.

F.W. Taylor

F.W. Taylor (1856–1917) is sometimes referred to as 'The Father of Scientific Management'. He was less concerned with workers as people than with the best and most efficient way of getting tasks done. He believed that by taking a scientific approach to the organisation of work he could maximise efficiency. Having started his career as an industrial engineer in the United States he had practical experience of the relative inefficiency of many factories. He was a man obsessed with efficiency—apparently he used to count the number of paces he took between home and work to ensure that he was taking the shortest possible route.

Taylor believed that there was a natural tendency for workers to protect their own interests by doing the minimum amount of work they could get away with. He regarded workers as inherently lazy, motivated only by money, and therefore requiring very close supervision. This is sometimes referred to as the concept of 'Rational/Economic Man' and is dealt with again in Chapter 10. Taylor drew a distinction between the concept of planning, which he saw as a managerial function, and the execution of tasks, which he saw as the workers' function. He did not expect workers to get involved in planning, as he felt their inherent laziness would prevent this.

Out of Taylor's work grew the various methods of time-and-motion study, or work measurement, which are still in use in some organisations today. When first introduced, these produced spectacular increases in productivity by analysing every step of a job, breaking it down into component parts, and making sure that each part was carried out with the minimum waste of effort, time or resources and with no duplication or overlap.

By training staff to be expert at one small task, very high rates of output can be achieved. Likewise, those with greater skill can be employed on more complex tasks whilst the less skilled are paid proportionately less for carrying out the more humble elements of the job. Factories run on these principles usually pay their workers piece rates to encourage maximum output.

The problem with this view of working man is that simplification of tasks results in monotony, boredom and lack of motivation. Paying piece rates may also result in poor-quality products as the workers strive only for quantity. There is no incentive for the workers to take an interest or a pride in their work.

Nevertheless, many production line jobs still operate under this ethos and, even in the clearing banks, the division of jobs into simple steps is prevalent in the more routine clerical tasks. Until very recently, all large organisations would have an 'O & M' (Organisation and Method) department whose role was to monitor the efficiency with which routine tasks were carried out. This became the butt of many a joke as the caricatured figure of a man with a clipboard and stopwatch, timing every movement of a shopfloor or office worker, down to the time it takes to erase an inch of pencil line, the distance walked to collect a piece of paper from a filing cabinet, or the time it takes to blow one's nose twice during a working day! However, there is a serious purpose behind such studies as they allow a standard to be set against which different departments, different branches, etc., may be measured. The important point is that such studies should be used as part of an overall appraisal of a situation, not as an end in themselves or a method of 'punishment' for workers seen to be lagging behind the 'norm'.

To some extent, if workers are treated as irresponsible and lazy they will tend to react by fulfilling this expectation. In one factory where absenteeism was very high, a group of workers was asked by a researcher why they came in, on average, only four days a week. The answer was 'Because we can't get by on the pay for three days'!

Key points of Taylor's theory can be summed up as:

— Reduction of all jobs to simple, defined tasks.
— Specialisation of workers to match tasks.
— Organisation of work layout for maximum efficiency.
— Motivation of workers almost entirely by pay.
— Rewards given according to quality and quantity.

Henri Fayol

A French engineer, Henri Fayol, was another management theorist who is considered a part of the Classical school. He developed a set of principles for organisation at the managerial level. These basically propose that an effective organisation requires:

— Clear objectives.
— Clear lines of authority and control.
— A rational division of work.
— An opportunity for subordinates to show initiative.

(The last is a departure from Taylor's ideas.)

Fayol was particularly concerned with spans of control and lines of communication. He felt that any employee should have only one boss, with a single clearly identified chain of command leading up to the chief executive. He tried to establish precise rules as to the number of staff one manager should be able to control effectively.

His principles have been criticised on the grounds of inflexibility. It is an oversimplification to state that all organisations can have clear objectives and that all work can easily be divided into simple tasks to achieve these. In practice, a complex organisation will have a variety of aims and objectives which will change over time, requiring flexible management to modify the organisational structure, job design, etc. to respond to these changes.

Many of the theories of Fayol, and of the Classical school in general, may have applied in the early days of the century when paternalistic management, ruling their employees with an iron fist in a velvet glove, was acceptable, when the economic climate was very stable and there was little need for organisations to change. This approach is far less satisfactory today, when workers have higher expectations of interesting jobs, an element of responsibility for their lives, etc. and they are no longer content to be passive, when the economy swings from boom to recession and back and when organisations must change quickly to survive.

■ The Human Relations school

The main proponent of this school of thought is Elton Mayo, whose 'Hawthorne experiments' are widely quoted in support of his ideas. The point of the experiments is often overlooked however, so it is well worth spending some time considering them.

Hawthorne experiments

Researchers at the Western Electric Company Hawthorne works in Chicago were interested in how changing lighting levels would affect the output of workers. They put similar groups of workers in two separate rooms. In one room the lighting level was increased; in the other it was kept constant. To their surprise, the productivity increased in both rooms. The researchers called in Elton Mayo, a consultant from the Harvard Business School, to try to explain their findings.

Over a period from 1924 to 1932 a series of experiments was carried out on groups of workers from the plant. Small groups of women from the relay assembly room were put in a separate room from the rest of the workers. Various changes in their working environment were made: the number of rest breaks, the length of the working day, the method of payment, and so on. With each change the rate of productivity increased. Finally the conditions were returned the those originally in place, and productivity increased yet again!

Clearly it was not the conditions themselves which were causing the increase in output. Mayo concluded that it must be the extra attention being shown to the workers by management which was responsible for the improvement.

A second series of experiments was carried out in the bank-wiring room. This has nothing to do with banks as financial institutions, but is a technical term for the type of electrical assembly work carried out in a section of the factory. By studying small teams of men at work in this room, the researchers found that, despite financial incentives, the teams were setting informal levels of effort beyond which they would not work. Another worker was put into the team as a 'plant' to work at a faster rate than the norm. Within a few days social pressure was brought to bear on this worker, building up to overt threats, to force him to slow down to the team's informally approved work rate. The same thing happened in reverse when a 'plant' was put in who worked at too slow a rate—the team applied pressure to bring his work rate up to the norm.

This study highlighted the importance of groups and of peer pressure. A manager in this situation must act as a motivator and facilitator rather than trying to 'rule' his subordinates. In such a branch or department a 'chargehand', someone who is regarded as a leader by the workers but is still one of the team, may be very useful from a management point of view, by influencing quality as well as the rate of work of the team.

Conclusions—Human Relations school

The conclusions which can be drawn from the Hawthorne experiments are that managers must consider their workers as human beings who need to feel that they belong to a group and to feel appreciated by management. This will be helped by encouraging horizontal lines of communication and a joint management/staff approach to discipline. These views are enjoying a resurgence of support in the 1980s/90s as managers are seen as motivators/team leaders/problem solvers who should get involved with the people they manage. These ideas are reflected in the importance many organisations now place on training their managers in interpersonal skills, so that they can interview and counsel their staff effectively, listen well and understand the needs of individuals and groups, and be able to persuade them to accept change. Underpinning this is the idea that the organisation will achieve its aims more easily if the workforce is happy and satisfied.

Some critics of Mayo's theories see his view of workers as too simplistic; they do not believe that workers will respond to false expressions of esteem, but feel they will be suspicious of attempts to foster a group spirit. Nevertheless, Mayo's work has been of great importance in the development of management theory and the establishment of the concept of 'Social Man' as a development from the Classical school's 'Rational/Economic Man'.

∎ The Systems approach

In 1948, Herbert Weiner published his book *Cybernetics* in which he developed the idea of links between communication and control in human beings and in mechanical and electrical machines (such as computers).

Weiner had been involved, during World War II, in the development of weapons control systems, and drew parallels between such systems and the living world.

The idea of the organisation as a complex system has been developed in an earlier chapter, so here we will concentrate on the theory.

Systems theory or systems analysis is a way of looking at a group of interrelated components which can be applied to many branches of science—both natural and social sciences.

The group of elements is regarded as a system. In theory there can be both closed and open systems. A closed system is one which is completely self-contained, cut off from any influence

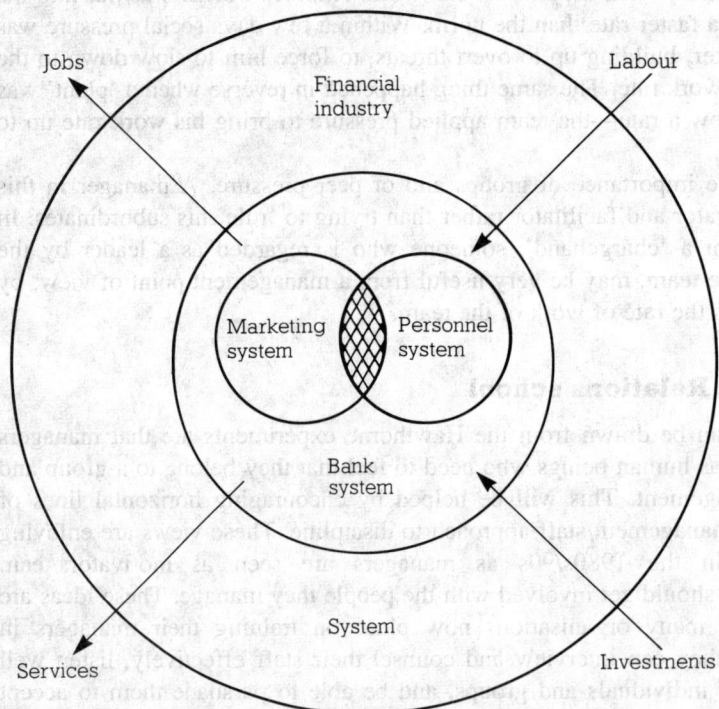

Fig. 7.1 The bank as a system and a sub-system

from outside. In practice this is almost impossible to achieve; most systems in the real world are open. That is to say they have boundaries which define the system but they are open to inputs from, and outputs to, the world outside the system boundary: see Fig. 7.1.

Many systems consist of a series of independent or overlapping subsystems. For example, a bank is a system but it is also a subsystem of the financial industry, which in turn is a subsystem of the economy of the country and so on. Conversely, within the system which is the bank, there will be subsystems comprising the various departments, branches and functional areas of the bank.

Inputs to a business system will include raw materials, labour, machinery, orders from customers, etc. Outputs will include finished goods and services, jobs, effect on the environment and so on. One of the features of any system is that it is capable of being analysed by a systems analyst so that the flows of information in and out of the system can be shown in diagrammatic forms, thus defining the system and its boundaries and interfaces with the outside world. In systems analysis it is the flow of data and information and the observation of where decision-making takes place, rather than the physical flow of goods, which are of prime importance. This can sometimes be difficult to assess for those actually involved in the business; therefore it is not uncommon for the systems analyst to be someone unfamiliar with the business, but an expert in systems, who will observe and question those involved in the business to track the information flows. This is a good example of the proverbial difficulty of 'not being able to see the wood for the trees' when one is too closely involved in something. Often a so-called business analyst, someone who is more familiar with the day-to-day operation of the business, will act as an intermediary, translating ideas from the workers to the systems analyst and vice versa, to ensure there is no communication barrier between them.

The purpose of systems analysis is to identify the real flows of work around the system, point up any bottlenecks, and suggest ways in which efficiency might be improved by redesigning work flows. Often this is carried out in conjunction with an automation or computerisation process but this is not always the case. 'Systems' has come to be synonymous with computer systems in some people's minds, but any set of operations defined by a boundary with interfaces to the outside world, as explained above, is a system.

Conclusions—Systems approach

The Systems approach requires a conceptual leap which not all managers find easy to achieve. As explained above, it is the difficulty of seeing the wood for the trees. Modern organisations are so complex that it can be very difficult and time-consuming to analyse their many subsystems fully. This is probably why the approach has really become common only when systems are being computerised, when a wholly different approach is easier to justify to sceptical managers.

■ Contingency theory

Contingency theory recognises that there is no single approach to the management of an organisation which will be appropriate in all situations. The main researcher associated with this approach is Professor Joan Woodward, whose work in the 1950s illustrated this idea.

By identifying key attributes of an organisation, it provides a framework on which to build an analysis of a particular organisation and its problems, before an attempt at solving these problems can be made.

These key attributes include:

(a) Size and structure of the organisation (larger organisations tend to be more formal, more complex, more standardised but less centralised).

(b) Task or mission of the organisation (a research laboratory or charity will require a different style of management from that of an aggressively profit-driven sales organisation).

(c) Technology of production (firms involved in mass production tend to be very formalised and hierarchical with unskilled operators and much forward planning; those involved in unit production have closer management involvement, shorter scale planning and skilled staff at all levels—leading to fewer industrial relations problems).

(d) Rate of innovation (highly centralised organisations with rigid hierarchies will tend to fare worse in times of rapid change than those with flexible, organic structures).

(e) People (the calibre of staff and their response to change will determine the best management style to adopt).

Conclusions—Contingency theory

Contingency theory does not, in itself, propose a way of determining the best way of managing an organisation, but it suggests that there is a variety of factors which need to be taken into account before such decisions can be made. It also recognises that these factors will change over time, even for the same organisation, and that therefore an on-going analysis of the organisation's needs is required if it is to remain successful.

▎Management functions or processes

Management is sometimes defined as 'Getting things done through people'. Put more grandly, the purpose of good management is to harness and coordinate the effort of many people and channel it into the achievement of organisational goals. Imagine the challenge of building the Channel Tunnel, or ensuring that the Olympic Games run smoothly, and you will have some idea of the management skill which is required if such massive undertakings are to be achieved. On a smaller scale, perhaps, that is what the managers in your own organisation are doing every day.

There are a series of general processes or functions which most managers carry out, whatever their specialist tasks. These general processes are considered in more detail in the next chapter, and are:

— Setting objectives.
— Forecasting.
— Planning.
— Organising and coordinating.
— Motivating.
— Monitoring and controlling.

Individual managers may also be responsible for specialist processes—for example, in a bank there will be managers responsible for taking credit decisions, for running the computer system, for forecasting economic changes, for devising new business strategies, and so on. However, all of these managers will also be involved in the main managerial processes, particularly if they have a team of staff reporting to them.

Clearly, managers at different levels in the organisation will have differing levels of responsibility. They may concentrate more on certain of the managerial functions than on others. For example, the chief executive will spend much of his time considering the long-term goals of the organisation, a branch manager will be more concerned with shorter-scale events (managing the branch staff and business, achieving monthly or quarterly targets, and so on) whilst the head of the securities department will probably be concerned almost solely with the day-to-day running of the department.

Nevertheless, all these people are managers and all are involved to a greater or lesser degree with the processes outlined above.

∎ Management roles

We all perform a variety of roles in our daily lives, at home and at work. At home we may be parent, husband or wife, child, friend, secretary of the drama society, goalkeeper in the football team, all in the same day in different situations. At work a manager may be called on to act as spokesman for the department one minute—and as confidant to a member of staff with a personal problem the next. In some ways these roles can be considered as equivalent to the roles an actor plays on stage—each requires a slightly different set of skills and competences.

Henry Mintzberg defined 10 managerial roles. Some have rather cumbersome names, but the ideas behind them are common sense so don't be put off by the jargon. They were grouped in three categories:

- **INTERPERSONAL:**   Figurehead
  Leader
  Liaison

- **INFORMATIONAL:**   **Monitor**
  Disseminator
  Spokesman

- **DECISIONAL:**   **Entrepreneur**
  Disturbance handler
  Resource allocator
  Negotiator

Not all managers will necessarily perform all of these roles; it depends on the type of job which they do, their position in the organisation's hierarchy, etc. Let us consider each role in turn

(a) Interpersonal

These are roles in which the manager is linking one group of people with another, or facilitating dialogue.

(i) Figurehead

This role is associated with senior managers. It involves representing the organisation or department to the outside world, for example at official functions such as dinners, conferences, presentations, etc. The manager can convey a good impression of the organisation by the way he carries out this role.

(ii) Leader

By inspiring his team to follow his lead and example, the manager works to achieve the goals of the organisation.

(iii) Liaison

It is frequently necessary for a team or department to coordinate their work with that of another team or department—to receive information or resources necessary for their task, or to supply reports, finished goods, etc. In order that this coordination should be smooth and to avoid any possible conflict, the manager should act in a liaison role with his opposite number in the supplier or customer department. This involves good communication skills.

(b) Informational

These roles are concerned with the transmission or receipt of information important to the successful completion of tasks. They all require well developed communication skills.

(i) Monitor

The manager must monitor the performance of the team members against their objectives and keep them aware of progress.

(ii) Disseminator

It is a responsibility of the manager to keep abreast of developments outside the department which will affect the team, and to keep them informed and up-to-date. This role also involves explaining the organisation's policies to the team and illustrating the importance of the department's work to the success of these objectives.

(iii) Spokesman

This involves explaining the nature and importance of the department's work to people in other departments, or even outside the organisation. In a large organisation, such as a bank, this can be very important as often the function of, for example, head office departments, can be unclear to others, even though the function may be vital to the success of the organisation as a whole.

(c) Decisional

As the name implies, these roles are particularly concerned with decision-making (although this may be involved in many of the other roles as well).

(i) Entrepreneur

In this role the manager is acting creatively—perhaps devising new ways to get things done, challenging the accepted routine, looking for new opportunities to advance the objectives of the organisation.

(ii) Disturbance handler

This is sometimes described as 'crisis management'. The manager is the person who must decide what is to be done when the daily routine is interrupted. There will always be things which go wrong; the challenge is to sort them out as quickly as possible and return to a smooth running operation.

(iii) Resource allocator

Resources (staff, machinery, raw materials, etc.) are very rarely unlimited. It is up to the manager to decide how to make the best and most efficient use of scarce resources to achieve the required objective.

(iv) Negotiator

Where it is necessary to put the department's case, for example when the organisational budget is being decided or targets set, the manager must argue the case for his department and negotiate with his superiors for the benefit of his department.

Almost all these roles require communication skills and decision-making skills, as well as more specific skills in each case.

Which roles a particular manager undertakes will depend on his job. A very senior manager will tend to spend more time on the figurehead, liaison and spokesman type of roles; whereas a middle manager may be more concerned with disseminator, negotiator and entrepreneur roles; and a supervisor may spend more time on the disturbance handling and resource allocating roles. There is no hard and fast rule about this.

If you have difficulty remembering the difference between 'roles' and 'processes' as applied to management, think of it this way:

— **Processes**, like a manufacturing process, are the operations carried out by a manager (planning, controlling, etc.).
— **Roles**, like the roles an actor plays on a stage, are the different ways a manager acts in different circumstances (figurehead, negotiator, etc.).

■ The transition from 'worker' to 'management'

For many people, one of the major steps in their career is when they move from the ranks of the 'workers' to the 'management' team. Most people have looked forward to this step but many regard it with apprehension for a variety of reasons.

For some, it is seen as moving from being 'one of us' to being 'one of them'; from being part of a friendly team to becoming rather distant and perhaps distrusted or even disliked by the friends they have left behind. There is no reason why this should be the case, provided that the person is well prepared for the jump in status and difference in approach which is needed from a manager.

Some new managers will be lucky in that they will be properly inducted into their new role. They will be introduced to their new boss, who will explain what the job entails and what is expected of the new manager. They may be lucky enough to meet their predecessor, and even have a handover period to ease them into their new job.

Unfortunately it is much more likely that, one day, you will simply be told that as from a certain date you will be the manager in charge of a certain branch or department. It will be up to you to find out, as quickly as possible, where the department is, what it does, how it does it and, perhaps most important of all, who the people are who staff the department and whom you will be managing.

This is perhaps the most difficult aspect of getting to grips with a new job. The staff all know each other, they know the previous manager and how he liked things done, they know the job (which perhaps you do not) and they will tend to be a little defensive when presented with a new and unknown manager.

This may be exacerbated if the new manager has been promoted from within their ranks—not only will you need to adopt a different approach, but the staff will have to get used to treating you in a different way. However much you may want to remain 'one of the gang' and be very friendly with all the staff, you must be prepared for a certain amount of 'distance' to build up between you. This is essential if you are to maintain the authority you need to direct or guide the staff, to take sometimes difficult or unpopular decisions, to deal with problems and nonstandard situations and to take responsibility for the performance of the section.

As the new manager, you must get to know the staff—their capabilities, their shortcomings and their potential. You must instil in them a respect for your competence as a leader.

Don't be too hasty to rush into changing everything about the department, or to accept everything that is suggested by the staff. A new broom may sweep clean, but it may also sweep away valuable longstanding procedures and methods without having anything better to put in their place. The arrival of a new manager is sometimes the cue for workers with a grudge to try and settle an old score against a fellow-worker. On the other hand, they may have very sensible suggestions to make, so equally you should be open to ideas. Give yourself time to consider suggestions, work through them in your own mind and perhaps discuss them with other members of the team, then let the person who made the suggestion know whether you have decided to act upon it and why.

An effective way to establish the confidence of your team is to discover and solve some of the minor but longstanding irritations which plague any office. If the daily circulars are taking two weeks to reach the people who need to see them, arrange for a second copy to be received and halve the length of the circulation list; if the light bulbs are always failing in the ladies' cloakroom, plunging the girls into darkness, get an electrician in to cure the problem and install long-life bulbs; if the leaflet display stand in the banking hall gets in the way of opening the enquiries window, get head office to supply an alternative variety of a different shape. These are the sort of irritations which people complain about but do nothing about—show that you are the person who gets things done and you will inspire respect and confidence without having to shout about it.

▎Action points

(a) Consider your own organisation. Do you feel you are treated according to the Classical school or the Human Relations school of management theory?

(b) The answer will probably be a bit of both—list examples of each type of management in your part of the organisation.

(c) Consider your own office or department as a system. Could you explain to an outsider what the boundaries of that system are? What are the inputs and outputs?

(d) How does your office or department fit into the larger system of the branch or division, and how does that fit into the bank as a whole?

(e) Work through the section on Contingency theory and see if you can define your organisation in those terms.

(f) Consider your own job. Do you carry out any of the management processes? What about your immediate superior?

(g) Now consider roles. List all the roles you have played today, or over the past few days, both at work and at home. You will probably be able to think of at least five or six.

(h) Considering roles at work, choose one of your managers and list the roles you feel that manager plays. Identify situations where each of these apply.

(i) The Chartered Institute of Bankers has produced an excellent video, *Appointment with Change*, which follows a new manager as he takes over responsibility for his first branch.

See if your Institute Local Centre or local college is planning to show the video at one of their meetings—if so, make sure you go along. Otherwise, perhaps you could get together with some fellow students and borrow a copy from the Institute. You will find it very interesting and useful.

Questions and answers

Question 1

What are the major roles performed by managers and what are the key managerial processes in which they are involved?

[Total marks for question—25]

Question 2

Describe the major characteristics of the 'Classical' school and the 'Human Relations' school of management thinking. [16]

Critically review the contributions of these two schools to the development of management thinking. [9]

[Total marks for question—25]

Question 3

What contributions did F.W. Taylor make to management thinking? [10]

What contributions did Elton Mayo make to management thinking? [10]

How relevant are their ideas to banking today? [5]

[Total marks for question—25]

Question .

You are the manager of a branch of your bank. Six months ago you promoted Dawn Reeves to a first-line supervisory position.

You are sure she was the best candidate for the job.

She undertook her new duties enthusiastically with appropriate guidance from you. The output of the section has increased.

Dawn, however, is not as happy as she used to be when she was an ordinary member of the section.

'I'm not sure I'm the type to be a supervisor', she confided to you recently. 'There seems to be so much to do, but not a lot of it is what I call proper work.'

This seems to be an ideal opportunity to talk to Dawn about 'managerial roles'.

(a) Write brief notes on what you would say to Dawn about managerial roles in general. [20]

(b) List the **key** roles which Dawn should play in her current job. [5]

[Total marks for question—25]

(*Hint:* There is a lot of positive information in this question, so don't waste time suggesting Dawn was badly selected—the question states she was the best candidate; or that she is a complete failure—the output of the section has increased; concentrate on what the question actually asks.)

Question 5

Guy Brent was appointed to his first supervisory post six years ago. He had been an outstanding performer at his last job which required a great deal of technical expertise. You have been his manager for a year and you are disappointed in him as a supervisor.

He spends as much time as possible immersed in the detail and the technical work, and does not venture out of his office very much. He manages by writing long memoranda which set out what should be done, the methods to be used, and a clear timetable. If the results are not achieved the offender is called in for a good dressing-down.

Guy's results are barely adequate because of the rapid turnover of staff in his department.

(a) What is your analysis of the current situation?

(b) What steps would you take to help Guy improve?

[Total marks for question—25]

(*Hint:* This time the question gives more negative information—but don't fall into the trap of thinking that sending Guy on a course will be the answer to all his problems! After all, has a course ever had such a dramatic effect for you?)

Answer 1

Refer to the text of this chapter, and of Chapter 8.

Answer 2

Classical school

Main features are:
— belief in one central authority and one focus of loyalty,
— well defined views on span of control,
— clear division between line management and staff,
— the need for equal responsibility and authority,
— importance of delegation of authority,
— division of work into rational work assignments,
— well established policies and rules,
— close control,
— ignores the role of nonwork activities, and
— very manipulative.

Criticism usually centres on:
(a) The neglect of the importance of people—subsequently stressed by many authorities, e.g. Elton Mayo and his followers, the Tavistock Institute, the Glacier Institute; those believing in the pluralism of organisations and the importance of collective bargaining.

(b) The universality of the school. Subsequent work has shown how organisations vary significantly according to overall technology, objectives, type of market, nature of the environment, etc.

Human Relations school
Main features are:
— focuses on the paramount importance of people in organisations and stresses the relationship between good human relations and productivity,
— the role of managers is thought to be of key significance, particularly their managerial style,
— involvement and participation of employees in matters that affect them is stressed,
— communication and managerial skill in interpersonal relationships and relationships with groups of workers is important,
— managers are regarded as an élite who will play a pre-eminent role in the development of a stable industrial society,
— conflict is regarded as damaging.

Criticism:
(a) Evidence on the correlation between good relationships and productivity is unclear. Many regard the beliefs of this school to be derived from the needs of the managerial class to manipulate employees in the managers' interests.
(b) Subsequent investigations have stressed the importance of understanding the sociotechnical system as a basis for grasping the complexities of managing people in organisations. Others have drawn attention to the existence of conflict in organisations and the importance of poor relationships between employer and employee in the real world.

Answer 3

F.W. Taylor
Concerned with operational efficiency. Made important contribution to productivity increases through the application of the following principles:
— the separation of planning from doing,
— breaking each job into its basic elements,
— careful selection of people to do one element of the task,
— thorough training,
— reward according to output and quality.

In other words, he was concerned with standardisation and simplification of work. This is still important in banking especially in areas of highly routine tasks. It is one way of improving processing. O & M departments owe a great deal to Taylor. The adverse consequences of his ideas can also be seen—dull, monotonous work resulting in low morale and high labour turnover.

E. Mayo:
His ideas were revolutionary at the time. He observed that:
(a) Man is not only rational—he has feelings as well as being logical. This means:
(b) He responds better if he knows of matters going on outside his own area of work but which nevertheless affect him. Hence the importance of employee communication.
(c) Managers must understand these needs to acquire appropriate leadership skills, and
(d) To develop the interpersonal skills which enable them to understand the needs of their employees.
(e) Particular stress should be placed on listening skills and interviewing skills.

These ideas are still influential—particularly in the management development programmes of banks, in which interpersonal skills training and leadership training play an important part.

Answer 4

Mintzberg identified 10 managerial roles which he grouped into three categories:

Interpersonal roles
- (a) Figurehead—representing the organisation, branch, department or team to the outside world.
- (b) Leader—the person responsible for motivating the team towards the achievement of its common objectives.
- (c) Liaison—whereby the manager develops and maintains communication links with other teams, departments, etc.

Informational roles
- (d) Monitor—whereby the manager measures the progress towards the achievement of the objectives.
- (e) Disseminator—the person responsible for passing information to the group.
- (f) Spokesman—the person who represents the group and explains its views, etc., to other units.

Decisional roles
- (g) Entrepreneur—the person who is charged with making sure that things get done.
- (h) Disturbance handler—whereby the manager ensures that following disruption the work processes return to normal as swiftly and smoothly as possible.
- (i) Resource allocator—the manager has the prime responsibility to marshal and use his often limited resources to best effect towards the achievement of the objectives.
- (j) Negotiator—there will inevitably be competition between units for resources—the manager is responsible for bargaining on behalf of his group.

Although these roles give an indication of the totality of management it is unlikely that they are found to be performed at all times by all managers. Dawn may find that she is likely to spend most of her time as a monitor, resource allocator and disturbance handler. In talking with her it may be necessary to emphasise the point that the performance of these roles is vital to the success of the operation; it is important for her to operate in this managerial capacity rather than as one of the 'faceworkers'.

Answer 5 (outline only)

Analysis

The problem seems to be that Guy has continued to behave as a supertechnician rather than as a supervisor. This is because either he has not been told what being a supervisor means, or no-one has given him feedback on how he is behaving, or he is incapable of performing as a supervisor. Your first job is to find out which of these is true. He clearly has a very limited view of leadership and he does not understand the relative merits of oral and written communication.

Next steps
(a) Explain what you expect of a supervisor. Spell out the performance standards that you require.
(b) Through discussion and observation over the next three months try to work out whether he has the ability to become a supervisor.
(c) Give him help in:
 (i) understanding the range of possible leadership styles,
 (ii) practising the use of the appropriate style in specific situations,
 (iii) understanding the ways in which he can delegate work to subordinates, and
 (iv) training of subordinates.
(d) Counsel him to help him decide when to use oral and written communication—their relative advantages and disadvantages.
(e) Make arrangements to:
 (i) set him short-term goals to improve his supervisory skills,
 (ii) give him frequent feedback to let him know how he is getting on,
 (iii) coach and counsel him and arrange appropriate training, and
 (iv) if he fails to respond, warn him that you will have to take action to transfer him to other work.

CHAPTER 8

Managing the system

● The management job ● Henri Fayol ● Forecasting ● Planning ● Organising ●
Monitoring ● Controlling

▌ The management job

In Chapter 7 we examined the management roles—the way a manager must act—and touched on the management processes or functions—the things a manager must do. In this chapter we will examine the latter in much more detail.

Research has shown that there is a series of characteristics which distinguish managerial jobs from, say, clerical office jobs, or shop-floor jobs in a factory.

Typically management jobs will be characterised by:

(a) High activity levels—up to 200 different activities per day.
(b) Brief encounters, interruptions and discontinuity.
(c) Variety of forms of work—paper, phone, meetings, etc.
(d) Location of work—more time spent away from the department or organisation.
(e) Up to 90 per cent of work time is spent in oral communication.
(f) Networks of contacts, inside and outside the organisation, are important for information gathering.

Clearly every management job will be slightly different, but most will exhibit many of these characteristics. This gives a picture of a person who is always busy, under pressure, making swift decisions, rather than the stereotype sometimes presented of the manager as a cool, aloof individual, observing from afar and never harassed or flustered. If managers do appear that way, they are probably either not very effective, leaving others to do their work, or they are good actors!

In order to manage the system, in other words to manage an organisation or a department within it, the manager will normally be involved in a series of functions or processes as described below. Figure 8.1 shows in diagrammatic form a summary of those things which a manager must understand or be skilled at in order to manage the system and the people in it effectively and efficiently. We shall consider the people in more detail in Chapter 9; here we shall concentrate on managing the system itself.

▌ Henri Fayol

Henri Fayol was a French mining engineer, later managing director of his company, who lived from 1841 to 1925. He was in his seventies before he published his ideas on management in

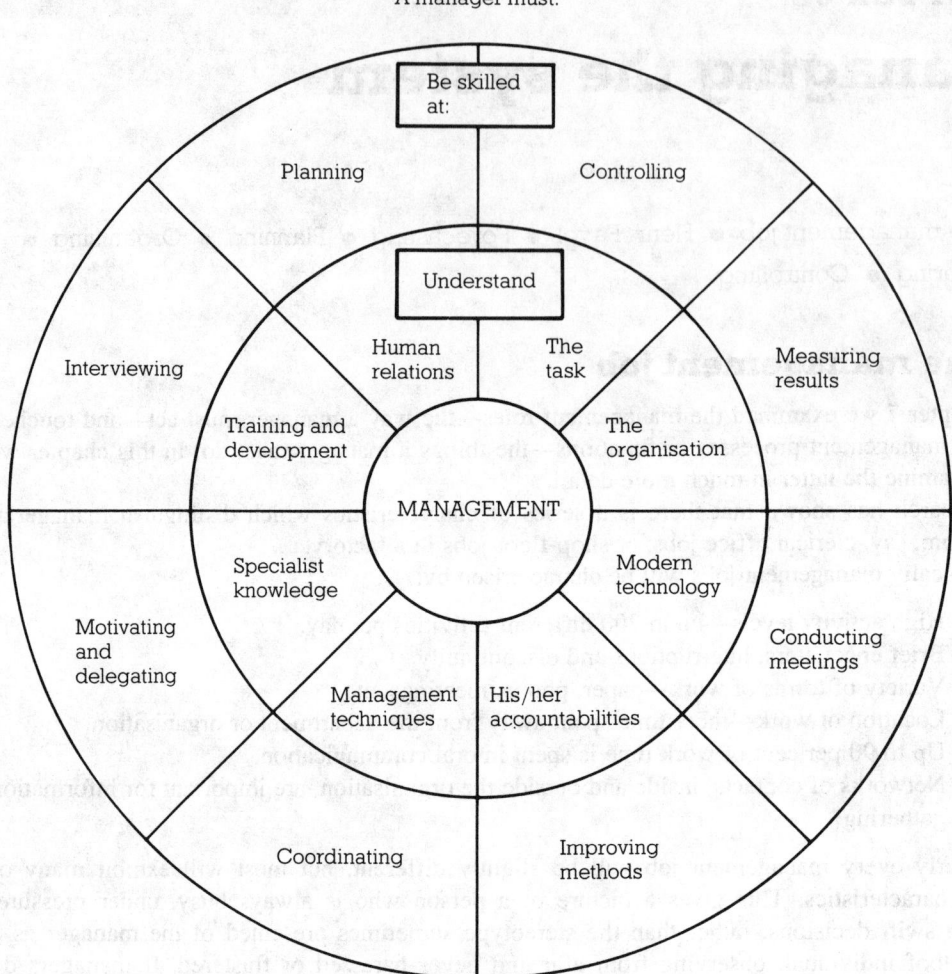

Fig. 8.1 A manager's essential skills and knowledge

1916. It was not until 1949 that his work was translated into English by Constance Storrs and published as *General and Industrial Management*.

Fayol is the earliest known proponent of a theoretical analysis of managerial activities—an analysis which has withstood over half a century of critical discussion. He suggested that all activities of organisations can be divided into:

(a) Technical activities (production, manufacture, adaptation).
(b) Commercial activities (buying, selling, exchange).
(c) Financial activities (search for and optimum use of capital).
(d) Security activities (protection of property and persons).
(e) Accounting activities (stocktaking, Balance Sheets, costs, statistics).
(f) Managerial activities (planning, organisation, command, coordination, control).

At the time, Fayol's definition of management was unique. He described it as comprising five elements:

(a) To forecast and plan (in French, *prévoyance*): 'examining the future and drawing up a plan of action'.
(b) To organise: 'building up the structure, material and human, of the undertaking'.
(c) To command: 'maintaining activity among the personnel'.
(d) To coordinate: 'binding together, unifying and harmonising all activity and effort'.
(e) To control: 'seeing that everything occurs in conformity with established rules and expressed command'.

Fayol regarded management as being essentially looking ahead, so planning and forecasting are a central business activity—the essence of planning being to allow the optimum use of resources.

Organising means building up an organisation which will allow the basic activities to be carried out in an optimal way. Central to this is a structure in which plans are efficiently prepared and carried out. There must, in Fayol's view, be unity of command and direction, clear definition of responsibilities, precise decision-making, backed up by an efficient system for selecting and training managers.

Fayol's third element, command, follows logically after the first two. Through an ability to command, a manager will obtain the best possible performance from subordinates. The word command is less popular these days, carrying as it does a connotation of unthinking obedience on the part of staff. It may be appropriate in the military, but a more consultative style of management is preferred in today's more participative organisations. Nevertheless, the manager must still motivate and lead his staff by example, knowledge of the business, knowledge of the subordinates, and continuous contact with staff, and by maintaining a high level of activity by instilling a sense of mission.

Coordination is necessary to bind together all activity and effort, making sure that one department's efforts are in line with those of the other departments and with the overall aims of the organisation. This requires a constant circulation of information and regular meetings of management.

The logical final element is control, checking that the other four elements are performing properly. Fayol believed the best way to ensure quick control and effective sanctions was to separate the inspection functions from the operating departments whose work they inspect.

Since Fayol's time, command has become an unfashionable word; control is seen as a function of monitoring followed by corrective action in a less rigid way, and motivation has become a prime management activity. This has led to a variety of alternative lists of the 'five management functions': for example, Bill Braddick in his book *Management for Bankers* listed: setting objectives; planning and forecasting; organisation coordination and decision-making; motivation; and control.

However, the Chief Examiner for Management in Banking, Ian Whyte, has listed his preferred five as: forecasting; planning; organising; monitoring; and controlling. These are the five we will concentrate on here.

Forecasting

No one would claim that managers should be able to foretell the future—the crystal ball is not yet an obligatory item on a manager's desktop! However, if plans are to be as accurate as possible, managers must be able to make educated guesses about what is likely to happen in the future, for example how the market for the company's products and services is likely to develop, the major forces at work in the country's economy, trends in the labour force, etc.

A forecast is a prediction of future events, as opposed to a plan, which is a predetermined response to the anticipated future events. Thus a forecast is an essential precursor to the process of planning.

All forecasting is difficult; in management, accurate forecasts are notoriously difficult to achieve. Environmental changes can occur very quickly; employment and other laws may alter; new agreements may be negotiated with unions; production techniques may be made obsolete by a new invention; consumer tastes may change overnight; suppliers may suddenly increase their prices, and so on. Generally, the shorter the time period of the forecast, the more chance there is of it being accurate.

In addition, forecasts are usually based on experience of the past and there is no guarantee that past trends will continue in the future.

Many firms therefore prepare both long- and short-term forecasts: the short-term forecast in detail, the long-term one in outline only (more a statement of intent than a prognostication) as it is not worth expending money and effort on detailed long-term predictions of highly uncertain events. There may even be a range of forecasts, each based on a slightly different set of assumptions about the future. These are sometimes called 'What If' analyses, as they examine **what** would happen **if** a certain set of circumstances prevailed.

Over time, the forecasts should be compared with plans or budgets and actual events or results so as to monitor the accuracy of the forecasts. If these prove to be highly inaccurate, the source of the error may be identifiable (inadequate or inaccurate data, faulty forecasting techniques or poor judgement on the part of the forecasters) and appropriate correction should enable more accurate forecasts to be prepared in the future.

Planning

Planning is looking ahead and making provision for the future. In more technical terms it is the selection of goals or objectives and the definition of policies, procedures and resources for achieving them. In order to plan, management will require internal information from the business (e.g. reports on current and forecast levels of production, staffing, etc.) and external information from the environment of the business (e.g. current and forecast levels of interest rates, prices of raw materials, etc.).

Planning can be divided into two types: long-range planning is concerned with the strategy of managing an organisation, whilst short-range planning is concerned with tactics, usually changes in components of the total plan, and often takes place at a lower level in the organisation.

Long-term planning (corporate)

Strategic planning is carried out by the highest levels of management in an organisation. In a major clearing bank, for example, it will be done by the executive committee or the board of directors, often supported by a corporate planning department. This will result in a corporate strategy, sometimes called a 'mission statement'. At this level, specific objectives may also be set—the precise things which are being aimed at.

Examples of the objectives of a large company might be to survive, to make a profit, to provide a service, to grow, to be efficient, to increase market share, to avoid being taken over, and so on.

Any planning process must start by identifying the objectives, continue by defining the activities which are involved in achieving these objectives, and setting targets for achievement in the key result areas. It is usually best not to plan in too much detail at a high level, but to leave the next level of management to work out more precisely how plans are to be achieved, since they are closer to the business and more able to make realistic, workable, detailed plans.

It is essential that all levels of management are committed to the planning process if it is to be worthwhile. Equally, plans must not be so rigid that they are incapable of modification in the light of changing conditions—the plan should be a tool in running the business, not a weapon of punishment for managers whose performance fails to meet planned targets when the underlying assumptions prove to be way out of line.

Short-term planning (departmental)

The departmental or branch manager will be required to make plans for his own office, based on the strategy laid down by the senior executives but incorporating the local conditions and objectives. These are often called targets or goals—the actual numbers being aimed at.

For example, a part of the corporate strategy may be to increase the small-business customer base; the branch plan will be to gain, say, an extra 50 business accounts in the year, whereas a similarly sized branch in a different type of location may plan to take on 100, or only 30, new accounts, depending on forecasts of local conditions (a branch near a developing new industrial estate in the first case, a branch in a predominantly residential area in the second, for instance).

Targets set must be measurable, otherwise it is impossible to tell if they have been achieved; they must be as specific as possible (e.g. reply to all written customer queries by the next working day, rather than 'deal with queries promptly'), and they should be challenging but attainable. Unrealistically high targets simply result in frustration and demotivation amongst those required to aim for them. In practice, the unattainable target will tend to be ignored and a more reasonable one will be set informally by the workers themselves. This emphasises the importance of involving staff at all levels in the planning process if it is to be realistic.

The manager's job, then, is to devise a plan to achieve the agreed target. This might involve allocating resources (money and staff) to particular tasks, devising a timetable of events (telephone calls to likely local firms, following up with a visit to their premises, etc.), fitting these activities in with other pressures of work on the branch, making sure sufficient stationery is in stock to supply 'welcome' packs and ordering more if necessary, and so on.

The manager will also need to plan his own time and work schedule. This is covered in greater detail in Chapter 14, but meanwhile, consider how well you plan your own work—do you keep a detailed diary showing regular meetings, when reports are required from you, which days to keep free for expected urgent work, etc.?

Organising

Organising (also referred to as coordination) is the management activity of putting the plan into practice—putting all the elements together in such a way that the overall plan succeeds as effectively and efficiently as possible.

In the example of the branch manager targeting new small-business accounts, it will be the steps he takes to ensure that the plan is feasible—taking on or training staff, ordering stationery, obtaining the names and addresses of contacts in possible customer firms, etc. He will need to ensure that all the departments of his branch are working in an integrated way (i.e. without conflict, or duplication of effort, pulling in the same direction) towards the common goal.

Mintzberg on organising

It is tempting sometimes to think of all management theorists as having been dead for years. This is far from the case; many are relatively young men and women who are alive and kicking and actively writing on their subject.

A case in point is Henry Mintzberg, currently professor of management at McGill University in Montreal. In a recently published collection of his speeches and papers (*Mintzberg on Management*) he emphasises that it is not enough for companies to develop plans and strategies; they also have to implement them. In rather a tongue-in-cheek way, he defines implementation as: 'dropping a solution into the laps of people informed enough to know it won't work but restricted from telling anyone in power what can'.

Mintzberg attributes the success of some Japanese companies, such as Honda, to the fact that senior executives were prepared to listen to their employees who were closer to the market place, and modify company strategy accordingly. British managers might argue that they too have done much to improve communication with their workers, through team briefings, company newspapers and videos to explain corporate strategy to the workforce. However, Mintzberg would counter that while these devices enable management to talk to their employees, they do little to help employees talk to management.

Since it is the employees who have to put management's plans into practice, who know most about the production process and the preferences of customers, who run the company's equipment and sell and service its products, management would do well to seek their contribution and advice. Whilst there are some UK companies which make efforts to use their employees' intelligence and experience, to most executives the idea that their subordinates might know more about aspects of the business than they do is anathema.

Mintzberg instances one UK employee who, on a trip abroad discovered an ideal market for his company's products. Arriving back in the office filled with enthusiasm he telephoned the director responsible. The director's secretary demanded to know what he wanted, and then went off to speak to her boss. On her return she announced: 'He says to put it in a memo.' As Mintzberg points out, we tend to build our organisations so that they cannot learn. In his words: 'The formulators lack the information, the implementers lack the power.'

■ Monitoring

It is realistic to expect that activities of the business will not necessarily go exactly according to plan. Management must therefore monitor, i.e. get information on the performance of the organisation relative to the plan.

All organisations keep records of various kinds, but these records must be in sufficient detail and accuracy to enable proper comparisons to be made. For example, if a small shop keeps records of total sales, but not of sales of individual products, the shopkeeper will be unable to identify which lines are selling badly when he finds his total sales are lower than expected. If he kept separate totals for sales of newspapers and magazines, sweets, cigarettes and groceries, he would be able to spot when cigarette sales dropped—perhaps because a rival shop has opened around the corner selling the same brands at lower prices.

Keeping these records and examining them is **monitoring**; deciding what to do about them is **control**.

A decision must be made as to how frequently information is required upon which to make comparisons. This will vary widely depending on the type of business, the type of information, etc. Two major considerations influence the decision. Firstly, what is the cost of obtaining the information? Secondly, how much time may be allowed to elapse before a variance from plan will begin to cost an unacceptable amount in terms of money, time or other resources?

With food products, for example, continuous monitoring of quality, weight and appearance may well be needed to maintain the required standard. With domestic appliances, on the other hand, the thickness of paint on a fridge door may be checked by sampling one machine out of each batch, but is not so crucial as to require every item to be checked individually.

Similarly, in banking, the manager targeted to increase small-business accounts may well review the figures each month to see that the branch is on line to meet the target, but checking twice a day would be unnecessary.

On the other hand, the amount of cash in the branch safe will be checked at least once, and possibly several times a day, since the less frequent the 'monitoring', the greater the chance of a serious loss going undetected. It is all a question of degree—how far is the manager (or the organisation) prepared to risk the possibility of loss, balanced against the cost of carrying out checks?

This introduces the concept of a 'significant variance'. There is no fixed rule to determine what constitutes a significant variance; this must be left to the experience of the manager. To take a personal example, if your home telephone bill is usually around £50 per quarter, would you regard a bill of £55 as showing a significant variance? Probably not. What about a bill for £325? This would probably send you straight to the telephone company to complain that there must be a mistake; however, it could be perfectly acceptable if your sister in America had just had twins and you had been telephoning daily for news of the mother and babies. The point at which an increased bill became significant would therefore be a matter for judgement—say, a 20 per cent increase on the previous reading, combined with knowledge of any changes in circumstances.

It is quite easy for managers to be swamped with too much information from monitoring systems. To get around this problem, the concept of 'management by exception' has gained favour. Once the manager has decided what constitutes a significant variance, he will be informed only of variances which exceed this level; everything else is assumed to be OK. Some managers find it very difficult to do this as it requires trust in subordinates to tell them when something **is** wrong. It also requires detailed, agreed plans so that it is clear what constitutes a variance.

Within retail bank branches, much of the monitoring is done by computer—printouts are received regularly detailing accounts which are operating unusually in some way—for example, where no credits have been received in a certain period, where a deposit account is showing a debit balance, where a loan account has not received a regular repayment, where a borrowing limit is overdue for review, and so on.

Controlling

How often, in a film or television play, have you heard one of the characters cry, in some emergency: 'Don't just stand there, do something!' In the film, the person who responds is often the hero or heroine, taking the necessary action to save the day. In business, it is the manager who is responsible for taking action when a situation gets 'out of control'.

Having obtained information on results relative to plan by monitoring the business, management must take action to control any deviation. Information for this purpose must be timely and accurate; there is little value in information about a deviation from plan if it is too late to do anything about it.

Basically, there are three courses of action which the manager can take when presented with evidence of a variance from plan: do nothing; change the plan; or adjust the operation in some way.

In a retail bank branch, the manager or his deputy will examine a warning list each morning, showing accounts which will go overdrawn or over an agreed overdraft limit unless action is taken. The manager may decide to permit the overdraft (do nothing), to arrange an overdraft limit or other facility with the customer (change the plan), or he may decide to 'bounce' a cheque received in the morning clearing to bring the account back into order (change the operation).

Controls can be devised to operate on any element of an organisation: money, materials, equipment and even people. With inanimate objects like money and materials, the question is how much control is needed to avoid significant loss; with people it is rather more tricky. Excessive control over staff can lead to a feeling of not being trusted and a lack of motivation—too little control can encourage abuse from those looking for an excuse to be idle. The degree of control is therefore linked inversely to the degree of trust (more trust, less tight control) although there must come a point where the question has to be asked—if there is no trust between manager and staff, is that a reasonable basis on which to operate at all?

Figure 8.2 takes a light-hearted look at monitoring and control, suggesting options for the incompetent manager. By pointing out the dangers of messing about with things unnecessarily, it illustrates the wisdom of a well-known American saying, applicable to almost any walk of life: 'If it ain't broke, don't fix it!'

Managing the system

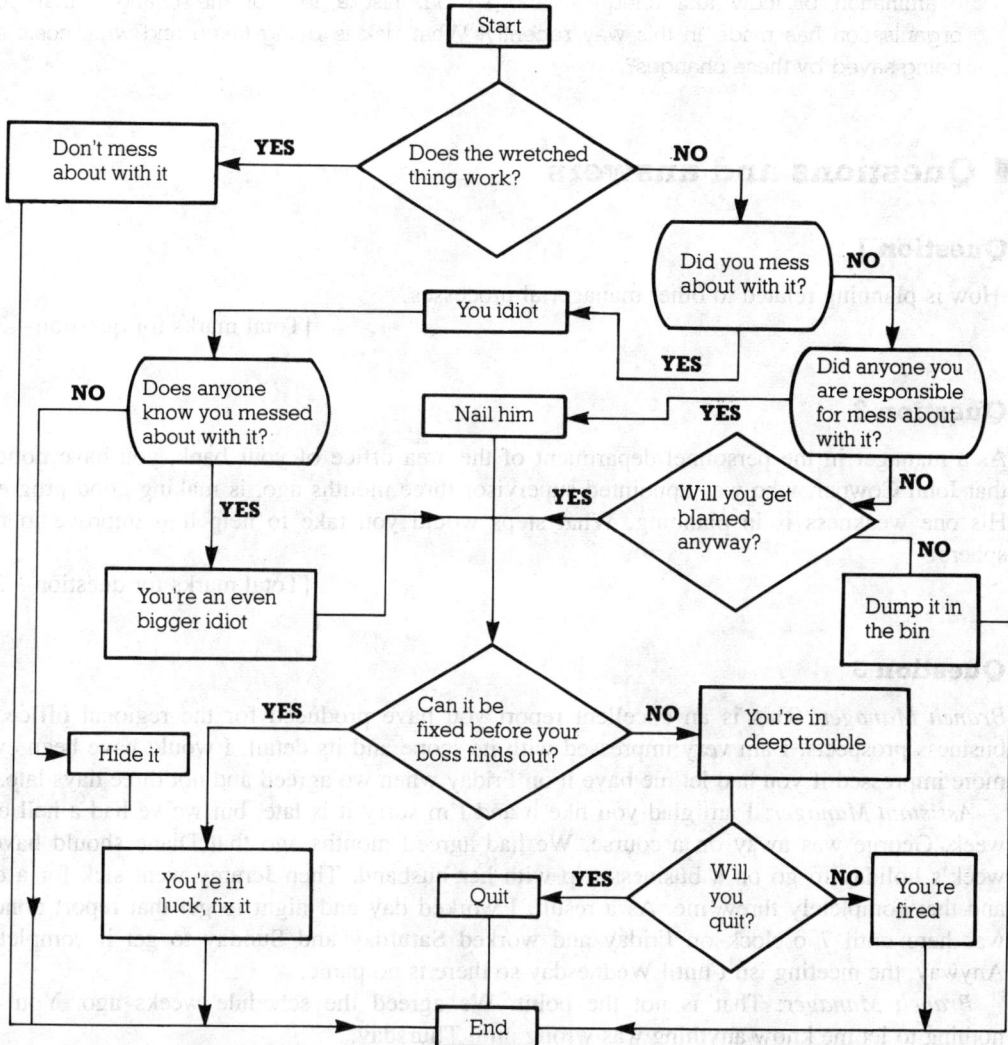

Fig. 8.2 Troubleshooting flowchart (how not to monitor and control the situation!)

Action points

(a) What is the corporate strategy of your bank? Has it been clearly communicated to you? If you are not sure what it is, get hold of a copy of your bank's Annual Report and Accounts and read the Chairman's statement.

(b) If you had a good idea for promoting the business of your branch or bank, how would you inform your management? Do you think you would be listened to? Is there a system for staff suggestions in your organisation, and do you think it works?

(c) Most banks have been reducing the level and frequency of checks on clerical procedures, examination of individual cheques, and so on. List a few of the changes that your organisation has made in this way recently. What risk is being taken and what costs are being saved by these changes?

Questions and answers

Question 1

How is planning related to other managerial processes?

[Total marks for question—25]

Question 2

As a manager in the personnel department of the area office of your bank, you have noticed that John Cowper, who was appointed supervisor three months ago, is making good progress. His one weakness is in planning. What steps would you take to help him improve in this sphere?

[Total marks for question—25]

Question 3

Branch Manager: This is an excellent report you have produced for the regional office on business prospects. I am very impressed with its scope and its detail. I would have been even more impressed if you had let me have it on Friday when we agreed and not three days late.

Assistant Manager: I am glad you like it and I'm sorry it is late, but we've had a hell of a week. George was away on a course. We had agreed months ago that Diane should have a week's holiday to go on a business trip with her husband. Then Jeremy went sick for a day and that completely threw me. As a result, I worked day and night to get that report done. I was here until 7 o'clock on Friday and worked Saturday and Sunday to get it completed. Anyway, the meeting isn't until Wednesday so there is no panic.

Branch Manager: That is not the point. We agreed the schedule weeks ago. You did nothing to let me know anything was wrong until Thursday.

Assistant Manager: I must say I don't feel I have received much reward for working flat out for a week. I'm completely exhausted and this is all the thanks I get.

Branch Manager: I'm not complaining about your ability or your hard work, but I do think you could organise better.

Required:
(a) Your analysis of the problems of this case. [15]
(b) How can the manager help his assistant do his job better? [10]

[Total marks for question—25]

Question 4

Things seem to go wrong unexpectedly in the department of which you have recently been appointed supervisor. You have been caught out several times and made to look rather foolish because it seems as if you do not know what is going on. What should you do to ensure that this situation is corrected?

[Total marks for question—25]

(*Hint:* This question is not just about planning—there is another equally important and inseparable element).

Answer 1

Planning is one of the main processes of management. The others include the setting of objectives, forecasting, organisation and coordination, motivation and control. All these are related and the omission of any one will impair the efficiency of the others.

Setting objectives:	Objectives must be set otherwise planning will take place in a vacuum.
Forecasting:	Forecasting is concerned with making an estimate of the likely market and its potential growth so that plans can be made to achieve an appropriate share.
Planning process:	Planning itself operates at several levels. Strategic and long-term plans are made for a specific future period—say 4/5 years. Corporate and departmental operating plans are usually developed on an annual basis. These are very specific and quantifiable.
Organisation and coordination:	The purpose of organisation is to provide the structure to enable objectives to be achieved. It is clearly related to planning in that poor organisation and coordination will reduce the possibility of succeeding in hitting a planned target.
Motivation:	This relates to planning because plans can be achieved only through people, and careful thought must be given to creating conditions under which they will work to achieve corporate objectives. An important part of motivation concerns the involvement of people in the planning process.
Control:	It is useless to plan unless one has knowledge of how far one's day-to-day activities relate to the planned course of action. Control information is therefore vital to monitor and detect any deviation from plan as a basis for corrective action.

These processes should be regarded as a cycle of related activities, all of which are critically interdependent.

Answer 2

Discuss with John the importance of planning as a managerial process. Explain the need to anticipate future workload, identify short-term goals, and have clear performance standards in mind for the department and individuals within it. Impress on him the need to monitor progress and to modify the plan accordingly. Explain the importance of involving his staff in the planning process and get him to appreciate the importance of making plans in the light of information concerning the wider organisational goals.

Explore with him whether he experiences any of the following problems:
(a) Does he try to keep too many options open so that he is unlikely to set realistic goals?
(b) Is he afraid of being judged? If a goal is set and plans are made it is possible to measure success or failure. For some, this is a frightening prospect. Is it for John?
(c) Does he really understand the organisation? Effective goal setting and planning involves a knowledge of organisational goals and the work of other departments to be fully effective. Lack of knowledge of these might cause conflict or duplication. Can you help him?
(d) He might lack information on the outside world. If John does not understand the needs of his clients, competitors, etc., the goals he sets will be confused and inadequate. You should check this.
(e) He might not be convinced that the organisation will provide the resources to achieve plans or that he can achieve them if the resources are available. Explain what help he can expect.

Explore ways of overcoming difficulties:
(a) Make sure that all possible information is available to him about the wider plan (including environmental information) so that he can understand his department's contribution.
(b) Make sure he involves all levels of staff in the planning process.
(c) Reward him when he makes a successful contribution to the planning process and its implementation.
(d) Set him clear goals in this area—identify the standards you require.
(e) Support him, coach him and give him feedback about progress.

Answer 3

Symptoms/issues
— High-quality work.
— Everyone away simultaneously.
— No real concern with deadlines.
— Did much of drafting himself.
— Comparison between technical work and management.

Analysis
The root of the problem is that the work is badly scheduled and handled. The case suggests that the need for this report has been known for some time; but everything seems to have been left until the last minute in spite of the fact that two of the absences were known about in advance.

The assistant manager seems to think that management means doing what he was doing before but working harder at it. He seems to have no conception that managerial work is quite different in kind from non-managerial work.

To help the assistant manager, the branch manager should think about setting a good example. He appears to have let the assistant manager get on with very little supervision so that he was taken by surprise when the report was late.

Action

The manager should explain to his subordinate that successful management involves:
  (a) The setting of objectives.
  (b) Careful scheduling and planning of work, taking into account known difficulties, to achieve deadlines.
  (c) The organisation of his department so that each person is clear about his responsibilities and has well defined goals and tasks.
  (d) The motivation of his staff by making clear what is expected of them, keeping them informed of progress, etc.
  (e) Monitoring of progress of projects, controlling deviation from plan by taking corrective action.

The manager should:
  (a) Help the assistant manager to set targets for himself and his staff.
  (b) Review progress with him regularly.
  (c) Help him with difficulties.
  (d) Reinforce his strengths with appropriate rewards (e.g. recognition, encouragement, praise—as well as financial rewards).
  (e) Counsel him about areas for improvement by coaching, example, and appropriate training.
  (f) Check that his resources are adequate.

Answer 4

Symptoms
  — Unexpected happenings.
  — Manager taken by surprise.
  — Does he know what is going on?

Analysis
He is not planning and, particularly, not controlling the work of his department.

Planning
The first step is to establish a plan for the department so that the manager can see what his aim is and how he intends to get there. It is very helpful if the plan is quantified and specific as this helps at other stages of the control process.

Monitor and Control
Comparison: Records must be kept to allow a comparison between the plan and actual progress. If these records are to be useful they must be in sufficient detail to allow useful comparison, e.g. if a range of different items is being produced, an overall output figure will not be sufficient to monitor detailed progress.

Frequency: A key element in any control system is to determine how frequently information must be made available to enable corrective action to be taken. Many management information systems provide information far too late; others supply so much information that the relevant cannot be separated from the irrelevant.

Variations: When comparisons are available it is important to alert the responsible persons about significant deviations so that they can take appropriate action.

Speed: The sooner the information is available, the more likely it is that appropriate action can be taken.

Decisions: The control system must supply information which is specific enough, and in sufficient time, to allow a manager to take the appropriate action to:

(a) change the organisation to meet the plan, or
(b) modify the plan.

This feedback process must be continuous, accurate, timely and cost-justifiable.

CHAPTER 9
Managing the people

● Choice of management/leadership styles ● Blake Mouton grid ● Ashridge model (tells, sells, consults, joins) ● Action-centred leadership (John Adair) ● Summary of leadership styles ● Relationship with internal and external customers, bosses, peers and subordinates ● Delegation

■ Choice of management/leadership styles

Management style

Management has been defined as 'getting things done through people'. The newly appointed manager might have been a very good clerk, salesperson or whatever, but he is now required to acquire new competences in interviewing, delegation, influencing people, negotiation, performance appraisal, setting objectives, etc. Refer back to Fig 8.1 to remind yourself of the range of managerial skills and knowledge required.

Effective managers must be good communicators, able to turn their hands to a variety of activities, able to work easily with others and to adopt a flexible approach, quick to respond to change. Introspective individuals who are happiest working alone are rarely successful and effective executives.

When you become a manager (or if you already are one) how you manage your team will depend on your personal inclinations, your training and environmental factors, such as the culture of your organisation. You should also make a conscious decision about your management style, and in particular your leadership style, in the same way as you choose your style of dress or the type of house you live in—it is essentially something personal to you.

Managers are not judged so much by the work they produce as individuals as by their ability to achieve results through the efforts of their team. You will therefore want to choose a style which has the best influence on the morale and hence the productivity of your department.

Leadership style

I have mentioned before that one of the key attributes of a manager is the ability to act as a leader—to take decisions, to suggest solutions, to resolve crises and to direct the activities of the team.

Early studies concentrated on the idea that leaders were born not made, and tried to identify personal traits which would predispose a person to be a good leader and therefore a good manager. Although the studies failed to demonstrate a consistent pattern, the armed services still adhere to this notion to a considerable degree, selecting potential officers on the results of interviews and exercises (written and physical) designed to identify 'leadership material'. Some of you may have undergone similar selection procedures when joining your bank, or when applying to join an accelerated management development programme.

Modern thinking is that, whilst certain personalities will find leadership more natural than others, good leadership techniques can certainly be taught and improved. Peter Drucker, who has been economic adviser to various banks and insurance companies and is one of the leading contemporary writers on management policy issues, has said that all executives can learn to be effective, if they practise hard enough.

The remainder of this chapter runs through three of the major theories of management/leadership style, discusses relationships with the various groups with whom you will interact as a manager, and concludes with a consideration of one of the important skills which flow from leadership—the ability to delegate effectively to your subordinates.

■ Blake Mouton grid

Robert Blake and Jane Mouton are American psychologists, currently running a company providing behavioural science consultancy services to industry. Their work is based on the assumption that managerial competence can be taught and learned. They see a manager's job as involving fostering positive attitudes and behaviour among staff, stimulating creativity, encouraging innovation and promoting efficient performance to get the task done.

Their 'grid' provides a theoretical framework against which managers are able to understand their style of organising people to achieve the task. The managerial grid has been

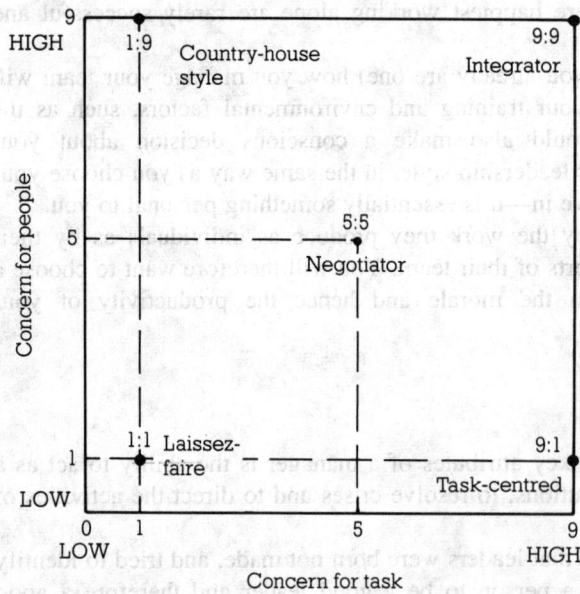

Fig. 9.1 Leadership styles: the Blake Mouton grid

successfully applied in a variety of different countries, types of organisation, and functional departments within organisations. It is equally applicable from the supervisory level right up to senior executive levels.

The Blake Mouton grid is illustrated in Fig. 9.1. It relates the strength of two basic elements of managerial behaviour: concern for people and concern for production. In this context 'production' means not just physical products, as in a factory, but all types of output: accounts processed, volume of sales, quality of service given, etc. Likewise concern for people implies concern for their self-respect, their right to fair and equitable treatment, their aspirations, etc., as well as their physical wellbeing.

Every manager will exhibit more or less of these two attributes (concern for production, and concern for people) in their approach to managing their staff. The manager may show a high degree of concern for production and a low degree of concern for people, or vice versa, or may demonstrate a low degree of both, or a high degree of both, or (more probably) a middling degree of concern for each aspect. In practice, successful managers may fall in a variety of places on the grid, depending on the circumstances in which they are operating. The same manager may also adopt a different approach in differing circumstances, placing himself in a variety of points on the grid on different occasions.

Any point on the grid is feasible but, for the sake of simplicity, we shall look at the four corners and the centre of the grid in more detail.

1:1 Laissez faire manager

A manager who shows very low concern for production combined with low concern for people is virtually abdicating all responsibility. He will do just enough to keep his job and stay out of trouble, but in effect is leaving his staff to 'get on with it'. Staff of such a manager will tend to be lazy and apathetic, and output will be minimal.

1:9 Country house manager

The manager who scores 1 on concern for production but 9 on concern for people likes to maintain a cosy 'country house' (sometimes referred to as 'country club') atmosphere, valuing friendly relationships more highly than productivity. People are encouraged and supported and their mistakes overlooked, because they are 'doing the best they can'. The deficiency is that people try to avoid disagreements or direct criticism and production problems are glossed over.

9:1 Task-centred manager

In contrast to the 1:9 manager, the 9:1 manager values high productivity whatever the cost in human terms. Individual needs are ignored and people are regarded as units of production, being told exactly what to do to maximise output. This style of management can achieve high output in the short term, but individual creativity will be directed to defeating the system rather than improving it and resentment may simmer under the surface—this style can easily lead to union/management confrontation.

9:9 Integrator

The 9:9 style manager obtains high productivity through gaining commitment from his staff. This style harnesses individual and group motivation to the common task and so makes fullest use of the energy contained in the whole system. This manager does not accept that there is any incompatibility between the two concerns and attempts to integrate people around production. Problems are confronted directly and openly, not as personal disputes. The 9:9 style is regarded by Blake and Mouton as the best, since it builds on long-term development and trust. Some would see it as rather idealistic—it requires a very skilled and energetic manager to maintain the high level of staff morale necessary to keep production at the highest levels at all times.

5:5 Negotiator

This is perhaps the commonest style for reasonably successful managers. It is a compromise position. This type of manager sticks to rules and procedures and aims at producing as much as possible without upsetting people. Managers sometimes alternate between 1:9 and 9:1—tightening up to increase output, then softening when human relationships begin to suffer. The middle-of-the-road 5:5 manager shifts only marginally around the 'happy medium'. He pushes enough to get acceptable production but yields enough to maintain acceptable morale—fair but firm.

▋ Ashridge model (tells, sells, consults, joins)

A second model of leadership styles was developed at Ashridge Management College in England in the 1960s and 1970s. This identified four styles of leadership:

- Tells
- Sells
- Consults
- Joins

Tells

The manager makes his own decisions and tells his subordinates what he has decided and what they must do. They are expected to carry out the manager's instructions without question.

Sells

The manager in this case has also made his own decision, but instead of simply announcing it to the subordinates, he tries to persuade them that it is the best decision—he sells the decision to them to reduce any potential resistance.

Consults

A manager using this style does not make the decision until he has consulted with his staff. He gives them the opportunity to contribute ideas, suggestions and advice—recognising that they may in fact know more about certain subjects than he does himself and may have valuable specialist knowledge to share. The decision is still finally the manager's, but it will not be taken until he has listened to the views of his staff, who thus feel much more involved and important.

Joins

In this style, the manager joins with the rest of the group on an equal basis to make a democratic decision. The manager defines the problem and may indicate limits within which the decision can be made (for example, budget limits). The problem will then be discussed freely among the group and the final decision will normally reflect the majority decision.

This set of four styles is easy to understand and apply in real life. No doubt you can think of examples in your day-to-day work. Most managers will adopt different styles in differing situations. If the building is on fire, the manager will tell you to get out—there is no time for a democratic decision! On the other hand, if the rest room is to be repainted, he may well adopt a 'joins' style, allowing free discussion to decide the colour scheme, furnishings, etc. In between these two extremes, there will be occasions when rules or instructions from above will mean that a decision (e.g. to introduce wordprocessors) has effectively already been made, but your manager may try to 'sell' the decision to you, to gain support as far as possible. On the question of how to organise the introduction of the wordprocessors, and the training which will need to take place, the manager may be willing to 'consult' with you, taking advice from the team on the best way of arranging the changes.

Thus, while some managers will tend to act in a particular style most of the time, many managers will in fact adopt all four styles from time to time in differing circumstances.

▌Action-centred leadership (John Adair)

Dr John Adair, in the 1970s, developed a model to illustrate how people and the work they do interact (see Fig. 9.2). His model is known as 'action-centred leadership'. Three overlapping circles represent the three important elements which a manager (or any leader) must take into account—achieving the task, building the team (or group) and developing the individual.

The circles overlap to indicate that each of these aspects interacts with, and has influence over, the other two. For example, team morale and individual job satisfaction will be high when the task is seen by all to have been achieved (as, for example, when a sports team wins a match). Similarly, a well-knit team can influence the degree of success in achieving a task by all pulling together; this can be more successful than a collection of isolated individuals, however highly skilled. Conversely, a succession of failures in the task can reduce team and individual morale, or a lack of team spirit can lead to task failure.

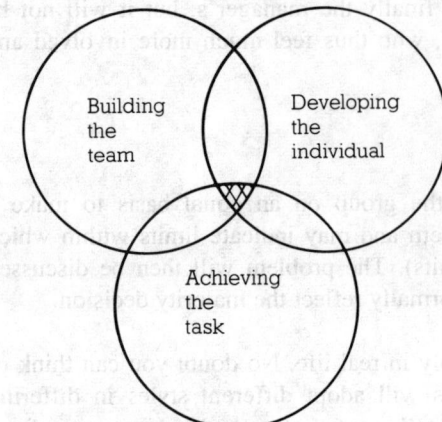

Fig. 9.2 Action-centred leadership

Supervisors who concentrate too much on the task fail to achieve optimum output when compared with similar teams. Supervisors of the high-producing teams were more employee-centred, but this too can be taken too far, in which case productivity suffers. The correct balance calls for the harnessing of individual motivation and group spirit to the performance of a common task.

Summary of leadership styles

Reading through the sections above, you should have noticed something—all the theories of management/leadership styles are really just different ways of saying the same thing. It is not enough to manage one element (people or task) very well; there must be a balance between them for the most effective and efficient result.

These ideas are not new. Admiral Lord Nelson is quoted as saying: 'You can't have a happy ship unless it is an efficient ship; you can't have an efficient ship unless it is a happy ship.'

There are many other models and theories for leadership and management styles, but the three above should be ample for the Management in Banking syllabus. Other phrases you may hear are 'contingency theory,' which simply means that managers should adapt their style contingent on the particular circumstances, and 'trait theory'—which was mentioned at the start of the chapter—the idea (now discredited) that leaders are born not made, so that it is personality or psychological traits which define a good manager.

Make sure that you can understand fully the major theories outlined above, but even more important, make sure you understand how these theories apply in practice.

∎ Relationship with internal and external customers, bosses, peers and subordinates

In the working day, a manager will interact with a variety of different people: subordinates in his own or other departments, colleagues in the same department or elsewhere in the organisation, superiors, suppliers, customers, perhaps representatives of the local community, the press, government departments (e.g. the Inland Revenue), and so on.

Whilst his approach to each of these groups will be slightly different, a common thread runs through all interpersonal relationships: in all cases work relationships should be polite, well mannered and even-handed (firm but fair). If the manager allows personal preferences to influence business relationships this is a recipe for friction, noncooperation and even outright conflict.

Interpersonal skills are vital for effective management; they can be learned and improved but they will have been developing since very early in our lives. The attitudes we develop in childhood act as a frame of reference against which we judge and resolve new problems. Thus, drives, emotions and unconscious ideas are as much a part of our attitudes as rational thought. Powerful forces are at work to make an individual conserve his existing attitudes, which may make his approach so rigid that it builds barriers between himself and others. Managers must therefore be willing to question their ingrained attitudes, to be objective and retain a flexible response to experience. It is all too easy to see only what we want to see; to rationalise or forget what does not fit in with our world view; to ignore or distrust reality.

Just as important as what we do is what others see us doing or hear us doing (or think they see or hear us doing!). The way we behave has a direct influence on the way others respond: we smile—they smile; we get angry—they get angry; we show a willingness to compromise—and so do they; and so on.

As managers, we should try to maximise effective behaviour patterns, for example by:

— listening perceptively,
— seeking information/suggestions/solutions,
— suggesting alternatives,
— disagreeing constructively,
— clarifying,
— summarising,
— offering solutions, etc.,

and minimise ineffective or destructive behaviour such as:

— showing our feelings (irritation, annoyance) at the wrong time,
— talking too much or too little,
— boasting,
— moaning,
— not listening, and
— losing our temper.

Transactional analysis

A useful way of analysing and understanding our own and other people's behaviour is called transactional analysis (TA). If you are interested, many books are available which will give you far more detail than is possible here, but in essence the ideas are as follows.

We all contain three states within us—the child state, the adult state and the parent state. Developing from our infancy, these are ways of feeling, aspects of our ego, accompanied by patterns of behaviour. They can be visualised as three video tapes running in our brains. At any one time, or in any one situation, there may be elements of all three tapes running but one or two will probably predominate.

The 'child' ego reacts spontaneously and emotionally with the feelings and instincts of childhood, using phrases like 'You always try to ...', 'I will in a minute ...'; 'If she can, so can I ...', 'It's mine ...'.

The 'adult' ego is mature and deliberating, making decisions based on facts but almost devoid of feelings, asking questions and seeking out facts: 'Why did it happen?', 'What are the choices?', 'Let's find out.', 'Let's define it'.

The 'parent' ego corrects and criticises, but also nurtures and takes care of people, reflecting our experiences of parents and teachers. The controlling parent uses phrases like: 'Why haven't you ...', 'What will people say ...', 'Never ...', 'Always ...', whilst the caring parent says: 'Take care ...', 'Don't be late ...', 'Remember to ...', 'I'll help you to ...'.

It is possible to take a test, consisting of answering a series of questions on your attitudes and behaviour, which will give you a reading of the relative strengths of your 'child', 'adult' and 'parent' egos. An example of someone with strong 'adult' ego would be a judge; a strong 'parent and adult' ego would make a good airline pilot; a campaigner for good causes would probably have strong 'parent and child' egos whereas an actor or TV presenter would probably have strong 'adult and child' egos.

Reacting skilfully to others depends on recognising which 'tape' is being played, i.e. what ego state they are in, so that you can respond appropriately. In a work environment, an 'adult'-to-'adult' communication is probably the safest in all situations unless you are sure that the other party will respond positively to an alternative approach.

The following paragraphs run through a few commonsense points about the way a manager should interact with the various groups he meets during the working day.

Customers

Customers, both external and internal (other departments in the organisation) can be notoriously difficult to handle, but the manager should never allow irritation to lead him to losing his temper or becoming abusive. Relationships between the various parties listed above are too important to the success of the business to allow them to be jeopardised by personal grievances, hurt pride or a clash of personalities. If the manager genuinely finds a certain client impossible to handle effectively, it may well be better to allow one of his staff to conduct business with the customer.

As explained in a previous chapter, effective cooperation between departments of the organisation which rely on each other to pass work on or to provide input to the task can be made much easier by frequent liaison between departmental heads. It is also valuable for staff at lower levels to be encouraged to spend some time seeing how the other department works, to get a perception of their problems and pressures.

Bosses

I suggested right at the start of this book that we all need to be able to manage our boss—to make sure he does what is needed to make our job possible, looks after our interests, keeps us informed of things that affect our work and so on. Good communications between manager and boss are essential for this to happen.

A frequently heard complaint is 'My boss doesn't listen'. There is a variety of possible reasons for this—assuming that he understands what you are saying to him, but still will not do anything about it; it could be that his own problems are more pressing, or he is not interested, or he thinks the problem can be solved without his interference.

Since the boss's time is precious, make sure you are not long-winded or uninteresting when you write or speak to him. Be clear and unambiguous, stick to facts or well supported theories to convince him that your solution or recommendation is the right one. If you are presenting him with a problem, make an attempt, at least, to suggest a solution so that he does not need to think the thing right through from the start—do as much of the work for him as possible and you are more likely to get acceptance for the course of action you want to follow.

Peers

For many managers, lateral relationships with managers of equivalent status in other departments or organisations, or diagonal relationships with their superiors or subordinates are frequent and important.

The difficulty in lateral relationships is that you have no authority over the people with whom you are dealing, so you must rely on persuasion, negotiation, and trading something you need for something you can offer the other party. You may be seeking information, a favourable decision, or a speedier delivery, or you may have made a mess of something or put another manager in a difficult position and you are looking for exoneration or to make amends. You may need to use a variety of social skills—from sympathy, through cheerfulness to sparkling charisma!

Favours given at one time may be called in at a later date and it is always worthwhile cultivating good relationships with your peers so that, when you do need to call on them for help in an emergency, they are willing at least to listen to your plea.

There is an old saying in business—'Treat people well on the way up—you may meet them again on the way down!' (In other words, if you trample on people around you in the rush to gain promotion or power, beware—they may be in a position to make life very difficult for you if you fall from grace in a few years time and they are in a position of power over you.)

Subordinates

Relationships with subordinates are considered throughout this book. Suffice it to say here that you should establish a high degree of trust and goodwill between yourself and your staff. This will ensure that your subordinates are willing to come to you with problems before they become crises and will enable you to call on your staff for that little extra effort when the task requires it.

▊ Delegation

No manager can do all the work himself. The skill of management is to get the job done, but to do so through the best possible use of the skills of the people in the team. To do this it is essential that work is delegated to staff who are willing and able to carry it out.

Delegation does not mean that the manager abdicates his responsibilities for seeing that the job is well done. He will need to agree clear objectives with the staff, perhaps to see and agree their plans for getting the work done, and then to leave them to do it in their own way. It is wise to ask for regular reports of progress against these plans. The manager must be available to listen to problems and to provide advice and guidance when necessary.

Delegation is an important tool in building trust between boss and staff; the challenge and achievement associated with it will encourage and motivate staff.

An inevitable result of delegation is that some mistakes will be made. This is an important part of learning for the staff and the manager must be prepared to accept responsibility for these mistakes personally—allowing the staff to develop and learn from their experiences but ensuring that no really damaging mistakes are made.

Good communication skills are essential for good delegation. Rather than dogmatically issuing criticism and instructions, the manager should discuss plans and progress with the staff, encouraging them to draw out the weaknesses themselves.

It is essential that managers delegate some of their work; there are not enough hours in the day to allow them not to—but what is more difficult is to decide what to delegate. There is a tendency for only the boring, uninteresting work to be delegated, with the manager keeping the exciting parts of the job for himself. This will quickly be spotted by the staff, who will resent being asked to do only the 'dirty work'. More sensibly, the manager should delegate those elements which he knows his staff can do better than himself—but also he must delegate tasks which will stretch the staff, offering opportunities for training and development. The manager should give personal coaching to an employee in this situation so that in future the task may be delegated regularly.

It is not unknown for employees to try to delegate upwards, to pass problems to the boss when really they should sort them out themselves. This is often achieved by the use of subtle flattery: 'I'm sure Mr X would take it better, coming from you'; 'I don't really think I can deal with this, but I know you solved it very easily last time'. The danger is that the manager will find it easier to deal with the problem himself than to coach the subordinate to do so, but when this has happened once or twice, the problem will always rest with the manager rather than the subordinate who should be dealing with it in the first place.

Barriers to delegation

Many managers find it difficult to delegate, even if they know that they should do so. There is a variety of reasons for this:

(a) The subordinate is not competent or trained.
(b) The subordinate is not trustworthy.
(c) The subordinate will complain.
(d) The manager enjoys that job too much.
(e) The manager fears loss of status.
(f) The manager thinks only he can achieve a high enough standard.
(g) The manager fears the wrath of his boss if there is a mistake.

The manager may also find that subordinates are reluctant to accept delegated work, especially if they are already fully employed and are offered no extra reward for additional responsibility. They may also be afraid of making mistakes and being punished for them.

The organisation itself may also put up barriers to delegation by insisting on certain tasks being the personal responsibility of certain grades of management or by restricting the circulation of essential information.

Good delegation

It may be that some of the barriers to delegation are genuine, but in that case it is up to the manager to coach or counsel his subordinates to ensure that they are willing to accept delegated work and understand the extent of responsibility which comes with it.

Delegation is a sign of strength, not weakness, in a manager. The manager should:

(a) Make sure the task is well understood by the subordinate.
(b) Give him the authority necessary to complete the task.
(c) Make him responsible for the successful completion of the task.
(d) Not interfere but be ready to give advice and guidance when needed.
(e) Reward the subordinate adequately (by praise or in a more tangible way) for success.
(f) Not punish mistakes but treat them as learning opportunities.
(g) Pass on some of the good things as well as the less interesting.

Now try to answer Question 3 below. The suggested answer gives a few extra ideas about good and bad delegation and the reasons why some managers find it difficult.

▎Action points

(a) Think about the person who manages you at the moment. How would you describe their most usual management style? Do you think it is effective? Does it inspire you to want to do well? Do you think another style might be more effective?

(b) Who was the best boss you ever had? What was it that made them special? Was that person also an effective manager?

(c) Think of the worst boss you ever had—why was he or she bad? Did they get the work done at the expense of the staff?

(d) In the section on transactional analysis, examples (pilot, actor, etc.) are given. Can you work out why these examples fit the type of ego profile described?

(e) What profile do you think you show? What about your boss? What does this say about the best way for you to communicate with him or her?

(f) Does your boss delegate to you? If not, why not? If yes, is it done well (do you understand exactly what is required and what authority you have)?

▌Questions and answers

Question 1

George Boxer joined the bank when he left school. By persistent hard work, he became branch manager at the age of 50. He says he came up the hard way and thinks that young people today have a very easy life—but not in his branch. He keeps a very close eye on all aspects of the branch's activities and staff. No one comes in late or goes early. No one gets away with poor work. If a mistake is made, a reprimand swiftly follows.

What are the possible consequences of this style of management? [6]

What other possible styles would you draw to George's attention? What are their advantages and disadvantages? [19]

[Total marks for question—25]

Question 2

Describe the major leadership styles and their characteristics. Assume that you are a newly appointed supervisor. What factors might influence the leadership style you adopt?

[Total marks for question—25]

Question 3

Your fellow manager, John Birch, finds that he seems to work day and night and the strain is beginning to tell. You have concluded that John does not delegate and is doing everyone's job as well as his own.

Why are some managers reluctant to delegate? [10]

Explain to John the advantages of delegation. [8]

What guidance would you offer to John about when he should and should not delegate? [7]

[Total marks for question—25]

Question 4

Reg Reynolds was promoted to supervisor of his section in the bank when Makebridge was a small country town. In recent years it has become an overspill town. It has developed around the nucleus of the original town which still forms the centre of the new development. The building in which the branch is housed was large enough to accommodate more staff and it has become the central branch for Makebridge. Staff increased as business boomed and Reg found himself running a very large section.

At first he coped but recently he has been showing increasing signs of strain. Once punctual, he now sometimes arrives late. He often stays late in the evening, takes work home, worries his boss for decisions on matters referred to him by his staff. As a result, work piles up and this makes him more anxious. Staff are demoralised; one or two key people have left and this has increased performance problems.

As the manager of the branch:

(a) Identify the main problems. [5]

(b) What action would you take? [20]

[Total marks for question—25]

Answer 1

(*Note*: although this suggested answer uses the Ashridge model, any of the main theories of leadership style would have been acceptable, provided the question was clearly answered.)

Leadership styles are generally classified under four headings: tells; sells; consults; joins. George is using only the 'tells' style.

Characteristics of the 'Tells' style

The leader:
— sets goals;
— tells people what to do;
— expects obedience;
— supervises closely;
— leaves little initiative to individuals;
— punishes rather than supports;
— does not encourage participation in decisions.

Advantages:
— Decisions are clear cut and rapid.
— Everyone knows who is boss.
— Things get done.
— Orderly atmosphere is maintained.

Disadvantages:
— Little initiative left with individuals.
— Work is often uninteresting as boss does not delegate.
— People do not innovate or take risks because of fear of punishment.
— Encourages 'yes' men.
— Can result in low motivation and high turnover.

It would be necessary to explain to George that the disadvantages listed above can be overcome if he is more flexible, using some of the following styles, choosing the most appropriate for the circumstances.

Characteristics of the 'Sells' style
This style is a disguised form of telling:
— The leader uses persuasion rather than direct orders.
— More supportive than 'tells'.
— Parent/child relationships generated.
— Dependence on boss emphasised.

Advantages:
— Similar to 'tells' but generates more pleasant relationships.

Disadvantages:
— Many employees do not like being treated as children.
— They like independence and autonomy.
— Can also result in low motivation and high turnover.

Characteristics of the 'Consults' style
— This is the problem-solving style:
— Manager sets goals, but
— Employees are involved in decision-making through consultation on matters affecting them.
— Opinions are sought.
— Open discussion is encouraged.
— Employees are given freedom to make own decision on what to do and how to do it within an agreed framework.
— Mistakes are accepted.

Advantages:
— People feel involved.
— People feel committed.
— Employees have opportunity of learning through discussion and making mistakes.
— Motivates people.

Disadvantages:
— Decisions take longer.
— Sometimes employees have nothing to contribute because a decision does not allow it, or
— They do not have the knowledge.

Characteristics of the 'Joins' style
— The group (including the manager) makes the decision.
— Manager defines the problem.
— Members jointly solve it.
— Decisions reflect majority opinion.
— Free discussion encouraged.

Advantages:
— Everyone involved.
— Everyone committed.
— High morale.
— Open atmosphere.

— Stimulates learning.

Disadvantages:
— Decision-making is slow.
— Ambiguity about leadership.
— Sometimes, a compromise decision is reached.
— Time sometimes wasted because of unnecessary discussion.

Answer 2

For the first part, see the text of this chapter and Answer 1 above.

Influences

(a) The personality and experience of the leader. A manager's values, background and experience will have a powerful influence on his style. For example, a 'Theory X' person will believe that he has to coerce and control people, and a 'Theory Y' person will believe in the need to create the conditions under which people will wish to work (see Chapter 10). A leader who values freedom and the ability to learn will adopt a more democratic style than the manager who distrusts employees. The latter will wish to control their work in detail and adopt a more authoritarian style.

(b) The behaviour which a superior rewards is very important in influencing the style of the subordinate manager. For example, if the subordinate is rewarded if he gets results at any price, whilst he is punished for showing consideration, he will probably become more authoritarian in his attitudes. Lower-level managers will tend to model themselves on their superiors so that it is unlikely that they will develop a dramatically different style.

(c) Expectations of subordinates. Subordinates can influence the style of a superior in many subtle ways because he is ultimately dependent on them for performance. For example, he will be influenced by the number of skilled employees. Skilled staff usually need less supervision than new or untrained personnel. The attitudes of staff differ. Some prefer an authoritarian style, others prefer a more participative one. Expectations also play a part. The new manager might be expected to behave like the one he replaced.

Subordinates have a wide variety of ways of letting their manager know about the acceptability of his style and he will often take their wishes into account.

(d) The nature of the task. Jobs which may require precise **instructions**—such as landing an aircraft—demand a more authoritarian approach than **teaching,** where much is left to the discretion of the individual. Getting people to work in a team involves a much more people-centred approach than that required in managing isolated individuals.

(e) Organisation culture. Every organisation has its own 'personality' which influences the behaviour of its employees. For example, managers in an organisation governed by norms of strict accountability will be closely supervised and controlled. In times of economic prosperity, many organisations will leave much more freedom to individual managers than in times of recession, when much tighter controls will probably be introduced.

(f) Expectations of colleagues. People at one's own level are an important point of reference and their opinions usually matter. It is not surprising, therefore, that a manager will be very much influenced by what his peers feel is an appropriate style of management.

Answer 3

Reluctance to delegate

Many subordinates complain that their boss clings to work which he should pass down to them. Reasons are varied but they often include:

(a) The manager's attitude:
— He does not trust his subordinates to do a good job.
— He has not trained them to take over the work.
— He is worried about their ability to achieve a high standard.
— His own sense of security compels him to do the job himself.

(b) The subordinates may not respond to his wish to delegate because:
— They are frightened of making mistakes because of the boss's attitude.
— They are insecure people.
— They have not been adequately trained.
— They are given no reward if they take on extra responsibility.
— They are perfectly content with their current level of work and do not wish to accept further responsibility.

(c) The organisation's attitudes may prevent managers delegating because:
— Senior managers expect more junior ones to know a lot of detail.
— Top managers keep decision making to themselves and so set a bad example to their subordinates.
— Jobs are very rigidly defined and do not leave flexibility for delegation.
— For status reasons, certain types of work (e.g. sitting on certain working parties or committees) can be done only by the boss.
— Some customers will deal only with very senior managers.
— The structure of organisational decision-making will not allow delegation.

Encouraging delegation

To get managers to delegate means:

(a) Creating a climate in which making mistakes is recognised as an essential part of learning.
(b) The recognition that delegation can help senior managers to concentrate on the key problems at their level and help more junior staff to learn new and useful skills.
(c) The acknowledgement that there is more than one way of doing something and that the subordinate can get as good a result as his boss by a different method.
(d) That they should realise the importance of trust, and should offer a challenge and the prospect of achievement to encourage and motivate subordinates.
(e) Managers must understand the advantages of delegation, which
   (i) motivates staff to higher performance,
   (ii) creates learning opportunities,
   (iii) frees time of manager,

(iv) creates climate of trust, and
(v) gives flexibility.

When to delegate

Conditions for delegation are best where there are well trained subordinates who are:
(a) clear about the standards expected of them,
(b) given information about their progress towards goals, and
(c) given frequent feedback about how well they are doing and encouraged to try even harder.

The manager should be cautious of delegating:
(a) to untrained staff,
(b) to insecure staff unless he has briefed them carefully, and
(c) work for which his boss holds him personally responsible.

Answer 4 (outline only)

Analysis

The job has grown, yet Reg has not grown with it. He is becoming increasingly indecisive, delegating less, and his behaviour is affecting staff and causing a deterioration in performance.

Action
(a) You have to decide whether he can be helped to manage the increasing load or whether the job is now too big.
(b) Discuss the declining performance with him.
(c) Get him to express the problem as he sees it. Counsel him on how he can improve.
(d) Get him to establish targets and standards for himself and his staff.
(e) Make sure that these are designed to result in more delegation—explain the advantages.
(f) If he refers to you decisions which he should take himself, help him towards a decision, but make sure he takes it.
(g) Check that he is delegating work and not taking it all on himself.
(h) Review progress regularly, and give him feedback on his performance and that of his team.
(i) Make arrangements for appropriate off-the-job training.
(j) Review the situation after six months to decide his future.

CHAPTER 10

People as individuals

- Differences between individuals • Motivation • Selection • Induction •
Learning • Coaching and development • Feedback and appraisal • Counselling

■ Differences between individuals

If you think of the people you work closely with every day, it is easy to see that people can be very different from each other (in physique, in intelligence and in personality) even when they are all members of the same small group, performing similar tasks.

Physique

Physique is of little importance in placing individuals in appropriate jobs in the modern workplace. The advance of technology has greatly reduced the number of jobs in which physical endurance or strength is required; modern technology and instrumentation often decrease the need to rely on the senses of touch, hearing, etc. In banking, eyesight is perhaps the most important physical factor, although you will probably know of colleagues who are colourblind, or have poor eyesight, but still manage perfectly well to carry out normal banking jobs. Indeed, banks are often able to offer employment to blind telephone operators or audiotypists.

Some banks insist on a medical examination before taking on staff, so that no one is asked to do work for which he is physically unsuited (and also, more cynically, so that they do not take on someone who is likely to need a great deal of time off work for sickness).

Intelligence

Intelligence, or mental ability, can be defined as the capacity to make effective use of the intellect—the sum total of the mental functions of understanding, thinking, learning, observing, problem-solving and perceptual relationships.

To some extent, previous success in general education and examinations can give a guide to intelligence, although some employers will also require prospective applicants to sit intelligence or aptitude tests. For example, computer programmers require a particular combination of mental abilities which can be tested in specially designed aptitude tests. This avoids expensive training being wasted on staff who are unlikely to benefit from it.

Personality

In the context of selection for work, personality is usually taken to mean a combination of emotion, motivation, interests and social qualities, as well as the more common usage of the term, which tends to equate personality with the degree of charm and dominance. If you were asked to describe the personality of someone you know well, you would probably recall their behaviour in different circumstances, describing them as sociable, tolerant, enterprising, inspiring, friendly, submissive, cooperative, honest, reliable, etc. Many of these traits may vary with circumstances: for example, someone may appear submissive in dealing with his boss but dominant in respect of subordinates.

A variety of tests are available to define an individual's personality traits, although they are not usually regarded as a very good predictor of success in a given job.

Theory X / Theory Y

In the past, there was an assumption that the working man was naturally lazy, avoided responsibility, soon became uncooperative and was often rather stupid (Douglas McGregor called this 'Theory X man'). As research continued, a more promising view of human nature emerged. This suggests that, in suitable circumstances, the majority of people can become committed to a cause they value; they will not only accept responsibility but will positively seek it out. This view sees work as a natural function, not a penance, and finds creativity and innovation scattered throughout the population, not confined to a narrow 'management' class. This is McGregor's 'Theory Y man'.

Clearly, this more modern view of working man has major implications for the way people should be treated to gain the best performance from them. The rest of this chapter considers these implications as they apply to selection, training and overall motivation of staff.

∎ Motivation

Chambers Twentieth Century Dictionary defines motive as: 'an incitement of the will; a consideration or emotion that excites to action', and motivation as 'motivating force, incentive'.

In the management sense, by motivation we mean the stimulus which will encourage a worker or group of workers to give of their best, with good will, and for the good of the organisation or the project in hand.

Different people will be motivated by different things (and by different things at different stages of their lives).

When you left school or university and began your first job, the greatest motivator was probably to get that first salary slip—real money to spend as you wished, after years of pocket money or having to ask your parents for cash. At that stage, a good pension scheme or private health insurance would probably not have been high on your 'want' list. However, in a few years time, recently married, with a huge mortgage, and a new baby on the way, insurance would probably have seemed a much more attractive perk. Later in your career, promotion to a high-status job, perhaps with a smart company car, might be a powerful motivator.

Looked at in reverse—what are the things which would act as demotivators to you, which would make you want to leave your present job? Probably cutting your pay to one-third of its present level would be a strong demotivator, as might be increasing your working hours so that you never got home before 11p.m. at night and didn't see your family. If your boss started blaming you publicly for every mistake in the office, even when it had nothing at all to do with you, or spread rumours about your private life, then you might well feel fed up and demotivated. It might be something as simple as a boring job or an unpleasant working environment.

Positive motivators might be an interesting, challenging job, a friendly team to work with, a magnificent place of work, set in acres of beautiful countryside, excellent rates of pay, or the prospect of rapid promotion and recognition of your talents.

You can see that it is not just one thing which motivates an employee but a whole range of elements, and the balance between motivating and demotivating factors.

There are two main theories of motivation: Maslow's hierarchy of needs and Hertzberg's hygiene factors. We will now examine these two theories in more detail.

Maslow's hierarchy of needs

A.H. Maslow, an American psychologist, developed his theory of human motivation in the early 1940s. He identified a variety of human needs and postulated that motivation comes from the individual's desire to satisfy these needs. He grouped the needs into a hierarchy, a series of ascending levels, which are usually represented in a triangle (see Fig. 10.1). The various levels of the hierarchy are as follows:

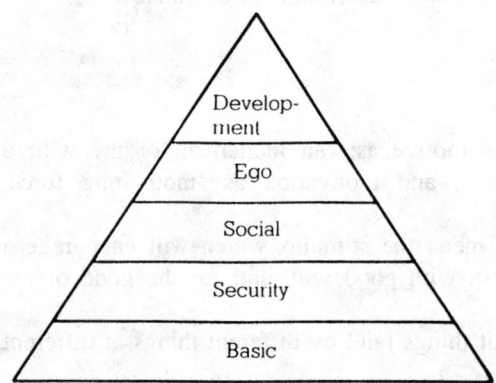

Fig. 10.1 Motivation: Manslow's hierarchy of needs

(a) **Basic**: the basic or physiological needs are the fundamental needs of hunger, thirst, and sleep. In the industrialised western societies, these needs are almost always satisfied, but there are still some parts of the world where they are the overwhelming motivator. At work, the fundamental purpose of pay is to satisfy these basic needs—it is the extent by which pay exceeds this basic requirement which may be a motivator.

(b) **Security**: the need for safety or security covers not only the physical aspects: shelter, warmth and protection from hostile attack, dangerous machinery, or fire—but also the psychological needs for security: pensions, insurance, welfare benefits and unemployment payments. In the current economic climate, the need to avoid redundancy can be considered a need at this level.

(c) **Social**: sometimes described as affiliation needs. These cover the need for friendship, love and affection, a sense of belonging to a group (at work and socially). Ties to work groups can be very strong and can influence attempts to reorganise a working environment—strong motivators may need to be employed to overcome this need to belong.

(d) **Ego**: also called esteem needs. This includes the need for self-respect, independence, status, responsibility, to feel that one has achieved something worthwhile and that this is recognised and acknowledged by peers and particularly by superiors. There are clear opportunities here for managers to utilise these needs as motivators at work.

(e) **Development**: also known as self-actualisation needs. This is rather a mouthful but refers to a need for self-fulfilment and creativity. This is seen in people who have chosen to devote all their time and energy, even if it results in reduced income, to following a personal passion—such as art, music, sport or writing. Not everyone will feel such a need and it is not often easy to satisfy such a need at work; hence it is often those who have achieved considerable material success at work who can then afford to indulge such a desire.

Since Maslow first put forward his theory, it has been acknowledged that people are rather more complex than the hierarchy allows. Individuals will not necessarily satisfy all needs in the first level, then move on to satisfy all those in the second, and so on. Most people will have a mixture of needs, from more than one level at any one time. They may also move back down the hierarchy at certain times in their lives when their circumstances change (as described in the introductory section, on motivation, on p. 43).

Nevertheless, Maslow's ideas helped to put motivation into perspective and are still a valid starting point for managers to consider how best to motivate their staff. Managers should try to avoid, for example, putting employees into a position where they suffer a conflict of needs—for example, if an employee is offered a promotion which will require moving to a part of the country that neither he nor his family likes, he will be torn between the desire to advance his career and the desire to remain in a certain location. This type of conflict is difficult to resolve without some bitterness resulting, which is not beneficial either to the employee or to the company.

Hertzberg's hygiene factors

Dr Frederick Hertzberg, in the 1950s, investigated job satisfaction among a group of several hundred accountants and engineers. He studied the results of interviews in which these professionals were asked what events at work increased or decreased their job satisfaction. As a result, Hertzberg developed a theory that there are two classes of factors which determine job satisfaction:

- **Hygiene factors**—whose absence is demotivating (i.e. reduces job satisfaction).
- **Motivators**—whose presence is motivating (i.e. increases job satisfaction).

Hygiene factors

These are so called because, like good sanitation or refuse collection, they make the environment fit to work in. They have also been called 'maintenance factors' because they will tend to maintain the employee in the job.

Hertzberg listed pay, working conditions (standard of furnishings, space, lighting, etc.), pension funds, perks, and quality of supervision as hygiene factors. He believed that these factors have to be present and adequate, otherwise there will be dissatisfaction. However, increasing the level of, for example, pension provisions will not act as a positive motivator.

Motivators

These are the factors which positively motivate people to work harder and with more commitment. They have to be present if there is to be job satisfaction. They include achievement, recognition, creativity, responsibility, and challenge. Without them, however good the hygiene factors, there will be no improvements in job satisfaction, productivity or efficiency.

Thus Hertzberg suggests that managers must choose rewards from the list of motivators, rather than the hygiene factors, if they want to improve output. Not everyone has agreed with his findings, especially as they have not been related to manual workers, only to professionals, but they do seem to have considerable relevance in an industry such as banking.

You may, at first glance, feel that pay must be a motivator, but consider how long a pay rise actually motivates you to work harder? You might well be encouraged to strive for a good increment at the end of the year, but once this has been received, do you really keep that in mind in your daily work?

Hertzberg's theory may be summed up by saying that earning a living is just one aspect of work; deriving satisfaction from the work itself is another. The hygiene factors affect the first aspect, the motivators contribute to the second.

Expectancy theory

One further view of motivational theory which is worth mentioning is expectancy theory. This states that the effort which an individual puts into trying to satisfy a need will be proportional to his expectation that the effort will produce a certain desirable outcome. His experience of rewards in comparison with expectations will influence how motivated he will be in similar situations in the future.

For example, if a bank employee sees passing the Chartered Institute of Bankers' examinations as the route to promotion he will probably put a good deal of effort into his studies. On the other hand, if he is convinced that his bank is unlikely to promote him even if he does well in the exams, he is unlikely to put in so much effort. If the employee has passed some of the papers but his boss is unimpressed, he is likely to feel there is nothing to be gained by passing the rest and will probably give very little effort to future studies.

■ Selection

The organisational issues associated with recruitment and selection are tackled in Chapter 13, but here we will look at the issues raised by individual differences as they have impact on selection procedures.

Selection can, of course, include people from inside the organisation who are recruited from a different department as well as people from outside the organisation.

It is the personnel specification which defines the type of individual who is most likely to fit the vacancy. The personnel specification must always be based on the job description and be realistic. A phrase such as 'must possess outstanding initiative' is both too vague, and unlikely to relate to the actual demands of the job. The specification should describe the person who is capable of doing the job adequately, not an impossible ideal.

The seven-point plan

A system devised by the National Institute of Industrial Psychology suggests that a personnel specification (and the subsequent assessment of candidates) should be arranged under seven headings:

(1) Physical make-up.
(2) Attainments.
(3) General intelligence.
(4) Special aptitudes.
(5) Interests.
(6) Disposition.
(7) Circumstances.

For each of these headings, the personnel specification should state those elements which are **essential**—without which the candidate cannot be acceptable; **desirable**—to achieve a satisfactory standard; **negative**—characteristics which will rule out a candidate at an early stage.

(1) Physical make-up

As explained above, physique is not usually a major factor these days, but this heading also encompasses first impressions, which may be important for a salesman, for example, when customers will gain an impression of the company from the rep's dress and physical appearance.

Age, health and speech characteristics may also be important for certain jobs. Great care must be taken if specifying sex, marital status or nationality, since these are governed by strict discrimination legislation. There are some instances in which such specifications are permitted, but these are restricted. (See p. 196.)

(2) Attainment

This covers academic qualifications, professional or technical qualifications and training, experience in other jobs, etc.

(3) General intelligence

As discussed on p. 142.

(4) Special aptitudes

Such characteristics as manual dexterity, facility with words or figures (literacy and numeracy), analytical skills or creative artistic skills come under this heading.

(5) Interests

A person's interests outside work may give important clues to his likely behaviour at work. For example, someone who runs the local football team successfully obviously has skills in leadership and organisation, and perhaps in administration, negotiation and persuasion as well. It is worth asking candidates to list their interests in an application so that these features can be explored in the interview.

(6) Disposition

This fits with the personality issues discussed above. It covers factors such as: self-reliance and ability to work independently; willingness to work under pressure; willingness to fit into a strict hierarchy or to be part of a very unstructured team; degree of reserve or outgoing nature; ability to relate to staff at all levels, e.g. to feel at ease speaking to very senior managers; willingness to undertake very routine tasks; and so on.

(7) Circumstances

The job may require extensive travel, a house move to a different area, long working hours, shift work or weekend working. A candidate's suitability for such jobs may be affected by whether he has small children who need to be cared for, or older children at a crucial stage of schooling, or aged or disabled relatives living nearby, and so on. However, one should never make assumptions about peoples' circumstances without giving them a chance to give their point of view. It used to be assumed that a married woman, for example, would be unable to accept a job involving a house move; these days it may well be the woman who is the major breadwinner and her husband may be willing to move with her. Conversely, it is no longer taken for granted that all ambitious men will be willing to up-sticks and move around the country five or six times in their careers.

▌ Induction

We all depend on other people in our working lives. How this dependence is rewarded affects our behaviour. If a new recruit is ignored by the existing staff and expected to find his own way around, he will tend to adopt a self-centred attitude to his work. If, on the other hand, he is welcomed, introduced to everyone and helped at all stages until he settles in, it is likely that he will become an equally helpful and cooperative team member.

Induction is the process of introducing a new employee to the company, his colleagues and the work he is to do. It can be regarded as the final stage of selection, or as the first stage of training.

When a new employee joins the department, the manager should ensure that someone is nominated to meet the newcomer and look after him on the first day. He should be shown the cloakroom, the canteen and any other staff areas; he should also be shown the fire exits and first-aid point and have the fire drill and any other health and safety rules explained to him. If this is not done at the outset, it is likely to be forgotten and it is important that all employees are aware of the safety aspects of their job—if there is a fire on the employee's first day it is no help saying you intended to show him the fire exits tomorrow!

The newcomer should be shown round the department (by a colleague or by his supervisor) and introduced to his immediate colleagues, the manager of the branch or department (if they have not already met at selection) and any staff who will be working for him. On the first day, it is probable that not all the names will be remembered, but it is equally important for the existing staff to meet the newcomer, so that they know who the new face in the office is, where he fits in, and that he will probably need help to find things, etc., in the first few weeks.

An employee new to the company should also undergo some form of induction to the company itself (by way of a short course, lectures, films or visits) so that he understands its culture, aims and philosophy. This is most effective if undertaken a couple of weeks or months after arrival, when the employee has had time to get used to his own department and will begin to be interested in the wider view. In a small company this may be done by the immediate supervisor but in large organisations, like the big banks, centralised induction courses may be run at intervals, bringing together newcomers from across the organisation.

The new employee should have his own job clearly explained to him, together with any training plans, and be given an idea of the standard of work expected from him at various stages of his training. He should also begin to understand how his job fits in with the others in the department and where the department fits into the organisation as a whole.

Many of us have had the experience of joining a new department or branch and being 'thrown in at the deep end', being left to find things out for ourselves, to make mistakes and feel foolish with little or no help from other staff. This 'sink or swim' approach is seen by some managers as a good way of making staff think for themselves. On the contrary, it can alienate the newcomer and engender a feeling of distrust and resentment against the new department which helps no-one and which simply prolongs the period until the new member of staff is productive and well motivated.

Learning

The wider issues of training and career development are again examined from an organisational viewpoint in Chapter 13. Here we look at how people differ in their requirements and expectations of training and in their style of learning.

The first thing to do before training someone is to establish what skills and knowledge they need to do their job, what skills and knowledge they already possess, and what is their preferred style of learning.

Assessing training needs

A good starting point is the job description and personnel specification. It should be possible from these to identify the skills and knowledge required and, by observation of the work produced, by examining the staff file, or better still by discussion with the member of staff concerned, to establish any mismatch between skills and knowledge required and that already possessed.

A decision must then be taken on the best way to achieve the training needs. This may be by on-the-job training or coaching, by formal off-the-job training courses, by computer-based learning, by studying for a professional qualification, and so on.

Learning styles

For training to be effective, the trainee must be motivated to undertake and complete it. This would normally mean that the trainee must see some benefit to be gained (e.g. promotion, higher pay, increased status). Training in groups so that there is an element of competition may assist motivation, as may the setting of intermediate goals, e.g. tests to be taken and passed at intervals throughout the training period.

Depending on such factors as age, previous educational experience, cultural background and personality, different people prefer to learn in different ways. Some are frustrated by theory or classroom lectures—they are eager to 'have-a-go' and get stuck into a task straight away. Some like a very structured and orderly approach, wanting to understand the theoretical concepts behind a job before tackling it. Yet others will prefer to watch someone else do the job first, thinking through the process themselves before methodically beginning the task. A fourth group consists of pragmatists who dislike abstract learning for its own sake and can learn best if they can relate to a real problem.

These differences in learning styles should be taken into account when planning training. For example, someone who prefers a very practical approach will not be best suited to training which involves a detailed research project. Usually it is best to fit in with a trainee's preferred style (if this is possible) although there is something to be said for breaking away from routine patterns sometimes and confronting the trainee with something completely novel in a fresh way.

You can observe differences in learning style in practice. Are you studying for this examination in a class with the support of others? Or are you studying by correspondence course, or entirely alone by private study? Does the method you are using actually suit you best, or were you forced to choose it for some other reason? What does this imply for your chances of success or for the degree of difficulty you will have in seeing the course through to the end?

Coaching and development

Coaching is a particular type of training which helps people to learn the job while they are doing it. Whilst formal training courses may teach skills and impart knowledge they are always carried out in a rather artificial environment. Only by actually carrying out a task or doing a job full-time can one gain the experience which will eventually result in high levels of performance.

Unfortunately, all too often in organisations, an employee will be set to work at a particular job and expected to learn as he goes along, with some haphazard assistance from colleagues or from his boss. This often leads to unnecessary mistakes being made, as the learner is unwilling to pester his colleagues all the time, feeling they are too busy with their own jobs to spare him much time.

A better and more structured approach is for the boss to make conscious and planned use of the work to create learning opportunities. It can vary from the trainee simply sitting next to an experienced worker, asking questions as often as necessary, to more formal sessions in which an experienced employee (often the trainee's boss) explains the job. The coach will ask questions to ensure the trainee has understood what has been said, then set tasks for the trainee to perform, monitoring progress and gradually increasing the complexity of tasks and reducing the level of supervision.

Although frequently successful and a relatively inexpensive method of training, coaching does depend on the manager being able to explain how he does the job. Sometimes an experienced manager may take decisions so automatically that he finds it difficult to explain how or why he has taken them. In some organisations, managers will be unwilling to share their knowledge for fear of being overtaken by young high-flyers; sometimes they will simply be under too much pressure to get results to spare time for coaching. Success also depends on the manager being willing to take risks by allowing the trainee to learn by his own mistakes.

Feedback and appraisal

The details of a successful appraisal system have been discussed in Chapter 6 and the interview itself is covered in Chapter 11.

Appraisal is an important opportunity for the boss to praise the member of staff for successful work and to counsel him on areas where he can improve his performance. However, this process should not be confined to the annual appraisal interview.

Feedback is the continual two-way communication between boss and subordinate by which each is aware of the other's feelings and level of satisfaction about work projects. Feedback differs from formal appraisal in being short-term: it should follow immediately after the event or project concerned, so that both parties have the task fresh in their minds. It is a most important means of improving a subordinate's performance.

The manager should be sure to praise and give credit for a job well done—a verbal pat on the back can be a very powerful motivator, provided that it is sincere. The subordinates' strengths should be emphasised—sometimes we are not aware of our own strengths, or do not see them as such, and it is valuable to have this reinforced. If there are areas where the subordinate is weaker or could perform better, these should be pointed out, but always with constructive ideas on how they can be improved. If possible, the worker should be encouraged to identify these areas for himself, and suggest ways of tackling them. If necessary, the manager should be willing to spend time on counselling the employee or offering advice and guidance from his own experience. It may be valuable to plan a timetable for action to build on strengths and reduce weaknesses, with a follow-up in a few weeks time to check on progress.

The manager should also be open to approaches from staff who have a work problem and request assistance; he should be willing either to advise them himself or make sure that an experienced worker or supervisor does so.

Provided that this type of feedback is a regular part of manager/staff relationships, the annual appraisal should be a much easier affair for both parties, with no nasty shocks on either side.

▌Counselling

As well as a purely working relationship between boss and subordinate, most managers have a 'pastoral' or welfare responsibility for the staff they manage. In some organisations this role is undertaken by the personnel function, but even so, the manager should be aware of any serious problems which his staff have, which might affect their work.

There is a fine line to be drawn between prying into other people's affairs and having a genuine interest in and concern for their welfare. It is perfectly legitimate for a manager to want to be aware of the personal circumstances of his staff so that he understands any impact these have on their work. He should also be sufficiently sympathetic (whilst not becoming a 'soft touch') so that his staff are not afraid to go to him with work-related or personal problems.

This covers such things as advice on career planning—perhaps a member of staff is considering applying for an internal vacancy and would welcome advice on what the new job might entail and whether the manager sees it as a sensible career step.

It might be the case that a member of staff has a medical problem which could result in the need for frequent hospital visits or extended time off work; a female member of staff may become pregnant and need time off for prenatal check-ups; an employee may have worries over a sick relative, an unemployed spouse or an injured child which will certainly make it more difficult for him to concentrate at work. If the manager is to react sympathetically to such circumstances he will need to be aware of them. The employee must therefore feel able to consult his manager and explain the situation, secure in the knowledge that the manager will treat the information in strict confidence as far as the other staff are concerned.

This latter point is vital—no member of staff will confide in a manager who is known to spread gossip, or to discuss one member of staff with another without the permission of the first. Company rules and business necessity might mean that the manager will need to inform the personnel department, but if so he should make this clear to the member of staff concerned.

∎ Action points

(a) List the names of four or five of the people with whom you work and whom you know pretty well. Now list their characteristics under Physique; Intelligence; and Personality. Is there a wide variety of differences between them? What does this imply for management of this group of people?

(b) What motivates you to work harder? Is it higher pay, the chance of promotion, praise from your boss, the lure of a company car? Do you think you may be motivated by different things in five years time, or in 10 years?

(c) Think back to when you joined your branch or department. Were you made to feel welcome? What induction did you receive? Did this help you settle in and start to work effectively?

(d) What do you think is your learning style? Is this ever taken into account in training in your organisation? Do you think you would learn better or more quickly if it were?

(e) Does your manager give you regular feedback? If not, why not try suggesting it? After your next work project, explain to your boss that you would find it helpful to know how well you have performed, so that you can try to do better next time.

(f) Would you feel able to go to your manager with a personal problem? If you have staff reporting to you, be sure that you give them praise when due, help and advice when needed, and that you listen to their problems and counsel them when necessary. It is all too easy just to let people get on with things unnoticed.

∎ Questions and answers

Question 1

You are the manager of a small team. Brian Craven is about to join your team from another department of the bank. You are sure that he was the right choice from amongst the candidates for the job, but you recognise that he knows very little about the work he will be required to do.

What points would you consider in planning Brian's induction and his initial training—both on and off the job?

[Total marks for question—25]

(*Hint:* the question makes clear that Brian **was** a good choice for the post, so do not waste time speculating on his suitability but get on with answering the question.)

Question 2

You have been asked to coach a new member of staff. Describe how you would ensure that your coaching was successful. [Total marks for question—25]

Question 3

You are concerned about the attitude and performance of Ian Dalgleish, a member of your section. Since your appointment as supervisor of the section a few months ago, you have been able to come to terms with the rest of the team. Performance was mediocre when you arrived but you have obtained improvements by discussing and agreeing new ideas, by establishing clear short-term goals for all your staff, and by giving them frequent feedback. It has not worked with Ian. His work is sloppy and untidy. He misses deadlines. He sometimes comes in late and goes early. He seems to resent you and to take perverse pleasure in thwarting your intentions. You know he has considerable potential. He is honorary treasurer of two local societies, both of which are full of praise for him. He runs a football team very successfully and is popular with his colleagues.

What will you do now? If your proposed actions fail, what will be your next step?

[Total marks for question—25]

Question 4

David Newton's work as a bank employee meets the standards which you, as his boss, have set. You still see David as something of a problem, because you believe he has the capacity to produce even better work.

You have observed him in the workplace and find that he gets on well with his colleagues. He seems to be happy with the job he has at present and appears to enjoy the work. At his last annual appraisal, although you gave no indication that he would be promoted, you discussed the subject of promotion. David gave every impression that he would welcome promotion.

You know that he is married and lives in a house which he and his wife bought three years ago with the assistance of a bank mortgage. His first child was born three months ago.

You believe that it is time you gave some thought to David's motivation.

(a) Give a brief description of expectancy theory. [5]

(b) Describe briefly the ideas of Maslow. [5]

(c) Outline how you would use expectancy theory and Maslow's ideas to develop an approach to the problem of motivating David. [15]

[Total marks for question—25]

Answer 1

Induction
(a) Brian is already a member of the bank's staff and so will not need to know about the bank's history, objectives, policies, etc. However, he will need to know relevant details of his new department.

(b) To make Brian's transition from inductee to fully productive worker as easy and quick as possible, it is vital that he is made to feel comfortable in his new environment.
(c) His first day (or few days) should be carefully planned to ensure that he is expected, will be welcomed, and will be occupied.
(d) He should be introduced to his work colleagues, one of whom should be asked to take responsibility for settling him into his new environment.
(e) Brian must be given a clear understanding of his role in the department and of the department's role in the organisation.
(f) He should understand what output is required of him and the standards of performance which he will be required to produce. Coupled with this there should be an agreed training plan designed to enable Brian to produce that output to those standards within a specified period of training.
(g) It is often important to give an inductee the opportunity to relate his work to that of his colleagues who affect or are affected by his output. If this is not to be accomplished by job rotation it should be incorporated into Brian's induction plan.

Training
(a) Where off-the-job training is available, it should be:
   (i) appropriate as to content,
   (ii) appropriate as to participants (people from whom Brian can learn as they describe their experiences),
   (iii) appropriate as to timing (to maximise the cost benefits of the training).
(b) Brian should be fully briefed before attendance to help him to understand why he is being trained and to identify his learning objectives.
(c) Similarly, he should be debriefed after the training to check the extent to which his objectives have been met and to plan how his learning can be reinforced through his work.
(d) On-the-job training should be planned to take account of Brian's predominant learning style but also to ensure that all stages of the learning cycle are accommodated.
(e) Clear, short-term objectives should be set and accurate feedback given on areas for improvement and on performance which is good or acceptable.
(f) Brian's manager should monitor Brian's progress to ensure the effectiveness of the training and that Brian is moving towards being a fully productive member of the team.

Answer 2

Coaching involves using opportunities in the work itself to help job-holders to learn.

It is more effective if the culture of the organisation is conducive to employee development.

Similarly, the attitude of the coach will largely determine the benefit of the coaching.

The coach should be prepared to take the risk that jobs will not necessarily be accomplished to the highest of standards—recognising that the organisation will ultimately benefit from the improvement of the subordinate's skills.

The coach should seek opportunities within the work under his control with which to develop the subordinate.

These could include such tasks as preparing reports, making presentations, representing the department, developing a project, etc.

Coaching is more effective if it is planned. This involves the coach in identifying the training needs of the subordinate and in matching those needs to the learning opportunities.

The coach should also identify the learning style of the subordinate and choose methods appropriate to that style.

On the other hand, the subordinate's learning style could be enhanced and itself developed by supporting him while using an apparently inappropriate method.

The coach should set goals which are clear and agreed with the subordinate.

Goals should address both the work aspects of the coaching (outcomes and standards) and also the learning aspects of the coaching (what knowledge and skills have been acquired, and how can they be used in the future?).

The coach should ensure that all aspects of the learning process are covered, e.g. an activity should be undertaken, then reviewed. Conclusions should be drawn and plans made to ensure that lessons learned are carried forward to future activity.

The coach should manage the problem of the amount of attention to be given to the subordinate. The opportunities for learning are likely to be lessened, both if too much direct assistance is given and also if too little support and guidance are offered.

The coach should monitor progress towards all goals and feedback to the subordinate on aspects which are being well done (so that they may continue) and on those which could be improved.

Answer 3 (outline only)

Ian Dalgleish has the ability to do the job (witness his outside activities), so the problem is one of motivation.

Does the problem lie with the job, i.e. is it not stimulating and motivating? See whether the job can be changed in ways which would offer more scope. Alternatively, can Ian be moved to a more challenging job?

Does the problem lie in the relationships? There are hints that Ian is rather independent and might not like close supervision. Would a variation of style be useful? Do you need to tell him quite plainly what to do and let him get on with it?—Clearly, only occasionally.

If the proposed actions fail, you should warn him of the consequences of poor performance, explain the disciplinary procedure and explain that you intend to take him through it, if necessary, having given him the necessary coaching, guidance and feedback.

Answer 4

(a) Expectancy theory suggests that an employee contributes effort to his job. He does this because he believes that ultimately his effort will be rewarded.

The quantity and quality of the effort which he is prepared to contribute will be determined by:
 (i) the value he places on the reward, and
 (ii) the likelihood that his effort will lead to the achievement of that reward.

Rewards can be intrinsic (e.g. sense of achievement) or extrinsic (e.g. pay).

(b) Maslow suggested that humans are motivated in accordance with a hierarchy of needs.

He identified five categories of needs: Basic, Security, Social, Ego and Self-actualisation.

Man will always satisfy lower-order needs in priority to higher-order needs.

He will always attend to the lowest currently unsatisfied need.

Consequently, it is pointless to offer rewards which are designed to satisfy a higher-order need to anyone who has a lower-order need as yet unsatisfied.

(c) David is apparently contributing an amount of effort which is appropriate to the needs of his current job.

If it is necessary to motivate him to contribute more, then this must be with a view to his development, either to enhance his current output or to equip him for advancement.

In either case, expectancy theory suggests that any reward which is offered as an inducement must be one which is closely linked to David's performance and one which he values.

In 'normal' circumstances David would be concerned to satisfy needs in Maslow's Ego category.

Satisfaction of such needs is generally achieved by increasing responsibility, status, power and recognition, and most easily achieved by promotion.

This would seem to fit David's requirements—he is ambitious and would welcome a challenge.

However, David's current circumstances are not 'normal'. The birth of a first child often disrupts a normal motivation pattern, increasing the individual's concern for security and relationships.

This suggests that promotion—which would satisfy an ego need—may not be appropriate for David at present.

The most appropriate reward which could be offered is to increase David's pay for doing his current job. This would go some way towards satisfying his security needs whilst not disrupting his social environment at work. It also has the merit of satisfying ego needs by being an additional recognition.

It is unlikely that, within the bank's pay structure, it is possible to provide a sufficient reward through increased salary without promotion.

Offering the possibility of promotion for David has three drawbacks as a motivator:
(i) It does not directly satisfy his current needs.
(ii) It may not inevitably follow his increased effort; therefore the perceived link between effort and reward may be weak.
(iii) It may not be wise to increase the organisation's demands on David at a time when he is more orientated towards home life.

The manager is therefore left with a dilemma. How this is resolved is a matter of judgement. A possible approach would be to strengthen the relationship between the manager and David by a greater sharing of responsibilities and an increase in the amount of personal recognition given by the manager. This could be accomplished against the backcloth of possible promotion within the foreseeable future.

CHAPTER 11

Interviewing

- General interviewing techniques ● Customer interviews ● Selection interviews ●
Appraisal interviews ● Grievance interviews ● Disciplinary interviews ●
Counselling interviews ● Exit interviews

■ General interviewing techniques

All managers will be required to conduct interviews from time to time, whether interviews with prospective members of staff, interviews with customers, or interviews with existing staff for a variety of reasons.

Whatever the reason for the interview, there is a list of common factors to be borne in mind, before during and after the interview itself:

Before:
(a) Purpose. (b) Goals. (c) Plan. (d) Location. (e) Timing.

During:
(f) Introduction. (g) Questioning. (h) Listening. (i) Summarising. (j) Action points.

After:
(k) Notes. (l) Assessment of result. (m) Follow up.

Before the interview

Purpose

Always have in mind the reason for the interview before you begin. Is it a disciplinary interview, or an appraisal interview, or is the aim to give coaching and encouragement to one of your staff?

Goals

What do you hope to achieve from the interview? What outcome are you aiming for? In a selection interview, for example, your goal might be to choose the best candidate for the job, or it might be to form a shortlist by eliminating the worst candidates.

Plan

Before the interview commences you should prepare thoroughly. Read any appropriate background papers so the issues are clear in your mind. Consult with other managers if they have information which may be of assistance. Have a rough plan of how you want to conduct the interview—you will not want to stick rigidly to this plan, but it will help you to ensure that all the main points are covered and that you do not run out of time.

Location

Arrange for a suitable room to be available for the time of the interview. It is always better to conduct an interview in a private room, rather than in an open office, so that both parties will feel free to discuss confidential matters if they arise.

Ensure that there will be no disturbances. Have the telephone diverted or arrange for someone to pick up your calls. If tea or coffee is to be served (which is a good idea if you want to create a relaxed atmosphere) then try to ensure that the refreshments arrive before the interview begins. It can be very distracting, in the middle of a discussion, if a stranger walks in to deliver a tray. Take care of the obvious things like checking that the lights work, that the heating is satisfactory and so on, especially if the room is seldom used.

Consider how the room should be arranged. For an informal interview you may want to sit in easy chairs, with no desk between you and the interviewee. If this is not possible, one can usually move the furniture around, at least so that both parties are on the same side of the desk. In a more formal situation (a disciplinary interview for example), the traditional arrangement with chairs either side of a desk may be more appropriate.

If you are seeing several people and they may have some time to wait, make sure there is a suitable, comfortable waiting room, with something to read and a supply of tea or coffee, to reduce the tension.

Timing

Always make sure that the interviewee is given plenty of notice of when the interview will be. Have you ever been called in to see your senior manager, for an important interview, when you were feeling scruffy and wished you had had a chance to wash your hair/put on a clean shirt/wear your best suit/change those laddered tights, or whatever? It put you at a disadvantage straight away and made it harder to concentrate, didn't it? Well, bear that in mind when dealing with your own staff.

The other reason for giving adequate warning is so that the interviewee has time to collect his thoughts and prepare any questions **he** wishes to ask.

Be sure to allow sufficient time for the interview—it should not be brought to an abrupt halt just because the room is booked for someone else, or you have to rush off to another meeting.

Give thought to the best time to arrange an interview. Last thing on a Friday afternoon, when people want to get away for the weekend, is not a good idea. Nor is first thing on a Monday morning—even if the trains are on time and the traffic does not cause delays, most people like to get to their desks and make sure there are no crises to be dealt with first thing in the morning, before turning to other things.

Bear in mind how far the interviewee has to travel—for example, if someone is travelling for three hours on the train to reach you, make sure he has a chance to have a meal before or after the interview.

During the interview

Introduction

Make arrangements for the interviewee to be met and directed or brought to the interview or waiting room. Then, in any interview situation, the first thing to do is introduce yourself and make the interviewee feel at ease. Start with a few trivial questions (about the journey to the interview or, in traditional British style, the weather!) to break the ice while the interviewee settles down.

Make sure the interviewee understands the reason for the interview by restating the purpose and objectives. Give an idea how long you expect the interview to last (although this should not be too rigid).

Questioning

In most interviews, it is more important to encourage the interviewee to talk, and for you to listen, than the other way round.

An oft-quoted, but nonetheless valuable, verse by Rudyard Kipling is the clue to asking so-called 'open' questions:

> *I keep six honest serving men*
> *(They taught me all I knew);*
> *Their names are What and Why and When*
> *And How and Where and Who.*

If you start questions with one of these six words, it is impossible for them to be answered just by 'Yes' or 'No'. Thus the interviewee is forced to be more forthcoming and to give you information. For example, if you ask: 'Did you enjoy your last job?' you will probably get a one word answer. On the other hand, if you ask: 'What was it about your last job that you enjoyed?', you are likely to find out a good deal more.

You should also be wary of asking leading questions—that is, of making it obvious what answer you are expecting. An interviewee eager to please will simple follow your lead and you will have learnt nothing about them. For example, don't say 'You wouldn't mind some foreign travel, would you?', rather 'How would you feel about a job that involved foreign travel?'. Don't ask 'Do you think motivation is important?'—the answer is obvious; instead, ask 'How have you succeeded in motivating your staff?'

Don't allow the interviewee to steer the interview too much—be sure that you are in control all the time, even though you allow the line of questioning to follow a natural course, rather than rigidly sticking to your plan. The order in which you cover topics is not very important, so long as no important areas are left out.

Listening

As well as asking questions, it is just as important that you listen to the answers. You can pick up a lot of information about someone by 'reading between the lines' of their answers. Don't take everything the interviewee says at face value—ask more questions to make sure they are not exaggerating or trying to mislead you. Watch their body language and listen to the tone of their voice. Try to keep your own voice and emotions neutral.

Allow time for the interviewee to answer your questions—don't rush in to fill the silence. A pause can be very effective in forcing the interviewee to respond.

Pick up cues from listening to the interviewee to make sure your questions have been understood. Modify your language to the same level as the interviewee—don't talk down to someone, but beware of using language which is too technical or sophisticated with junior or inexperienced staff. Often they will be too nervous to admit they have not understood you.

Summarising

At the end of the interview, draw it to a conclusion by checking that there is nothing the interviewee wants to ask you. Then summarise what has been discussed or agreed. Be clear about what the next steps, if appropriate, are to be.

Action points

If any action is to be taken as a result of the interview, make sure this is noted and acted upon (whether by you, the interviewee, or some other person such as a personnel or training officer).

After the interview

Notes

You may well have made notes during the interview. If so it is courteous to explain to the interviewee that you would be doing so. If not, you should make notes as soon as possible after the interview while the details are fresh in your mind—especially when you are seeing several people one after the other. It is only too easy to confuse people in your mind afterwards. Even notes made during the interview will need to be tidied up afterwards.

Assessment of result

Consider how well the interview went from your point of view. Did you retain control? Did you cover all the points you wanted to? Did you tend to talk too much rather than allowing the interviewee to speak? Did you achieve your objectives?

Assess your own performance as an interviewer and plan how you can improve in future.

Follow up

If you have action to take, make sure you do so. Monitor to ensure that what was agreed is carried out. It may be appropriate to make a note to see the interviewee again in a few months to ensure all is going according to plan.

The points listed above will apply in almost all interview situations. However, there are differences in emphasis and specific points to remember in relation to interviews conducted for specific purposes. The following sections consider a variety of possible interview situations with which a manager may have to deal.

▊ Customer interviews

In interviewing customers it is particularly important to create the right first impression. You need to consider the type of customer in order to choose the appropriate approach. A personal customer who is having difficulty with his finances and is coming in to ask for a loan will probably be nervous and worried—he will respond well to an introductory chat on general topics to put him at ease. The managing director of a corporate customer, on the other hand, will probably have a busy schedule and will be looking for a businesslike approach, with little time wasted on pleasantries. He will expect you to know exactly what you are talking about (which requires good pre-interview preparation) and will want to be absolutely clear what has been agreed at the end of the interview. This last point obviously applies to the personal customer too, but the discussions leading up to the decision may require you to do much more questioning, as the customer will probably not have brought all the necessary information with him.

Always be sure to take notes of customer interviews. It may be vital, at a later date, to have a written record of what was said and agreed. It is sensible practice to write to the customer, following the meeting, setting out the action points on both sides (yours and his) so that if there is any disagreement or misunderstanding it can be settled at an early stage.

▊ Selection interviews

Selection interviews require thorough preparation. You will have the application form which the applicant has submitted and perhaps reports from previous managers (particularly for an internal applicant), so study these closely. They will give you a starting point for discussion—perhaps a topic from his list of interests—to start him talking naturally and freely, before moving on to the more serious part of the interview.

Don't rush the interview or try to stick too rigidly to a plan. Your aim is to find out more about the applicant than appears on the application form. An apparently free discussion between the two of you, subtly steered by you, will elicit information which the candidate will hardly know he is giving. You will discover things about him—the way he thinks, the way he expresses himself, the way he approaches problems—which might not otherwise come out. As the candidate settles down and relaxes, you will see him more nearly as he will be at work.

Remember that the candidate will be forming an opinion about you and your company, as well as the other way around. You must tell him enough about the job and the company to enable him to judge whether he would like to work for you and whether the job is one he wants to do. You are in effect selling your company—even if the candidate does not get the job, you want him to have a good opinion of the company. He will undoubtedly talk to his friends about the interview; you do not want him to give an unfavourable picture of the company to prospective applicants or customers.

On the other hand, beware of overstating the case. If you 'sell' the job by giving an unrealistic impression of conditions, perks, promotion prospects, etc., and the candidate joins on that basis, he may well be very disgruntled when he realises the truth.

At the end of the interview, be sure to ask the candidate if there is anything else he wants to ask you—some candidates will be shy of asking questions unless prompted to do so. Make certain the candidate understands the next steps. If you are interviewing other applicants for the position, it is only fair to say so. Give a realistic idea of how long it will be before he hears from you—try to keep this as short as possible: he may have other positions he wants to apply for if unsuccessful with you. It is usual to offer a refund of travelling expenses.

After the interview(s) assess your notes, compare the applicants (by the seven-point plan discussed in Chapter 10, for example) and make your decision. Then offer the job to the best candidate. If he accepts, make sure that all the unsuccessful candidates are informed as soon as possible. It is helpful to these candidates if you can give some indication of why they were not successful—it may help them to apply for more appropriate positions, or to approach future interviews in a different way.

Some employers prefer to use a panel of interviewers for selection. This enables a wider range of questions to be asked, from a number of specialists, as well as reducing the chance of personal bias. However, it can be very intimidating for the applicant—particularly for younger, less experienced candidates.

An alternative is for the candidate to be seen by a second, and even a third interviewer, having been shortlisted by the first. This is less intimidating but can be time-consuming and tedious for the applicant, since much of the same ground will be covered by each of the interviewers.

∎ Appraisal interviews

Appraisal systems were discussed in detail in Chapter 6. Remember that appraisal should be going on all the time, with feedback between manager and subordinate, but the annual appraisal interview is the chance to formalise these interactions and create a written record of progress, future plans, objectives and prospects, training needs, etc.

The employee should be given plenty of notice of the interview, usually being given a copy of the appraisal form and being encouraged to complete it himself as a form of self-assessment. This is a good starting point for discussion, as it establishes how much of a gap there is between the employee's perception of his performance and the manager's perception.

The best approach is a problem-solving one, where the subordinate is encouraged to talk openly about his successes and failures, strengths and weaknesses, and with the manager giving praise for achievement and offering help and counselling on the areas for development.

This requires a good relationship between manager and subordinate, so that the subordinate will not try to hide his shortcomings and the manager will have the skill and patience to spend adequate time on the discussions.

An important element of the appraisal interview is the action plan which comes out of it. This should identify training or coaching needs, set objectives for fulfilling them, and incorporate a follow-up interview in a few weeks or months time as appropriate.

▍Grievance interviews

Some employees always seem to be moaning about one thing or another, whereas others need a great deal of provocation before they are prepared to complain. When a manager is confronted with an employee who wishes to register a grievance, he should bear this distinction in mind in assessing the gravity of the problem. Very often the matter can be settled informally between manager and subordinate, but if this is not the case a formal grievance procedure is invoked (see Chapter 6).

Before the interview, the manager should try to find out as much of the background to the problem as possible. During the interview he should try to be as open-minded as possible. He should listen (and be seen to be listening!) to the employee's side of the story, questioning and probing to get as much information as possible. He should be wary of accepting what is said at face value—there may be underlying causes which the employee is unwilling to reveal (there are always two sides of a story).

At the end of the interview, the manager should summarise what has been said, ensuring that the employee agrees; explain to the employee what he intends to do to resolve the issue—he may need to gather more information from other sources, or interview other members of staff, for example; and give a date by which he will respond. The manager will then go away to consider the problem—checking facts, and considering the options open to him and the consequences of any proposed actions.

A second interview will need to be convened so that the manager can respond to the employee. He should support his decision with rational arguments and reasons, attempting to achieve a 'win – win' solution so that honour is satisfied on both sides.

▍Disciplinary interviews

Disciplinary procedures were considered in Chapter 6. The most common reason for disciplinary action is that the employee's work is well below standard, but other complaints might be harassment of other staff (racial or sexual), dishonesty, etc.

Before a disciplinary interview, the manager should check all the facts. At the start of the interview it is important to state exactly why it is taking place, emphasising the gravity of the situation, and outlining the form the meeting will take. If representatives are present on either side, they should be introduced and their roles made clear.

The employee should be told what the complaint is and he must be allowed to speak in his own defence. At this stage it may become clear that the original information was misleading, or that there are extenuating circumstances. It may then be appropriate to adjourn the meeting for further investigations, or to turn it into a counselling interview.

If, on the other hand, the manager considers the complaint is justified, he should tell the employee so. The employee should be told what he will be required to do to rectify the matter (e.g. improve his work performance, or cease certain activities which have been the cause of the complaint) and what help will be made available to assist him in this. A date should be set by which the improvement must be made, and a further interview arranged to consider progress.

The employee should be reminded of the appeals procedure, if he disagrees with the decision, and asked if he has anything he wishes to add.

At the conclusion of the disciplinary interview, the manager should summarise what has been said and agreed. The outcome of the interview must be recorded in writing, with a copy being given to the employee.

∎ Counselling interviews

A counselling interview is intended to give advice and information to an employee and to discuss (and if possible solve) problems. It is far less structured than other types of interview, with little preparation being necessary. The most important thing is for the manager to listen carefully to the employee's problems, probing for additional information and responding to the employee's needs.

In this type of interview, if the employee is to be encouraged to speak frankly, it is important to make the atmosphere as friendly and informal as possible. One way to do this is to remove the outward signs of the boss/subordinate relationship by conducting the interview in comfortable chairs, away from the manager's imposing desk, over a cup of coffee. The manager should try not to express his own opinions too early in the interview, but should draw the employee out, to express what is really on his mind and, if possible, to suggest his own solutions. Then the manager can join in, using his own experience (both of work and of life) to advise on the best way of handling the problem.

∎ Exit interviews

When an employee leaves a company, whether of his or her own free will (resigning to join another company, on retirement, or to have a baby, for example) or because he has been sacked, or made redundant, valuable information can be gained for the company by conducting a so-called 'exit' interview. It can be helpful for the personnel department, in particular, to know why people choose to leave the company (is it because there are seen to be no promotion prospects, or because working conditions are poor?). Although many employees are not entirely frank about their reasons for leaving, they may give hints about morale, or management practices which, if corrected, might help to reduce expensive staff turnover.

If the employee is leaving because he has been sacked, or made redundant, the exit interview is the company's last chance to offer advice or assistance in obtaining other employment—perhaps by pointing out what went wrong in this job and suggesting ways of improving in future.

Throughout this chapter, and indeed throughout management itself, one message comes through loud and clear—when you are dealing with your staff, behave as politely, as helpfully, and as fairly as you would like to be treated yourself.

∎ Action points

(a) Think of the last time you were interviewed. What went well and what went badly? How would you have organised things, given a free hand?

(b) Was your last appraisal interview successful, from your point of view—did you learn more about what your boss thinks of you and your work or has he always spoken freely with you throughout the year? Were you given plenty of opportunity to speak, or did you come away with a list of things you wish you had said? If the latter, why not ask your boss if you can have a counselling interview at a convenient time, to iron those points out?

∎ Questions and answers

Question 1

You have been given the task of interviewing candidates for a specific position on your branch's staff. All the candidates are from within your organisation.

Three of them have been short-listed. On paper there is nothing to choose between them.

You are determined to ensure a successful selection procedure. Outline what you would do:

(a) before each interview; [10]

(b) during each interview; [10]

(c) after the interviews. [5]

[Total marks for question—25]

Question 2

Douglas Wentworth is a very capable supervisor, who gets good performance from his staff by setting them clear goals, by telling them how they are getting on and by giving them help and advice when they need it. His staff say they learn a tremendous amount from him and they are never afraid of going to see him when they need help. All of them, however, without exception, dread the annual appraisal interview and so does he. He says that he is appraising his staff all the time and that there is no need to do an annual interview. He feels uncomfortable sitting down formally to talk over issues which he discusses frequently with each of his subordinates. He thinks it is a ritual and a waste of time and aims to get through the interviews as quickly as possible.

His subordinates agree that, as at present conducted, the interviews are a waste of time. Douglas seems to have no clear goals, is obviously ill-at-ease and so they become uneasy too. Most of them would like the opportunity for a longer-term assessment of what they have done and how they can develop, but it is never forthcoming.

How would you help Douglas to make the annual appraisal interview useful both to him and to his subordinates?

[Total marks for question—25]

Question 3

(a) Distinguish between feedback and formal appraisal in connection with staff management.
[2]

(b) When should feedback be given and how should it be structured? [8]

(c) What are the aims of a performance appraisal interview? [2]

(d) How would you advise an appraiser to prepare for, conduct and follow up an appraisal interview? [13]

[Total marks for question—25]

Question 4

Joan Greenwell, a recently appointed supervisor in your department, is still under training. It is your job to help her to understand the grievance procedure which is operated in your bank and you are also required to coach her in grievance interviewing. What are the major points you would make to her?

[Total marks for question—25]

Question 5

Brian North is a very bright young man. He obtained good 'A'-levels and has passed the Chartered Institute of Bankers examinations. But his performance at work is giving cause for concern. He is slapdash and argumentative. He wastes his own and other people's time in idle chatter. He often arrives late and has a worse than average sickness record. You have warned him orally that his work is unsatisfactory. Now you feel that you should have a formal disciplinary interview with him.

Describe and explain both the content and structure of this interview.

[13 marks for content, 12 marks for structure]
[Total marks for question—25]

Answer 1

Before the interview

Gather details about the job—job description, personnel specification etc.
Be clear as to the attributes for which you are looking in the candidate.
Gather information about the candidates. What documentation is normally supplied to you?—e.g. internal application forms, previous appraisals, managers' reports on candidates.
Determine your objectives for the interview. These should be (at least):

   (i)   To establish who is the most suitable candidate for the job.

(ii) To treat all candidates fairly to create in them a good impression of your branch and of your selection procedures.

Plan how to achieve these objectives—concentrating particularly on how to gather evidence about each candidate which is relevant to the personnel specification.

Attend to the usual details of setting up an interview—time; room; no telephone interruptions; furniture; ashtrays; coffee; reception of interviewee, etc.

During the interview

Establish rapport.

Put the interviewee at ease—talk first about a 'safe subject'.

State the objectives for the interview and the time it is scheduled to take.

Concentrate on exploring the areas you have planned to raise but be flexible and follow the interviewee's contributions when this is likely to be beneficial to your objectives.

Be careful with questions. Use an appropriate blend of open and closed questions plus reflections of the interviewee's words.

Deal with the question of note-making—if notes are to be made during the interview, agree this with the interviewee. If not, allow time for them to be made after the interview.

Allow time for the interviewee to question you.

After the interview

Evaluate your performance as an interviewer. Have the candidates been fairly treated?

Is there any bias evident?

Weigh the evidence gained during the interview against the personnel specifications to determine which is the most suitable candidate.

Make the decision. Offer the job to the successful candidate. If he accepts, advise the unsuccessful candidates.

It is helpful to those who did not succeed to be given feedback on why they were not successful.

Answer 2 (outline)

Help him to understand why informal and formal appraisal systems are necessary, e.g. informal—to give day to day feedback; to enable short-term goals to be decided, to help develop the required skills on the job; formal—to give both parties an opportunity to consider the subordinate's performance over a year, possibly to decide what this merits in terms of financial reward; almost certainly to identify training needs which will help longer-term development.

Make him familiar with the company system. He should know its purpose; how it works in terms of management; what benefits the employee is likely to get and when they are likely to happen.

Get him to warn the staff in plenty of time when the interview will take place. He should explain its purpose and its value. He should ask the employee to come prepared to discuss their own evaluation of their performance and their own feelings about strengths and limitations and how these can be improved.

Help him to prepare carefully himself by studying the subordinate's results and collecting evidence to help him evaluate performance.

Advise him about the interview itself:
— it should be in private;
— he should make the aim of the interview clear;
— he should allow plenty of time for thorough discussion;
— the interviewer should be positive and forward-looking rather than negative and backward-looking;
— he should adopt a supportive and helping, rather than judgemental role;

- he should tell the candidate what he sees as his strengths with supporting evidence;
- he should discuss areas where he can improve, producing evidence, giving tips and suggesting new approaches, training possibilities, etc;
- he should discuss and agree an action plan;
- he should follow up any action he has agreed;
- he should monitor future progress and give feedback.

Answer 3

(a) Both feedback and appraisal are concerned with performance improvement. Feedback is short-term and should be close to the event. Appraisal is longer-term and generally takes place on an annual basis.

(b) Feedback should be given shortly after the event to which it relates, whilst the performance is still fresh in the employee's mind.

The aim is to improve performance. This can be achieved by pointing out areas of strength and encouraging the employee to put them to full use.

Alternatively, the feedback can concentrate on areas for development, showing how performance in these areas can be improved. A useful structure is:

(i) state the aim of the feedback—to improve performance;
(ii) focus on the particular performance area concerned;
(iii) encourage the employee to recognise and articulate the merits or otherwise of his performance;
(iv) coach the employee;
(v) develop an action plan;
(vi) summarise—again best done by the employee.

(c) Aims:

(i) to review performance over the past period;
(ii) to formulate an action plan designed to improve performance;
(iii) to identify training and development needs;
(iv) to establish performance objectives for the next period.

(d) The interview

Preparation:

(i) Give appraisee plenty of notice.
(ii) Give appraisee an opportunity to contribute to the agenda.
(iii) Review appraisee's performance—identify areas of good performance and areas for development.
(iv) Set objectives and plan to achieve them.
(v) Ensure the interview will be private, uninterrupted, and that there will be sufficient time for the interview and for you to complete the documentation.

Conduct:

(i) Establish rapport.
(ii) Establish objectives.
(iii) Discuss performance over the period under review—encouraging the appraisee to talk about his performance.

(iv) Be specific about areas of strength (he may not recognise them as such).
(v) Plan for improvement in areas for development.
(vi) Encourage a forward-looking approach; establish goals, standards of performance and an action plan for the next period.
(vii) Plan to satisfy any training needs.
(viii) Be prepared to discuss agenda items contributed by appraisee.
(ix) Be prepared to listen.

Follow-up:
(i) Fulfil commitments made by you as part of the action plan.
(ii) Monitor performance and give appropriate feedback.
(iii) Review goals and standards in the light of changing circumstances.
(iv) Evaluate your own performance as an appraiser.

Answer 4 (outline)

Procedures will differ in detail but are usually designed as follows:
(a) The individual first complains to his supervisor.
    If not adequately dealt with at this level the complainant has a right to appeal to
(b) his supervisor's boss, who will usually interview both the supervisor and the complainant and any appropriate witness.
(c) Sometimes there is a further final level of appeal.
(d) Usually the complainant is allowed to bring a staff representative or friend with him.
(e) There is usually a limit on the length of time each stage of the grievance procedure may take.
(f) The personnel department is usually kept informed of the outcome of all grievances.
(g) Often the complainant is given a written as well as an oral reply.

The interview: A structure along the following lines is suggested:
(a) What is the issue?—background; circumstances; latent and manifest causes; procedural implications.
(b) Meet and get the picture—listen; probe.
(c) Consider the issue—implications; check facts; consider options.
(d) Reply—recap; develop reply; communicate decision; record.

Answer 5 (outline)

Before the interview: Get all the facts about the case.

Content

During:
Explain the purpose of the interview.
Describe your feelings about lack of progress or improvement.
Ask for employee's comments.
Set new standards of output and behaviour:
— be specific;
— quantify in output and behaviour;
— agree the help he will be given;
— agree review dates;

- warn formally;
- indicate consequences of failure;
- summarise;
- record.

After:
Follow up with help, guidance and feedback.
Formal review.

Structure

Before this formal warning:
The employee should have received at least one or more informal warnings.
He should be given notice of the interview.
He should be invited to bring a friend or representative.

During:
Make sure the warning is clear and unambiguous.
Give the employee an opportunity to put his case.
Allow the representative an opportunity to speak.
Explain rights of appeal.
Explain how the warning can be removed from record.

After:
Record summary.
Copy to interviewee and representative.
Review.

CHAPTER 12

People in groups

- Communication—methods and barriers • Group dynamics • Formal and informal groups • Team formation and roles • Successful and unsuccessful groups • Managing change • Meetings • Committees

Communication—methods and barriers

Communication can be defined as 'the transmission of information from one person, to create understanding in the mind of another, so that it can be acted upon'. Given our earlier definition of management as 'getting things done through people', communication is clearly a vital element of management.

The success of communication depends on four main factors:

(a) The sender: the ability of the sender to pass the message clearly and accurately.
(b) The medium: the choice of communication medium (oral, visual, written, etc.) to suit the message and the circumstances.
(c) The receiver: the ability and willingness of the receiver to understand the message and to act on it.
(d) The noise: any distractions or barriers in the communication system which might distort the message or hinder its reception.

The question of communication in organisations was considered in Chapter 4, so here we will concentrate on the mechanics of communication itself, and communication between individuals or in small groups.

Barriers

The first step in overcoming barriers to communication is to be aware of their existence. Frequently we speak of a 'breakdown in communications': the receiver has misunderstood what the sender intended to convey. Barriers may exist in ourselves, in our environment or in other people.

Let us consider spoken communication first.

(a) Barriers in the environment:
  (i) If a room is very hot or cold, or too noisy, a listener will find it hard to concentrate.
  (ii) A lack of privacy will distract both the listener and the speaker.

(iii) If the time and place are wrong (e.g. the listener is in a hurry to get to an appointment) concentration will be poor.
(b) Barriers to reception:
(i) Nervousness or anxieties on the part of the listener—these will make it hard for him to concentrate.
(ii) The attitudes and values of the listener – some senior executives would find it hard to accept information from a very junior member of staff, for instance.
(iii) Prejudices and preconceptions—about the person speaking.
(iv) Personality clashes—some people find it very difficult to listen or speak objectively to someone they dislike.
(c) Barriers to understanding:
(i) Jargon and technical language are confusing to someone from outside the group. You should always use language which you know will be understood by the receiver, avoid using 'big words' just to make your communication sound important.
(ii) Something as simple as a strong regional accent may make understanding difficult for the listener, and he may be embarrassed to keep asking the speaker to repeat what he has said.
(iii) A closed mind on the part of the listener will make it hard for them to consider new or challenging facts and ideas.
(iv) Length of communication—after about 10 or 20 minutes of speaking continuously, you will have passed the attention span of most people.
(v) Level of knowledge—talking down to someone will make him 'switch off' just as quickly as talking over his head.

Using written forms of communication may overcome some of these barriers, but adds further problems:

(a) How can you be sure the message has been read?
(b) How can you be sure that it has been understood properly?

In spoken communication you can at least check understanding by asking open questions (i.e. don't say, 'Now, do you understand how to do it?' — say, 'Now tell me, how are you going to do it?'). It is up to you, as the sender, to check the receiver's understanding. Many people will be too shy or nervous to ask questions and they will tend to say 'Yes' when they mean 'No' if you simply ask: 'Do you understand?'.

Good communications

The rules for good communication can be summarised as follows:

(a) Preparation: you, the sender must have clear objectives—what is to be communicated, to whom, and why. If the communicator clearly understands the idea he wants to get over, there is a better chance that the receiver(s) will too. You should try to anticipate the response of the receiver.
(b) Choice: of setting, timing, private or public, medium, etc. This should take into account

the type of message (formal or informal), whether a permanent record is needed, what the normal customs and practices of the organisation would suggest, and so on.

(c) Method: you should be conscious of tone of voice, nonverbal body language, the choice of words used, etc. You should anticipate and overcome any barriers to communication and pick up on potential benefits to the receiver in the message, in order to engage the receiver's interest.

(d) Feedback: by questioning, check for understanding. Listen (with the ears and with the eyes—watching for changes in expression, body language, etc.) to pick up signals from the receiver which indicate attentiveness, confusion, boredom, etc.

(e) Follow-up: make sure that your actions support the message you have given. Don't fall into the old parental trap—'Don't do as I do, do as I say!' If necessary, get training in how to communicate. However, the best training of all is practice—take every opportunity to watch good communicators at work and to practise and improve your own communication skills.

As a receiver, you also have a responsibility in ensuring that communication is successful. You should give your full attention, being aware of your own possible bias or prejudice. By your attitude, indicate to the sender that he has your attention; avoid interrupting or responding emotionally. Ask questions to clarify meaning and give helpful feedback to the sender. If both parties follow these rules, successful communication should be ensured.

In closing this section, it is worth reflecting that these guidelines for good communication are far from new. British Prime Minister William Gladstone (1809–1898) wrote that there were five rules for good communication: simple words; short sentences; knowledge of your subject; clarity of diction; and responsiveness to your audience. Gladstone was referring particularly to public speaking, but his formula applies equally well to communication of any kind.

∎ Group dynamics

Very few of us work entirely alone. Most of us are members of teams or groups (both at work and outside). Perhaps you attend evening classes, belong to a local community group, a sports club, an environmental group, or a parent/teacher association—and you probably play a slightly different role in each. Similarly, at work, a person may be a member of several different groups at the same time: a department, a committee, a working party, a temporary project team, and so on.

A group can simply be defined as a collection of people who interact with each other, who are pursuing a common goal, and who think of themselves as a group. A work group may be a small two or three person team, or it may be a large department in an office or factory. The former type is sometimes called a primary group, whilst the latter is referred to as a secondary group. In this section we are mainly concerned with smaller groups and teams, with say 2–12 members.

In the same way as the failure of one or two members of an orchestra to perform well will cause the whole performance to suffer, so, if one or two members of a work group fail to pull their weight it will reflect in the output of the group. Most of us have colleagues whose wishes and personalities we must learn to understand. When working closely with others we have to modify our behaviour to some extent in order to maintain harmony—acting in ways which are acceptable to the others rather than completely satisfying to ourselves.

These ways of acting become group norms. A new member entering the working group soon learns to conform to these norms if he wishes to become accepted as part of the group. In an earlier chapter, the Hawthorne experiments of Elton Mayo were considered in detail. One of the most important conclusions to come out of this work was the importance of the group and group norms in motivation.

Formal and informal groups

At work, there is a distinction between:

(a) formal groups—those which are part of the structure of the organisation, consciously set up for a specific purpose—and
(b) informal groups—those which form as the result of casual contact between people with similar interests. Although not part of the recognised hierarchy of the organisation, they can be very powerful and may even oppose its official aims.

Formal groups

Formal groups are generally created by management to satisfy an organisational need, with a structure related to the work the group is required to do, and the interactions with other groups which this demands. Other factors, such as whether the people like and respect each other, the power they wield, etc., should also be taken into account; sadly, this is often overlooked, the assumption being that the group will automatically bury their feelings towards each other in order to work towards the greater good of the organisation. In such cases, unless the group has a very strong and charismatic leader, the personal differences are likely to have a major detrimental impact on performance.

Informal groups

These may develop from people who just happen to work physically close to each other, even if they work in different functional areas of the organisation; they may also result from allegiances outside work itself, for example a group of people who belong to the company football team, or the music society.

The unofficial leader of such a group will often not be the senior person appointed by the organisation. This can create rivalry for the loyalty of the group, if the aims of the group and of the organisation are different. For management, this means that it is important to be aware of the existence of such groups, and to use them constructively where possible, rather than trying to destroy them (which is in any case unlikely to succeed).

Team formation and roles

Formation

When a team is put together (whether formal or informal) it will go through four distinct phases before settling down:
  (a) Forming—everyone tends to sit around in silence, waiting for a lead, wondering 'what are we supposed to be doing?'
  (b) Storming—someone takes the lead, discussions begin, conflicting ideas and opinions are put forward, the original leader may give way to another; this can be a very noisy phase.
  (c) Norming—the real task is brought into focus, there is more cooperation and listening than during storming, there is a growth of group feeling, roles are established and decisions begin to be made.
  (d) Performing—the initial 'sabre rattling' is over, roles have been accepted, energy is now devoted to problem-solving and achieving the group goals.

If you remember the last training course you went on, particularly one which was residential, away from your normal environment, you will probably be able to identify these stages. On the first morning you all sat in the lecture room, very quietly, waiting to find out what was to happen (forming). The first group exercise was probably rather chaotic, as you each wanted to make an impression, to give your point of view and so on (storming). The first evening, in the bar, you began to get to know each other better, to build friendships (or decide who you didn't get on with!) (norming). By the second day, a pecking order had probably been established, with certain people taking the lead, others sitting quietly adding well thought-out opinions when appropriate, and a successful course resulted (performing).

Knowing that this is the usual pattern, some courses will include a very participative exercise in small groups (syndicates) early on, so that the storming phase is facilitated. On a long course, the syndicates may be changed every few days, so that groups have to reform, allowing people to take new roles.

Group roles

The most effective groups seem to consist of no more than 10 or 12 people, who between them will be performing eight different roles. If the group is smaller, some members will be performing more than one role; in larger groups there may be conflict between people who each adopt the same role. An unbalanced group will not perform well. Belbin identified the following eight roles:

- **The Chairman**: this is the coordinator; he is not necessarily the cleverest or most experienced member of the team, but is respected, works well through other people, and is able to hold the team together, focusing its efforts on the task.
- **The Shaper**: full of drive and passion for the task, can be irritable, impatient and dominant, but is needed to spur the group into action.
- **The Plant**: the imaginative, intelligent member of the team who produces the original ideas. However, he tends to be inward looking and sensitive to criticism, so needs nurturing (like a real plant!).

- **The Monitor–Evaluator**: the analytical rather than the creative intellect. He has the ability to see the flaws in an idea and assess the practical problems—tending to work as a loner, dependable, rather cold, but a valuable 'quality check'.
- **The Resource–Investigator**: an extrovert, a sociable and popular member of the team, bringing in contacts and ideas. Makes a good ambassador, salesman or liaison officer.
- **The Company Worker**: a good administrator who can turn ideas into workable tasks; methodical, trustworthy and efficient but tends to be unexciting and not a leader.
- **The Team Worker**: a well liked, uncompetitive, supportive member of the team who listens to and encourages the others. Holds the team together; the sort of person who is not very noticeable, but is missed when he is not there.
- **The Finisher**: essential to tie up the loose ends, check details and push the others to meet deadlines—an important but not always a popular role.

These are roles into which most people fit almost without realising it, matched to their personality and preferences. It would be very difficult, for example, for a natural finisher to take on the role of resource-investigator, or vice versa. Thus, when choosing a new member for a team, it is important to consider the existing members and which roles are vacant before selecting a replacement. There is a danger that a manager will tend to choose staff in his own image, ending up with a very unbalanced (and therefore inefficient) team.

∎ Successful and unsuccessful groups

If a team is not performing well, there will often be many symptoms which can be observed, for example

- high labour turnover,
- high sickness rates,
- high absenteeism,
- low output,
- interrupted work flow,
- many customer complaints,
- unclear targets,
- low morale,
- low commitment to group goal,
- poor cooperation between members,
- negative attitudes,
- apathy and depression,
- few attempts at problem-solving.

On the contrary, a successful group is characterised by

- clear aims,
- individual motivation and concern,
- involvement in planning,
- good leadership,
- team building,
- openness,
- plenty of feedback,
- plus, of course, the opposite of each of the symptoms listed for unsuccessful groups above.

The effectiveness of a group will be affected by a variety of factors:

(a) organisational, e.g. size, status, composition;
(b) environmental, e.g. location, role in organisation, communication links;
(c) task, i.e. its nature, importance, amount of pressure, etc.

The manager's task is to overcome the difficulties presented by these factors in motivating the group towards its goal. This can be achieved by ensuring that all members of the group are aware of their individual and group aims, and how these fit into the organisations objectives. They should be involved as much as possible in planning how these aims are to be achieved. The Volvo experiments demonstrated that a team which is allowed to organise its own work as much as possible will gain a strong sense of bonding, and is usually more motivated and productive than a rigidly controlled team.

The manager must be wary of showing favouritism to any particular member of the team (in allocation of rewards, resources, targets, praise, etc.) as this can lead to conflict within the group.

Similarly, conflict between groups may arise through conflicting aims, lack of understanding of the other team's goals, competition for resources, differing standards or status, etc. (see Chapter 4).

■ Managing change

Almost everyone has a fear or distrust of the unknown. There are numerous everyday adages to support this: 'Better the devil you know than the devil you don't', 'Fools rush in where angels fear to tread', and so on. Often it is the very bosses who expect their staff to be willing to accept change who are most resistant to it themselves.

A CBI conference in 1989 studied the results of a survey of 3000 workers in British industry. This showed that whilst most employees feel free to express their opinions and come up with new ideas, only one-third find their bosses willing to act on them. Most feel that their companies are secretive, don't tell employees what they are planning, and more than 40 per cent believe they are fed misleading information by their bosses.

The company which carried out the survey found that, culturally, British managers don't see it as part of their job to look after the people who work for them. Of the managers surveyed, 41 per cent felt that their company gave them no reward or recognition for managing people. The result seems to be class consciousness, a desire to protect the manager's own position, a crippling fear of mistakes, and managers who feel threatened if good ideas do not come from them.

Whilst many companies realise that there will be a need for change with the abolition of European trade barriers in 1992, all too many blame the workforce for resistance, when it is really the executives who are the stumbling block. The research showed that trust between bosses and employees was the hallmark of an innovative company.

Change is essential if an organisation is to remain competitive and keep abreast of developments in technology, production, marketing, consumer tastes, etc. However, the very structure of a company which makes it stable and successful may hinder change because of the inertia which tends to build up.

Responses to change

People vary in their response to the prospect of change: some positively enjoy and encourage it, some accept it, some are indifferent and some resist it more or less strongly (see Fig. 12.1).

Many businesses begin with a single enthusiastic individual who is an entrepreneurial innovator (Clive Sinclair, Terence Conran and Freddie Laker are examples which spring to mind). As the organisation grows and the original entrepreneur retires, this type of individual becomes less popular as the structure becomes more fixed although, even in the most bureaucratic public service, there must always be some change to maintain efficiency (e.g. the introduction of computers to the Inland Revenue).

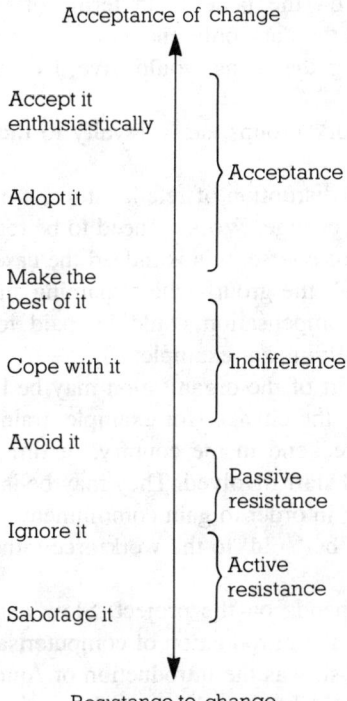

Fig. 12.1 Responses to change

Those who accept change range from those who quietly take new developments into their own area of influence, making sure they work, to those who are enthusiastic about anything new, always wanting the latest technology. The enthusiasm of the latter is infectious, and they can be a great asset in carrying more reluctant members of the group along with them.

Those who resist change may do so for a number of reasons:

(a) fear of the unknown;
(b) fear of loss of security or income (job, bonuses, overtime, etc.);
(c) reluctance to break up existing work relationships, relocate, etc.;
(d) the threat of new challenges—particularly older workers who may fear they will be unable to cope;
(e) fear of loss of freedom, status or power (e.g. if old skills become redundant);
(f) lack of explanation of the benefits of the change;
(g) expected difficulties (and lack of faith in management to overcome them);
(h) remembrance of previous bad experiences of change.

To overcome these barriers, managers and organisations must plan change well in advance. The staff or their representatives should be involved at as early a stage as possible, given information and consulted on the change itself and the means of introducing it. The change must be seen to have the full commitment of senior management.

Good communication is vital, explaining carefully to subordinates the need for the changes and their expected consequences, with the emphasis on the benefits in terms of reduced workload, more interesting jobs, etc. Keeping people in the dark only encourages rumour and speculation. The only reason for secrecy is if revealing the plans would give a competitor valuable information.

Where possible, it is best not to disrupt existing work groups, since loyalty to the group can be a powerful agent of change.

The fear of redundancy, or redeployment resulting in disruption of relationships, a move to a new area, etc., is a serious barrier to the acceptance of change. Workers need to be reassured that the organisation has their best interests at heart (if, of course, this is indeed the case—it is no good promising no redundancies and then sacking half the group—the remaining staff will never trust the management again). It may be that compensation could be paid to older workers who prefer to take early retirement rather than retrain, for example.

In some cases, running a pilot scheme in a limited part of the organisation may be helpful. It is often possible to offer rewards for cooperation with the change (for example, training for the use of new equipment may be combined with a weekend in the country, or time off in lieu). Training is very important and must be given to all staff involved. They may be involved in the planning of the timing and organisation of training in order to gain commitment.

In all cases the benefits of the proposed change must be 'sold' to the workforce rather than 'told' (to use the Ashridge model).

The pace at which change should be introduced depends on the project. Slow change is preferable where considerable retraining is required (e.g. the introduction of computerisation in the banks was done gradually, a few branches at a time; so was the introduction of Automated Teller Machines (ATMs), so that teething problems could be sorted out as the project went along). On the other hand, a swift change reduces uncertainty, makes the most of any competitive advantage to be gained, and is less likely to result in the new system being already out of date by the time the full introduction has been completed. For example, when Midland Bank introduced 'Free if in Credit' current accounts, the project had to be kept secret as long as possible, and was introduced very quickly in all branches at once. This led to training problems for the staff, and a massive increase in workload at the start, but it was 18 months before the other banks were able to introduce similar schemes. By that time, Midland had gained some 250,000 new accounts, so the problems were considered worthwhile.

The steps to achieve change are:

(a) **Unfreeze**—dissolve the present situation.
(b) **Change**—make the necessary change.
(c) **Refreeze**—consolidate the new position by problem solving and rewarding acceptance.

■ Meetings

Many managers find that a large part of their working day is spent attending meetings, writing up notes afterwards and actioning the decisions taken.

Such meetings can waste a great deal of time for all concerned if they are not carefully planned and managed; – if well run, on the other hand, they can be an excellent way of 'spending time to save time', leading to more effective management.

Meetings required by law (such as the Annual General Meeting of a company) and those on a very large scale (such as the sales conference of a large multinational, involving hundreds or thousands of people) are outside the scope of this book. Here we are concerned more with the everyday meetings called in all organisations to discuss work projects, to keep teams and groups informed about what is going on, to plan changes in the organisation, to solve a problem which has arisen in the running of the business, and so on.

For any meeting, there are several points which need to be organised in advance:

- Give people as much notice as possible.
- Advise the time and place of the meeting.
- State how long the meeting is expected to last.
- Provide necessary background papers and agenda in advance.
- Tell people who else will be there.
- Explain what they are expected to contribute.

If you are planning a meeting, remember that management time is valuable—don't invite too many people unnecessarily. At an average salary of say £15,000 – £20,000, a meeting involving six managers will cost your organisation around £100 an hour! Remember too that the more people are involved, the longer it is likely to take to reach a decision. As a rough rule of thumb, what four people could resolve in 20 minutes would take six people 2 hours and eight people 5 hours!

In deciding the time and place for a meeting, the subjects for the agenda and the length of time to allocate, similar considerations apply to those for planning an interview: choose a time when everyone will be fresh and enthusiastic (not last thing on Friday afternoon); choose a suitable room and arrange refreshments if appropriate; don't try to pack too much into one meeting, and do not plan to go on for more than $1\frac{1}{2}$ to 2 hours, or people will be tired and stale.

■ Committees

Committees are really just specialised forms of meetings. They may be standing committees, which meet regularly, or special working parties set up to study specific problems or to manage a particular project. The latter type will cease to exist once the problem is resolved or the project satisfactorily completed. Committees may also be set up to consider specific functional areas, such as health and safety, policy-making, social events, etc.

If the committee exceeds, say, 10–15 members, its size will be such that controlling the members and integrating their ideas will become a problem. However, it is sometimes necessary to include a wide range of people on a committee; for example, some people may have expert knowledge, others are there to represent their department or function, and some will be decision-makers who have the authority to commit the organisation. Some members may make only an occasional specialised contribution, others will wish to speak on behalf of particular causes or viewpoints, yet others will be chiefly concerned with relaying the outcome of the meeting to those they represent.

If a committee is very large, sub-committees may be set up, composed of a selected number of committee members, to pursue a particular topic more effectively and to report back to the main committee.

Formal committees

Some very formal committees will have a constitution—a written document which sets out the objectives of the committee, the authority it possesses, the membership and officials, and the decision-making procedures. The statement of authority should specify, for example, whether the committee is a consultative or advisory body, or whether it has a decision-making function.

The method of selection of members of the committee should be stated, together with the size of the quorum (i.e. the minimum number of members who must be present for any vote to be valid).

Committee procedures

The very formal procedures which used to be followed in committee meetings are becoming somewhat archaic nowadays. If you want to witness them in operation, listen to the proceedings of Trades Union Congress meetings or political party conferences.

Nevertheless, all committee meetings should follow certain procedures: a record of every meeting should be made, in the form of minutes, which are circulated to every member after the meeting and signed by the chairman at the following meeting as a true record of the proceedings. The minutes should record any decisions reached, any action points to be carried out by committee members, and the target date.

An agenda should be circulated before each meeting. This usually opens with 'minutes of the previous meeting' so that members can comment on any errors or follow up 'matters arising' from those minutes. The chairman may ask for motions to be proposed and seconded before each vote is taken, or this may be dispensed with in less formal committee meetings.

Duties of the chairman, secretary and members of a committee

The duties of the chairman are to control and steer the meeting, rather than necessarily taking a leading role himself. This is where many people fail as chairmen—they feel they must speak at length on every point, being the fount of all knowledge and taking all the decisions. If this were the case, there would be little point in having a committee; the better role for the chairman is to draw out the other members so that each gives of his best and each has a full chance to contribute. The chairman's role may be defined as follows:

(a) Before the meeting, ensure he understands its purpose.

(b) Choose an appropriate leadership style, bearing in mind the issues to be discussed and the status/knowledge/experience of the members who will be present.
(c) State the objectives at the start of the meeting and ensure all participants understand them.
(d) Act as a guide and facilitator, seeking to draw views from participants rather than impose views on them.
(e) Give everyone a chance to speak, but be prepared to cut short repetitive or irrelevant contributions. Allow only one person to speak at once.
(f) Ensure agenda items are adequately discussed, but avoid lengthy digressions keep to the agreed timetable as far as possible.
(g) Summarise at intervals as consensus is reached, or focus on points of dissension to avoid wasting time on areas of agreement.
(h) If a vote is needed, be sure that everyone is clear what they are voting for.
(i) If action is needed as the result of a discussion or decision, be sure it is clear who is responsible and by when.

The secretary's job is primarily to support the chairman by arranging the administrative details, ensuring paperwork is prepared and circulated, and taking the minutes of the meeting as it takes place:

(a) Liaise with the chairman on the purpose, timing and place of the meeting and who is to be invited (if not the standard committee membership).
(b) Make sure the chairman is fully briefed before the meeting.
(c) Ensure the agenda and any necessary papers are sent to participants well before the meeting, drawing their attention to any points which affect them specifically, or on which they are expected to speak.
(d) During the meeting, accurately record the participants' contributions and any decisions reached.
(e) Assist the chairman to follow the agenda and stick to the timetable.
(f) After the meeting, write up the minutes and distribute them swiftly.
(g) Follow up to ensure that any action points are carried out by the appropriate person.

Participants in any meeting can help it to run smoothly and be effective if they ensure that they are in fact the right person to be there (perhaps a subordinate would actually have more to contribute?) and follow some basic points themselves:

(a) Arrive on time.
(b) Come prepared, having read the circulated papers.
(c) Listen sympathetically to the other participants.
(d) Speak clearly, concisely and to the point.
(e) Avoid acrimonious arguments or personality clashes.
(f) Look for win–win solutions.
(g) Make positive contributions, designed to lead towards achievement of the objectives, rather than destructive comments.
(h) Ask for clarification if any points are not clear—others may be mystified too, but too shy to say so, leading to meaningless discussions.

Well run meetings, where all the participants come ready to make a positive contribution, can lead to well informed, effective decision-making. However, there are dangers, two of which were mentioned above: waste of time and money. Other dangers are that by adopting a committee approach, the final decision may be an unsatisfactory compromise. There is a well known description of a camel as 'a horse, designed by a committee'—in other words an ungainly beast, resulting from a whole variety of ideas thrown together, rather than an elegant if radical solution which might have been achieved by one person. A similar dilemma was faced by King Solomon when he had to decide how to divide a child between the two women who claimed him as their son—a committee would surely have tried to find a compromise, whereas Solomon was able to take a radical decision (in case you do not know the story, he announced his intention of cutting the child in two, at which one woman cried that she would rather he gave the child to the other woman than killed it. Thus Solomon deduced that this was indeed the true mother, as she could not bear the idea of the death of the child).

The point is that, whilst compromise may be a good solution in some cases (e.g. dividing resources between two departments in proportion to their needs), it can be inappropriate in others (e.g. allocating a specific piece of equipment for which two or more departments are bidding).

Another danger of committees is that they tend to be self-perpetuating: they spawn subcommittees, steering committees to coordinate the work of a group of other committees, etc., and if you are not careful, nothing is ever decided nor any action taken.

▌ Action points

(a) What role do you think you play in your work group? Think of the others who work with you and try to work out who takes each of the eight roles Belbin identified.

(b) How good is your manager at communication? Are there any barriers which you could help to break down? For example, do you always give him your full attention? Do you always check for understanding by asking questions, or do you wait until afterwards to discover you didn't really understand what was being said?

(c) To how many groups, formal and informal, do you belong? Make a list; you will probably be able to think of at least four or five, inside and outside work.

(d) Do you belong to any committees (work or social)? Next time you attend a meeting, watch the others to see how well they follow the guidelines given above.

▌ Questions and answers

Question 1

There are many barriers to communication. What can the sender of a message do to make sure it is clearly conveyed? [15]

What can the receiver do to grasp the meaning of the message as accurately as possible? [10]

[Total marks for question—25]

Question 2

Samantha Travers, who supervises a work group of six and who reports to you, has asked for your advice.

'I'm worried because my team doesn't seem to be performing as well as it did,' she confides. 'I know we've recently lost Eric and Christine and that has left a bit of a gap. Eric was the one who was bubbling with ideas and Christine could always be relied upon to look after the details. Iona and Keith seemed very suitable replacements but somehow Martina (who has been with me for six months) and Keith are constantly disagreeing and trying to wrest control from me. Iona is always analysing other people's ideas rather than contributing any of her own.

We now have to start on this really important project and I'm not sure that the team is capable of carrying it through.'

(a) Analyse what is happening in Samantha's group. [16]

(b) What steps should Samantha take to promote effective performance from her team? [9]

[Total marks for question—25]

Question 3

Jill Knight has been in charge of her group for three months. It appears to be completely demoralised. Productivity is low, absenteeism is high, no-one cooperates. As Jill's boss, what advice would you give her on how to improve the group's performance? [15]
What would be the signs of success? [10]

[Total marks for question—25]

Question 4

The regional manager was amazed at the hostility provoked by the introduction of word processors at his office. As far as he was concerned, they would make the job more interesting and take the drudgery out of secretarial work. He had arranged for training to take place and he knew that labour turnover would take care of any excess staff. He could see only advantages and yet there had been a terrific fuss and three secretaries had resigned to move to other organisations.

What were the possible reasons for the hostility which faced the regional manager? What could he have done to introduce the change more smoothly?

[Total marks for question—25]

Question 5

The unit of which you are the manager has been based some distance from its parent and this has caused many problems of communication. You are relieved to hear that a floor of the parent office building has now become vacant and that your unit can move in. It is 10 miles from your present site on the opposite side of the city.

(a) What issues will this raise for your staff and how will you deal with those issues? [15]

(b) When you get your new office space there is no restriction on how you organise it. What factors will influence your final decision about layout? [10]

[Total marks for question—25]

(*Hint:* This is not just a question about travel problems—think about the wider management issues raised.)

Question 6

As a manager in the personnel department of the area office, you are pleased to learn that a new supervisor, John Smith, who was appointed in another department a few months ago, is generally making a success of the job. His results are promising and he enjoys working with the individuals in his section. But he has one particular weakness: he finds it very difficult to run meetings of his group. He tends to dominate proceedings so that people leave feeling frustrated and irritable. Some say it would be better not to hold meetings if the results are so negative.

As a member of the supervisory team, John Smith also attends meetings with his supervisory colleagues. He finds these meetings very boring and shows his impatience, much to the annoyance of his manager, who needs to hold the meetings as the most efficient way of passing on information and coordinating the work of a large department.

John Smith recognises his weaknesses and wants your help. What would you do?

[Total marks for question—25]

Question 7

'That was the most effective meeting I have ever attended,' said Nigel Weston. 'We achieved everything we wanted. We fully discussed each item on the agenda and yet we finished on time. Sue Field did a marvellous job in the chair, everybody contributed positively, and Steve, as secretary, made sure that the administration was perfect.'

What preparations and contributions by Sue, Steve and the other participants are likely to have made the meeting so effective?

[Total marks for question—25]

Answer 1

See the text of this chapter.

Answer 2

Analysis
The membership of the group changed recently and, therefore, essentially a new group has been brought into existence.

Before a new group is likely to perform most effectively it needs to develop through the four stages of forming, storming, norming, and performing.

This group seems to be at the storming stage, as evidenced by bickering, criticism of ideas and attempts to challenge leadership.

The group lost two members who performed valuable team roles. These team roles do not, as yet, appear to have been filled.

Eric evidently acted as the group's 'Plant'—the ideas man.

Christine acted as a 'Finisher'—checking on details, following through.

Keith appears to be a 'Shaper'—competing with Martina in this role. Whilst a 'Chairman' (Samantha) can generally control one 'Shaper', two may be more than can easily be managed.

Iona is a 'Monitor-evaluator'—a valuable role, but one which may already be covered by another team member and which does not replace Eric's contribution.

The way forward

Given time, the norms by which the group members will regulate its behaviour will emerge and the group will mature naturally to the performing stage of development.

This process will be aided by an early emphasis on an important task.

Similarly—given time—the team roles necessary for effective group performance will be covered by members who will suppress their primary roles where otherwise there might be conflict, and promote secondary roles to cover those which would otherwise be missing.

Samantha should:
— focus on task needs (the project);
— clearly define the group's objectives and its short-term goals;
— set standards to achieve the required result;
— monitor and provide feedback on performance;
— encourage ideas for progress and integration;
— counsel, train and coach to help the team and its members improve performance.

Answer 3

Refer to the text of this chapter, and Chapters 8, 9 and 10).

Answer 4 (outline)

Symptoms and causes

The hostility is a symptom of the fear of personnel that they might be adversely affected by the change. The manager could have reduced such fears by much fuller provision of information and much more extensive communication and consultation.

The hostility will have arisen for some of the following reasons:

— No-one in the department understands word processors and their ramifications and they are seen as a threat.
— The advent of the word processor might lead to reorganisation which could break up existing relationships.
— The new equipment will require new skills which some people might not be able to acquire.
— On the other hand, the work might become less interesting and fewer skills might be required.
— Promotion prospects might be reduced.
— Redundancy might follow.

— Financial rewards might be affected.
— Some people might lose power and status.

The manager could have helped by:
— Providing information to enable people to understand the likely outcomes of the change.
— Making clear the potential benefits.
— Explaining how the word processors would be introduced and offering opportunities for consultation as the implementation proceeds.
— Explaining the training which would be given.
— Making sure that he understood peoples' fears so that he could take steps to allay them.
— Monitoring progress; checking feelings.
— Rewarding those who contribute effectively to the change.
— Arranging visits to other installations.
— Introducing a pilot programme.

Answer 5

(a) *Issues about the move*

Are there any savings in resources to be made in addition to better use of space, e.g. equipment, materials, people?

If there are savings in people, what will happen to those displaced—redeployment, redundancy (voluntary or compulsory)?

If compulsory redundancies, how will they be selected?

How is the group to be effectively integrated with existing staff?

Will change of organisation require new skills; if so, how will they be acquired and by whom? What planning needs to be done to ensure a smooth transition?

What is the timing of the move and what are the logistics? When should it be announced? How is work to be handled over the period of disruption, however long or short?

What consultation should take place? As the decision has been made to move, the consultation will not concern this issue, but will centre on the staff implications.

What happens to staff who do not wish to travel? Can they be absorbed into other offices in the immediate area?

If large numbers do not wish to relocate, what are the recruitment and training implications for efficient work at the new location?

(b) *Issues about the new office*

Layout for efficient working will include: work flow and communication; access to equipment, files, stores, etc.; ease of supervision; contact with other departments; and so on.

The degree to which the decision will be shared with staff will depend upon: the extent to which the staff can assist in ensuring an efficient working unit; the degree to which they will be motivated by participation in the final office organisation.

Answer 6

The problem is that this supervisor is in some respects still behaving as an individual worker and not as a supervisor. He does not share ideas with his staff, nor give them the opportunity to let him know their feelings. The result is that he runs poor meetings. He also does not understand his responsibilities in the management of the department so that he does not make useful contributions to meetings run by his head of department (who, it is possible, does not run meetings well either).

Courses of action

Explain the advantages of meetings in large organisations: their role as an effective means of passing and gathering information and opinions, as a way of gaining consultation and commitment.

Arrange training in the skills of chairmanship. Particularly, coach him to improve his skills to:

(a) state the purpose of the meeting clearly;
(b) have a clear agenda and schedule to help members to prepare;
(c) understand the appropriate leadership style for handling differing issues;
(d) act as a guide and facilitator rather than sole problem-solver;
(e) prepare before the meeting by studying the agenda and ensuring he has a positive role;
(f) during the meeting, listen; look for win–win solutions to problems; express himself clearly, concisely and logically; ensure there is training and positive feedback to members of his team.

Ensure that his manager has any help he needs in effective chairmanship and that he is aware of the reasons for the supervisor's difficulties. Ensure that the group of people he chairs are coached in good committee work and are prepared to be supportive.

Ensure that his manager gives him feedback on his role as a member of the meeting and that he is given feedback on the chairmanship of his own meetings.

Answer 7

See the text of this chapter.

CHAPTER 13
Organisational staff issues

- Recruitment and selection procedures
- Training and career development systems
- Equal opportunities
- Power

▌ Introduction

In previous chapters we have considered selection and training from the individual's point of view; here we will be looking at the wider organisational issues—the factors which lead to good practice in respect of recruitment and selection; training and development; and the impact of, for example, equal opportunities legislation.

▌ Recruitment and selection procedures

This is one area of the syllabus where I can guarantee you will all have first-hand experience. Everyone who is, or ever has been, employed will have gone through a form of recruitment and selection procedure and will be able to comment on how good/successful or bad/unsuccessful it was.

Below is a list of the major stages of the process of recruiting and selecting a new member of staff. Remember that selection may take place from within an organisation as well as by external advertisement, and the stages will be slightly different in each case.

- Job analysis
- Job description
- Personnel specification
- Advertisement
- Application
- Shortlist
- Tests/Interviews
- Choice of candidate

Job analysis. Job description. Personnel specification

These were covered in some detail in Chapters 6 and 10. Remember that job analysis is the process of determining what is done in a particular job so that a job description (a written statement of the tasks and responsibilities associated with the job) and a personnel specification (a statement of the type of individual most likely to fill the vacancy successfully—essential, desirable and unwanted characteristics) can be drawn up. Chapter 10 covered the features of a personnel specification, using the National Institute of Industrial Psychology seven-point plan.

When drawing up the description and specification for a new job, there will obviously be no existing job to analyse; nevertheless there will often be similar jobs, perhaps in other parts of the organisation, which can be used as models. If it is an entirely novel post, then the description must address the purpose of the job more than the tasks to be performed, and the personnel specification may be more loosely drawn, since it will be less certain exactly what type of person will best suit the post.

It is a mistake to define the personnel specification too rigidly; just because a certain type of person has successfully carried out a job in the past, this does not necessarily rule out a different type of person being just as successful in the future—one should try to keep an open mind. However, there may be definite requirements, such as a willingness to work in a small team, or without close supervision, if such is the case.

Advertisement

If the job is to be advertised (internally or externally), careful thought must be given to the wording, in order to attract suitable candidates, without either giving false hope to unsuitable candidates or putting off good potential applicants.

The medium in which to advertise must be carefully chosen. Internally, this will probably be fixed by custom—e.g. the circulars in a bank branch network, items on the noticeboard in a smaller firm, and so on. Externally, the choice of method is important.

If recruiting school leavers in large numbers, the mass circulation newspapers will be appropriate; there is no point using the *Bankers' World* magazine, for example, as this is not read by those who have yet to join a bank. Advertising in the local press is often very cost-effective in recruiting clerical or secretarial staff for a particular branch or area.

If recruiting a senior executive, however, advertisements in *The Financial Times* and the professional banking journals would be more appropriate than say *The Sun* or *Sunday Sport*. For specialist staff (e.g. computer programmers or accountants), the appropriate professional or trade journals would be suitable.

For junior management posts, banks may use specialist employment agencies; for the most senior posts, firms of 'head hunters' may be employed to contact identified individuals in other organisations who might not have actively thought of moving jobs, but who might be tempted by the right offer.

Application

The next decision is whether to use preprinted application forms, or whether to ask the candidates to write in.

The advantage of an application form is that one can ask a series of specific questions, appropriate to the type of job involved, and sort the applicants initially on the basis of their responses. It is usual to ask for the form to be completed by hand, rather than typed, to gain an impression of presentation, spelling, handwriting, etc. Someone who completes an application form for a job in a messy and slapdash way, with numerous errors and crossings out, is unlikely to prove to be a tidy, methodical worker.

The type of questions asked include: name, address, telephone number; date of birth, nationality and marital status; education; training and qualifications; medical history, e.g. any previous serious illnesses, any present disability; names of previous employers, jobs held and reasons for leaving; reasons for applying for this post and why the applicant feels he would be suitable; any other relevant information.

Clearly, the information needed from applicants for a manual job will be much less than that required for a managerial position.

For a more specialist or senior post, an application form may be less appropriate and one may simply ask for a letter of application enclosing a CV. A CV or *curriculum vitae* (literally the 'course of one's life') is a summary of a person's education, achievements and jobs to date, giving an indication of his preferences and successes. It should be taken with a pinch of salt in some cases, as it is quite possible to make very minor achievements and insignificant jobs sound most impressive if cleverly worded. One might well ask for documentary evidence of examination successes and for permission to approach previous employers for a reference. An honest applicant will have no hesitation in agreeing to both.

Shortlist

From the responses to questions on the application form it is often possible to reject some applicants straight away. For example, if the specification states that a degree is a requirement, applicants with no such qualification can be weeded out.

Rejected applicants should be sent a polite rejection letter immediately, so that they are not left in suspense and perhaps lose the chance of applying for other more suitable posts.

How many applicants are put on the shortlist will vary with the quality of response, the number of vacancies, how crucial it is to have exactly the right person (which may entail interviewing a larger number), and so on. Normally, a short list of two to six candidates will be ample for a single vacancy. Otherwise, whoever is interviewing them will be spending an inordinate length of time on the process and may well be losing concentration by the time the final candidates are seen.

Those applicants who are shortlisted should be advised of the fact and given details of the next stage (normally a one-to-one or panel interview—see Chapter 11).

Tests

For technical posts or those requiring particular skills, some form of aptitude or skill test may be appropriate. For example, for junior clerical posts, many employers carry out tests of basic mathematics, English and intelligence before final selection. Those entering the computer industry may be required to complete an aptitude test to ensure that they have the right mental abilities, and secretarial staff may be required to take typing or shorthand tests to check speeds and accuracy.

Such tests are less common where managerial jobs are concerned, although some firms employ personality testing or even graphology (analysis of handwriting) to select the type of person they are looking for.

Interviews

The shortlisted candidates will be interviewed, as discussed in detail in Chapter 11. It may be appropriate, when candidates come for interview, to show them around the office in which they would work, to allow the existing staff to spend some time talking to them. This both gives the candidates a better idea of the job, and allows the present staff to give some input into the selection procedure by commenting on their reaction to the prospective candidate. Someone who immediately rubs the existing staff up the wrong way is unlikely to fit well into the team. On the other hand, someone who asks intelligent questions and seems genuinely interested in the work is a more promising applicant than one who shows no interest at all.

Choice of candidate

Once the result of the interviews and of any tests are to hand, the applicants should be compared with each other (either by the person who carried out the interview, or in conjunction with his colleagues, and preferably including the person who will act as manager to the new recruit) to select the person best qualified and who best fits the job description and personnel specification. This will not necessarily be the person with the **highest** qualifications, as someone who is too well qualified may become bored by a routine job and quickly lose motivation and productivity, but the person who is **most appropriately** qualified.

The chosen candidate should be offered the job. This offer must include full details of pay, conditions (hours of work, bonuses, holidays, etc.), place of work, and any special conditions (e.g. conditional on passing certain examinations, or subject to satisfactory medical reports and references), and should stipulate a date by which a reply must be given.

Once he has accepted, the other applicants should be sent polite letters of rejection, if possible giving them some constructive guidance as to why they were unsuccessful on this occasion.

∎ Training and career development systems

It is a sad fact that, in British commerce and industry, we spend less per head on training than in many of our Western competitor nations. The government has initiated various schemes to try to rectify this situation, but without notable success.

This is a short-sighted view by senior management, since better trained staff should lead to greater productivity and therefore a more cost-effective operation, recouping the cost of the training itself.

Several theories have been put forward for this lack of enthusiasm on the part of management: that trained workers will be more easily 'poached' by rival firms; that in industries with a large female workforce, training is a waste of time as so many staff leave after a relatively short period of time due to family commitments; that formal training is unnecessary since people learn as they go along; that training soon becomes outdated with rapidly changing technology; and so on. None of these excuses really holds water and in this section we shall take a more positive approach to the various types of training and development available.

Relevant training

Training may indeed be wasted, if it is not carefully planned and monitored. Training which is inappropriate to the stage of development of the employee, is out of date or irrelevant, is seen by the employee as a punishment, or is given too early or too late (when the employee has no relevant experience or has already acquired bad habits through long exposure to a job), will be counterproductive—a waste of time and resources.

Managers should assess the training needs of their subordinates by looking for the 'training gap', i.e. the difference between the performance of the employee and the expected performance of a fully trained and fully competent employee. When this gap exists, it is probable that training will be beneficial to close it, provided that the cost of training does not outweigh the productivity benefits to be gained.

Organisational training needs

As part of the manpower planning process discussed in Chapter 3, an organisation must draw up a training plan. In a large organisation such as a British clearing bank, this may involve designing specific training programmes to be run in-house, either in the workplace or in a special training centre. In smaller firms, or for more specialist needs, external courses run by professional training suppliers may be more appropriate.

By estimating the likely changes in the size and composition of the workforce, it is possible to plan what kind of training will be required in the future, how many people are likely to require training, at what level, what the likely cost will be, what should be given priority, and so on.

There are several different reasons for training:

(a) Training for the immediate job to be done (e.g. how to deal with the duties of a standing-orders clerk).
(b) Training about the environment (e.g. the opportunity to learn about the bank as a whole and how it operates).
(c) Training as preparation for promotion (e.g. a clerk may be trained in management skills before taking up a supervisory post).
(d) Training to broaden outlook (e.g. a manager in a bank may be given the opportunity to see the other side of the coin, by learning how industrial companies operate so that he will understand his customers better.
(e) Training in specific skills (e.g. how to operate the branch computer system).

The organisational training plan must take all these types into account as well as the various possible methods of training (e.g. on-the-job; off-the-job; computer-based training; etc.).

On-the-job training

This is training which takes place in a normal working situation. The trainee is using the actual equipment, documents and materials which he will use when fully trained and can be regarded as a partly productive worker right from the start. The trainer is usually the supervisor, or another worker—which has led to the colloquial name for this type of training: 'sitting with Nellie'.

The advantages of on-the-job training are:

(a) It is less expensive as it uses existing equipment and staff in normal working hours.
(b) There is no problem of transferring skills from the training environment to a different working environment.
(c) It is useful for unusual skills which would not justify setting up special training courses.
(d) It is particularly good for practical skills training.

The disadvantages include:

(a) The trainer may not be a good teacher or may not have the time to train properly.
(b) The trainee may pick up bad habits and inefficient or incorrect methods of working.
(c) Mistakes and wasted work may result, particularly at the start.
(d) The stress of a noisy, busy office is not ideal for training.
(e) Theoretical training is not suited to on-the-job methods.

Off-the-job training

This is training which takes place away from the workplace, either at a training centre belonging to the organisation, or at a commercial training establishment, college, etc.

The advantages are:

(a) A specialist trainer should mean higher-quality instruction.
(b) Special exercises can be devised to lead the trainee through the course in planned stages.
(c) There is a more conducive environment for learning.
(d) The trainee will learn correct methods from the start.

The disadvantages include:

(a) There is a higher cost for premises, accommodation, instructors, etc.
(b) There is a difficulty, in some cases, in transferring skills to the working environment, perhaps with slightly different equipment.
(c) Some skills can only really be learned by experience, in the real business environment.

Other training methods

In recent years, a compromise between expensive off-the-job training and inconsistent on-the-job training has been developed with the various types of computer-based interactive training systems.

The trainee sits at a computer terminal or Personal Computer (PC) and works through a training course written as a computer software program. In most of these systems, the trainee must answer questions to show that he has understood what has been taught—by typing these responses into the computer. The program analyses the responses and can suggest a revision of the topic if the answers are incorrect. Once the correct answers are given, the trainee may move on to the next section of the course. This type of training allows trainees to go at their own pace, not held back by other students or pushed faster than they can cope with. It also allows a certain topic to be studied repeatedly if required.

Career development

The steps which the individual should take to enhance his career prospects are covered in the next chapter. However there are a number of things which the good employer should do to assist employees to make the most of their talents.

To begin with, the organisation should have a good management development and training plan so that the 'routes to the top' are clearly identifiable and logical. Within this plan, the organisation should offer work which will enable the ambitious employee to learn and to develop skills which will be appropriate to higher-level jobs.

The employer should offer appropriate and adequate training courses and development opportunities, and reward those who respond well to such training.

The managers of the organisation should themselves be sufficiently well trained in appraisal and counselling skills for them to be able to act as effective guides and mentors to the more junior employees working their way up through the business.

■ Equal opportunities

This topic has been touched on in various parts of the text already. I would hope that most people reading this book would agree with the proposition that discrimination on the grounds of sex, race or marital status is unfair. Nevertheless, in the face of complex legislation on these subjects, breaking the law unwittingly is easier than might be imagined.

All members of staff, and especially those responsible for managing and supervising other staff, need to be aware of unfair discrimination in the workplace and how to remedy it. There are two specific reasons for this: firstly, in certain circumstances the employee (rather than the organisation) can be held personally liable for his or her actions; secondly, ignorance of the law is no defence.

Both the Sex Discrimination Act 1975 (which covers discrimination on grounds of sex or marital status) and the Race Relations Act 1976 make a distinction between direct and indirect discrimination. Both are illegal, but indirect discrimination is more difficult to identify.

Direct discrimination

This is where a person from one group is treated less favourably than a person from another group is (or would be) treated. For example, if you encourage the boys in your branch to study for the Chartered Institute of Bankers' examinations, but not the girls (or vice versa), or if a coloured employee is not promoted to a management position because it is thought he would not be able to supervise white staff, this would be direct discrimination.

Indirect discrimination

This is where a requirement is set which cannot be justified, and although, on the face of it, it may appear to apply equally to all groups, in practice it can be met by far more people from one group (sex, marital status or race) than another. For example, by setting a height requirement of six feet for male officers, the police force is indirectly discriminating against men from the Asian races, who tend, on average, to be shorter than Caucasians. This could only be lawful if it could be shown that the height requirement was truly justified.

Another example is found in the Fire Brigade, where there is a requirement that recruits can carry a heavy load over a certain distance (in order to be able to carry a person out of a building, for instance). This requirement is clearly more likely to be fulfilled by a man than a woman, on average, but as it is a definite necessity for the job, it is not discriminatory.

However, if part-time employees were selected for redundancy before full-time employees, this would be indirect discrimination against women, since most part-time workers are women who would therefore be disproportionately affected.

Similarly, stating that good written English was a requirement for a labouring job would be indirect discrimination against non-English applicants, since it would not be a justifiable requirement. The same requirement for a job involving the production of high-quality written work (e.g. journalism) might, on the other hand, be justified.

Disabled employees

The Disabled Persons Acts 1944 and 1958 require that 3 per cent of an organisation's workforce is made up of people with a disability. Sadly, many companies are lawfully able to avoid this requirement by applying for exemption.

Exceptions

When advertising for job applicants, the only time that applications may be requested from a particular sex or race is if the job in question has a Genuine Occupational Qualification on the grounds of: authenticity (e.g. acting roles in the theatre); decency (e.g. for lavatory attendants one may specify sex); and welfare services to a particular group of people.

It is highly unlikely that any job in the banking industry would qualify for any of the above exceptions.

Good practice

To avoid the possibility of discrimination in the workplace, organisations and individuals should follow these precepts:

(a) Avoid assumptions. For example, do not assume that married women will be less mobile than single people or married men; do not assume that someone with a disability will be unable to carry out a particular job.

(b) Avoid biased questions. For example, do not ask women applicants about their plans for managing children and domestic commitments; this is probably not relevant to the job and is directly discriminatory, as it is unlikely that men would be asked the same question. If you need to ask about availability for unsocial hours of work, do so objectively: ask 'Will you be able to work on Saturday mornings?' rather than 'Won't you have problems with childcare facilities on Saturdays?'

(c) Stick to questions which are directly relevant to the job to ensure fair practice in selection procedures.

(d) Avoid assumptions about career patterns, e.g. encouraging men to look for promotion but women to stay where they are; or withholding training opportunities from a woman because she is due to go on maternity leave.

Positive action

Positive discrimination, i.e. choosing someone **because** they belong to a particular group, is unlawful.

However, the law does allow an employer to take measures to achieve equality of opportunity—this is positive action.

For example, several banks run courses specifically for women. Because there are so few women managers, these courses are designed to help them overcome the barriers that prevent them progressing. This does not mean that on completion of the course the women are automatically promoted—that would be positive discrimination. They still have to compete on merit.

▌Power

Within organisations, much of the interaction between people in different departments and of different status is based on the exercise of overt or implicit power. Leaders get things done through power. This is not necessarily a bad thing—without degrees of power, organisations would operate rather chaotically. We tend to regard power as a negative attribute—'Power corrupts; absolute power corrupts absolutely'—but in fact it is present in varying degrees in all of us, and in all situations where more than one person is involved.

There are seven identifiable types of power:

(a) **Coercive power**. This is power based on fear. Ultimately, it is power based on the threat of physical punishment, pain or even death. This is the power wielded by terrorists, by dictators and, to a lesser degree, by parents or teachers who use the threat of corporal punishment to command obedience.

(b) **Reward power**. This power is based on control over the rewards which an individual will receive, e.g. salary payment and increases, promotion, etc.

(c) **Legitimate power**. This is the power vested in a particular role or position. A manager automatically carries a degree of power by virtue of the status of the job; in any hierarchical system such as the military services, the church, the police, etc., the holder of a certain office has legitimate power over those junior to him.

(d) **Expert power.** Where one person possesses certain skills or expert knowledge, he will have power over those who do not and who have need of the skills or knowledge.
(e) **Referent power.** If one person is regarded as particularly successful or popular by others in the organisation, he will have an inherent power to get others to follow his example and model their behaviour on his.
(f) **Charismatic power.** Similarly to (e), this is the power to inspire others by example, encouragement and personality. This is a common attribute of the best managers and leaders.
(g) **Political power.** Expressed in phrases such as 'being in the right place at the right time' and 'It's not what you know but whom you know', this is the power achieved by understanding how the organisation works and using this knowledge to gain power in the system.

The amount of any of these types of power which a particular individual possesses is determined by the scarcity of the resource (charisma, skill, knowledge, rank, etc.) held by the individual. If you are the only person who knows how to operate the computer you have a great deal of power in deciding whose work shall be done on it first, for instance, but if everyone in the office shares this knowledge your power is diminished. Power also depends on the degree to which other people need your resource—if there are several computers available in another part of the office, people will be less dependent on your power as the possessor of scarce knowledge and again your power will be diminished.

If you feel you want to increase your power, there are a number of ways in which you might do so:

(a) Acquire a specific skill, or increase your knowledge in a particular area which you think will be valuable to others.
(b) Join a department within the organisation which has high visibility and high status and therefore confers political power on those who are part of it.
(c) Build up a network of contacts throughout the organisation; do favours for people in key areas so that, when necessary, you will be able to call on them for assistance.
(d) Identify who has power in the organisation; model your behaviour on theirs.
(e) Make sure you do first class work, and that it is seen by the key people in the organisation, so that they know who you are and are impressed by you. Then when they are looking for someone for a particular job, they should consider you favourably.
(f) Make sure you know where the power lies in your organisation (not necessarily with the top management—in many branches it is the messenger, the manager's secretary or the control clerk who wields the greatest power, not the manager!) Develop the skills to use this power base to your advantage.
(g) Get involved in outside activities which will attract your superiors' notice and gain their approval. For example, act as Education Officer for your Chartered Institute of Bankers local centre, get involved in the manager's pet charity, the local Rotary Club or other institutions through which you can improve the branch's (and your own) local reputation.

▮ Action points

(a) Think back to when you were recruited to your organisation. List the steps you went through. Identify areas where you think you could have been better treated, and those which you felt particularly good about.

(b) What training have you received recently? Do you know what is planned for you? If not, ask your manager if you can discuss your training plan at your next review.

(c) How many types of training have you received? Which did you find most successful?

(d) Do you know what your bank's policy on equal opportunities is? It should be available—ask your personnel department for details.

(e) Two helpful booklets are: The Equal Opportunities Commission, *Code of Practice* (£1.70 from HMSO, PO Box 276, London SW8 5DT); Commission for Racial Equality, *Race Relations Code of Practice* (£1 from the Commission for Racial Equality, Elliot House, 10–12 Allington St, London SW1E 5EH).

(f) What power do you have? Do not assume that, because you may be low down the hierarchy at present, you have little power. Think of the occasions on which people come to you for information or advice—could you increase this? What other steps could you, personally, take to increase your power?

▮ Questions and answers

Question 1

You discover, after a subordinate has been working with you for a year, that he has a medical condition which was not detected at his pre-employment medical and which means you should not have employed him in the first place. He did not tell you at the time. As he explained when challenged: 'If I had told you the truth you would not have given me the job. I lost seven jobs because I did tell the truth.' He is not only a satisfactory employee, he is first rate. He is very popular with his colleagues. Customers particularly seek him out and speak well of him. His conduct is exemplary and his results are outstanding.

What issues does this raise? What would you do now?

[Total marks for question—25]

Question 2

You have recently been made responsible for training in your bank's head office. This morning, six young graduates, all of whom are on a two-year management programme, have complained about the quality of the training they have been receiving. Departmental heads seem to be unclear as to what sort of training they are supposed to provide for the graduates. The graduates are given dull routine work which they could master in five days, but they are kept at it for a month at a time. They are not told whether they are doing well or badly. They are bored and dispirited.

(a) What is wrong with the management training programme? [10]

(b) What action should you take to improve the training of graduates? [15]

[Total marks for question—25]

Question 3

You want to become a senior manager in your bank one day. What steps would you take to advance your career? [13]
What do you think your bank should do to help you? [12]

[Total marks for question—25]

Question 4

All supervisors and managers exercise power, i.e. the capacity to affect the behaviour of others.

(a) What determines the amount of power a person possesses? [6]

(b) How can different types of power be described? [10]

(c) You have recently been appointed to a supervisory position. How would you set about acquiring the power to do your job effectively? [9]

[Total marks for question—25]

Answer 1 (outline)

Issues

How satisfactory is the selection procedure? Should it be modified to ensure that there is a thorough check to prevent repetition of this type of problem?

Do the interviewers need to improve their skills so that they can spot this type of problem?

What is the position of the employee? Should he have told you of his condition—even if not asked—or is it up to the organisation to discover the truth?

What are the company's disciplinary rules in relation to this situation?

Does it matter that the system failed if it resulted in a first-rate employee?

Should the medical conditions of employment be revised in the light of this experience?

Next steps

The problem is that you have a first-class employee who obtained his position by not telling you critical information which you failed to extract yourself.

Alternative courses of action are:
— dismiss the employee for not telling the truth;
— allow the employee to carry on—especially in the light of his record and the inadequate selection procedures of the company;
— ensure an overhaul of all selection and interviewing procedures is carried out.

The optimum solution is probably a combination of the last two steps, but the full implications for pensions and other benefits must be checked.

Answer 2

Analysis

It seems clear that:
 (a) Trainers have made the objectives of the exercise clear neither to the managers nor to the graduates concerned.
 (b) The training does not seem to have been planned. People are allowed to waste time on routine tasks.
 (c) No one is following progress, so it is difficult to help the group or individuals by developing plans to meet particular needs.

Action

 (a) Establish the aims of the management training clearly with your supervisors by the identification of the knowledge, skills and behaviour required by trainees by the end of the training session.
 (b) Produce a plan which will allow the knowledge and skills to be acquired—probably by a combination of formal and on-the-job training.
 (c) Break the plan down into detailed schedules, each with specific objectives.
 (d) Specify the performance levels required and indicate ways in which progress might be measured.
 (e) Make sure all concerned know the plan.
 (f) Make arrangements to review progress formally at each stage with the managers and the graduates concerned.
 (g) Take corrective action where necessary by modifying the plan or helping the person concerned to accelerate his learning.
 (h) Design a means of evaluating the effectiveness of the total programme to ensure improvements can be introduced subsequently.
 (i) Brief all graduates on the aims and expected outcomes of the programme. Give them a detailed plan with specific performance standards and deadlines for each stage. Make sure they get regular feedback.
 (j) At each stage the receiving managers should be told:
  (i) the training received hitherto;
  (ii) the knowledge, skills and behaviour the graduate is expected to acquire from his current phase of training;
  (iii) that regular monitoring of progress will take place.

Answer 3 (outline)

The first part of this question is covered in the text of Chapter 14, but the answer is also given here for the sake of completeness.

Self development

— Have clear goals, frequently re-examined and redefined.
— Make sure these goals are realistic by a careful analysis of personal strengths and limitations.
— Find out what the organisation requires of senior personnel. Acquire the knowledge, skills and behaviour which enable one to build on strengths and which help to reduce limitations.
— Watch for opportunities to develop, and accept them.
— Take on challenging assignments.
— Produce good work.

- Make sure your achievements are noted.
- Make sure the organisation understands your ambitions.
- Take training and development opportunities.
- Sit the Chartered Institute of Bankers' examinations.

The organisation's responsibilities
- To create career opportunities and plans.
- To offer work which will help people to learn and develop.
- To offer career development opportunities.
- To offer training courses and programmes.
- To reward those who respond to training.
- To offer realistic appraisal and advice on development.
- To make sure that managers are well trained as mentors and guides and that they know how to train.

Answer 4

(a) *Definition*

The amount of power a person possesses depends upon:
  (i) the resource the person commands, e.g. charm, knowledge, experience, etc.;
  (ii) the degree to which this resource is needed by others;
  (iii) the availability of the supply of the resource, i.e. the scarcer the resource, the greater the power of the person possessing it.

(b) *Types of power*
  (i) Coercive power—based on fear. It depends on the application of physical punishment such as pain or death.
  (ii) Remunerative power—derives from control and administration of the reward system, e.g. salaries, status, promotion, etc.
  (iii) Legitimate power—derives from the authority vested in position. Institutionalised power, e.g. managing director, Air Marshal, all managers.
  (iv) Expert power—derives from a particular area of knowledge or set of skills which others need.
  (v) Referent power—the power of the 'hero' to get others to model themselves on him.
  (vi) Charisma—the power to inspire others through presence and inspiration.
  (vii) Political power—achieved through an understanding of how the organisation works and the capacity to use this knowledge to gain power.

(c) *Acquisition of power*

Comes through a combination of the following:
- acquisition of a needed skill;
- joining a leading department;
- acquisition of the values, attitudes and behaviour codes of those who hold power;
- performing well;
- building an outstanding track record;
- increasing people's dependency;
- getting the backing of powerful people;
- increasing one's visibility;

- by personal charm;
- understanding and playing the organisational game;
- involving oneself in socially approved non-work activities, e.g. work for a charity.

CHAPTER 14

Managing yourself

- Problem-solving • Decision-making • Project planning and management • Time management • Stress management • Career management

▌ Problem-solving

Almost everything a manager does involves problem-solving in one way or another. This might be regarded as one of the differences between being a worker (who carries out instructions, repeats similar tasks and has little need to show initiative) and being a manager (who must deal with things which are out of the ordinary, must assist subordinates to cope with changes and is responsible for getting things done, whatever the circumstances).

Problem-solving may require split-second decisions in a real crisis but, where a little more time is available, a structured approach to problem-solving is to be recommended:

(a) Define the problem, identify the underlying causes as well as the outward symptoms.
(b) Gather all the available facts about the situation – speak to the parties involved, refer to management information reports, etc., as appropriate. Has a similar problem arisen before?
(c) Develop a series of alternative solutions; don't just accept the first one offered.
(d) Evaluate the alternatives. How well do they solve the problem? Are they compatible with the organisation's goals and the available resources?
(e) Select the best alternative solution.
(f) Analyse the possible consequences of the decision and plan to cope with them. What are the potential obstacles? Who needs to be consulted? What is the timescale?
(g) Implement the decision.
(h) Follow up and monitor the results of the decision, modifying it or taking remedial action if necessary.

▌ Decision-making

All problem-solving requires the manager to take decisions, although not all decisions are necessarily connected with problem-solving—they may simply be a natural part of the manager's daily work.

There are two main types of decision: programmed and unprogrammed.

Programmed decisions are those which can be made by following predetermined rules and procedures. Banks are full of such work-aids, manuals, and procedural instructions, designed to reduce the necessity for time-consuming decision-making over routine events.

Unprogrammed decisions are more difficult to make as they do not follow a set pattern. They are the decisions a manager must make throughout the day to solve customer queries, to avert crises, to deal with breakdowns in systems or equipment, and so on.

Decision-making faults

In making decisions, there are three main traps into which managers may fall:
   (a) **Too slow**—the manager may delay taking a decision in order to accumulate all possible facts. Whilst laudable on the face of it, this delay may result in higher cost, time wasted or opportunities lost. Even if the ultimate decision is of high quality, a quicker decision might have been equally good and more cost-effective.
   (b) **Too fast**—a snap decision, taken without weighing all the facts, may result in a poor-quality decision. Some managers take hurried decisions in order to reduce the stress of having the decision hanging over them, but if this is the reason, rather than a true need for a quick decision, it is likely give poor results.
   (c) **The safe option**—taking the easy way out by choosing the least controversial option may have the virtue of producing few errors. However, a well thought-out, more adventurous decision, with little increase in risk, might considerably improve the result.

Referring decisions downwards

Another danger is when the manager feels he must take all decisions himself. This is unnecessary, and can be counterproductive if it results in undue stress on the manager, demotivated staff and perhaps substandard decisions.

All decisions can be classified according to their quality and their acceptance. The quality of a decision is the extent to which it involves the consideration of complex technical data, the use of expensive resources, etc. The acceptance of a decision is the extent to which it relies on the involvement and commitment of subordinates for satisfactory implementation.

A high-quality/high-acceptance decision might be a major technological change in the organisation, a radical change in the salary structure or a change in working hours (having important technical and financial implications for the company and requiring support from the staff for successful implementation).

A high-quality/low-acceptance decision might be the selection of a new supplier of materials (involving large sums of money, but having little direct effect on the employees).

A low-quality/high-acceptance decision would be something like reorganising the seating in the office, planning the staff Christmas party, etc. (of lesser importance from the organisation's point of view, but capable of arousing considerable passions among the staff).

A low-quality/low-acceptance decision might be whether to fix the branch nameplate on the right or left of the door—a decision which someone must take, but which is trivial to management and arouses little interest among the staff.

The importance of this classification is that managers should take it into account when choosing how much to involve staff in a decision. High-acceptance decisions should involve consultation with subordinates whenever possible; if the decision is also a low-quality one, it can be left almost entirely to the staff (e.g. what colour to paint the staff rest room).

The rules for referring decisions downwards are similar to those for delegation, i.e. the manager should consult when the subordinate has specialist knowledge, when the decision is high-acceptance (see above) or where the subordinate will benefit from the experience of decision-making.

Referring decisions upwards

Similarly, there are occasions when decision-making should be referred upwards. These follow the rules for delegation upwards, i.e. one should consider the following criteria:

(a) Does the issue affect other departments?
(b) Will it have an important effect on the superior's area of responsibility?
(c) Does it require information only available at a higher level?
(d) Does it have important implications for the departmental budget?
(e) Will the superior be very annoyed if he discovers that a decision on the issue has been made without his authority?

∎ Project planning and management

A 'project' may be anything from a group of three people spending a couple of days organising an in-branch marketing event, to the huge team of people involved in managing the construction and financing of the Channel Tunnel.

Project management is really no more than the commonsense structured approach to planning, organising, coordinating, and controlling which a manager should apply to any task. A project team may be set up, drawn from a variety of different disciplines and functional areas within the organisation. They may work solely on the project until it is completed, then return to their own departments; or they may meet from time to time to progress project issues, but continue to work in their own areas at the same time.

If an organisation is involved in major changes (such as installing new technology, moving premises, merging with another company) a project group may be set up to manage the change from all angles.

Within a bank branch, projects might relate to marketing or sales initiatives, reorganisation of work flows, dealing with quarterly or year-end reporting requirements, and so on.

A successful project requires:

(a) Clear terms of reference—the scope, scale and budget of the project.
(b) A powerful project sponsor—someone in the organisation who can remove obstacles and get things done.
(c) An owner in the business—a manager or department who will 'own' the project once it is complete.
(d) A carefully chosen team of people with the skills and knowledge to make the project work and the ability to work together.
(e) Careful planning with realistic targets, periodic review dates and a timetable for reaching 'milestones' and for completion of the project.

There are a number of project management tools on the market. These usually consist of a computer program for planning and keeping track of the tasks and actions of the project team. For major projects, there are standard sets of documentation which can be completed to ensure that all stages are gone through, approved and signed off by the appropriate parties and that full records are kept.

▌Time management

Someone once said that there is nothing certain in life except death and taxes. There is one other certainty—that time, once used, cannot be retrieved.

Many managers feel that there are just not enough hours in the day, but one can certainly learn to use time more wisely, more economically and more productively.

The first thing to do is establish what exactly you are doing at the moment; then decide which things you **should** be doing, which are the most important, and how you can do them most efficiently.

How much control you have over the allocation of your time does, to some extent, depend on how high up the managerial ladder you are. If you have a secretary or personal assistant and a team of staff, it is easier to think in terms of delegation than if you are the sole person responsible for a particular area. Nevertheless, there are still steps you can take.

The 80/20 rule

It is generally accepted that, in most areas of business, the 80/20 rule holds good. In other words 20 per cent of your tasks constitute 80 per cent of the importance of your job and should therefore take up 80 per cent of your time. The remainder are of little or no importance and can be done in the time left—or not at all!

Find out what you do

Most of the books on time management (and there are many) recommend that you should keep a log for, say, a week showing what tasks you do and how long you spend on each. This is a tedious exercise in itself, but it does enable you to know how you are actually spending your time and then to make considered judgements about whether you are spending that time on the right things.

Your job description or objectives should tell you what the key areas of your job are—these are the ones which should take up most of your time and which should have priority. If you gave a hollow laugh at the idea that you should have a written job description, now is a good time to compile one for yourself, and get your boss to agree a set of objectives for you.

Don't imagine that you will be able to work at a constantly high rate all day. Work study experts expect around 15 per cent of time to be given over to 'personal needs', which as well as the obvious such as visits to the toilet, blowing your nose and drinking a cup of coffee, also allows for short periods of relaxation, which are essential to keep the brain alert.

Plan your time

Decide how you should spend your time over a normal week, giving most time to the priority tasks. You may like to set aside specific times for regular tasks such as reading essential journals and literature, answering correspondence or holding team meetings.

Allow contingency time for the unexpected, thinking time to prepare for meetings or interviews, writing time afterwards and, if necessary, travelling time to get there.

Make sure you are not doing things which are unnecessary, or which should properly be done by someone else.

Time-wasters

There are four classic ways of wasting time:

(a) Doing other people's work—don't get involved in things which need not concern you: if a colleague or subordinate ask your advice on something, give just that—do not take over the task yourself; do delegate (upwards or downwards) where appropriate.

(b) The ditherer—if you are being held up by another manager who is continually asking for more information or who wants to go over the same ground again and again, set a definite deadline—'If I don't hear to the contrary by Friday lunchtime, I will assume I have your full agreement.' That should provoke a swift response!

(c) The chatterer—don't allow others to delay you with incessant chat. Some chatting is necessary to maintain relationships, to oil the wheels of business, but it can go too far. If a phone call is going on too long, have an excuse ready—'Sorry, I have to go to a meeting', or 'The boss has just walked in'; in a face-to-face conversation say you are expecting an important call, or simply say you have an urgent piece of work and a deadline to meet.

(d) The meddler—some bosses just will not let their people get on with the job. Either they think they are helping, when really they are slowing things down, or they are always looking over people's shoulders, suspicious that things are going wrong. In either case, one must try politely to ask them to go away!

Of course the last three can also apply to ourselves—don't let your staff have occasion to accuse you of wasting their time.

The helicopter view

As a manager, you should not find your day so full of meetings, interviews and other tasks that you have your head down all the time. You should always have time to initiate action as well as simply respond—to take a fresh look at how the department's work is being done; to spend time with each of your staff to counsel and guide them; to read widely to keep yourself up-to-date, and so on.

This is sometimes referred to as taking the 'helicopter view', in other words not being so bogged down in your own work that you cannot step back and see how your team is functioning. This is essential if you are to act as a manager and not just another worker.

This approach can assist in anticipating crises before they arise, so that defensive action can be taken and, with luck and good judgement, the time-wasting crisis averted.

None of us is perfect (the world would be a much duller place if we were) so however carefully we plan our time, there will always be days when everything goes wrong: when you feel at the end that you have accomplished little or nothing, and that the in-tray will never get smaller. However, by following the suggestions given in this section, these days should be few and far between. You will know you have succeeded when they are outnumbered by the days when everything goes smoothly: the post has been cleared by lunchtime, your in-tray is empty, you have read that interesting article you kept putting to the bottom, and you have time to walk round the office (not meddling in your subordinates' work of course!) and congratulate yourself on how well the department is functioning.

Stress management

Stress is an inevitable part of any active life. In moderation it is beneficial—it is the bursts of adrenalin which the body produces in response to stress which give us the energy and enthusiasm to tackle a difficult task with confidence.

However, a build-up of stress can lead to a deterioration in performance and, at its worst, to physical symptoms of illness—headaches, migraines, irritability and depression or even ulcers and heart attacks. Research has shown that individuals who have experienced a dramatic change in their lives are more likely to be ill than those whose lives are more stable. Similarly, accidents at work are often associated with high levels of stress.

Stress does not only arise at work; moving house, divorce, bereavement and even stopping smoking can be very stressful events.

A sympathetic manager should be alert for signs of undue stress in his subordinates. If an individual is going through a traumatic time in his personal life, it is in the interests of the company as well as the employee that he should not be put under any more stress at work than is absolutely necessary for the time being.

One should also be aware of one's own stress levels. There are a variety of techniques to help cope with stress, such as relaxation exercises, yoga and meditation, but one can also try to minimise stress in the first place. If you find the journey to work in the morning particularly stressful, try setting out a little earlier, so that you have time to unwind when you arrive at the office, before you have to launch into the business of the day. Consider lunching from noon to 1p.m. rather than 1 to 2p.m.: you will find that you have a very peaceful hour from 1 to 2 when the phone hardly rings, as everyone else is rushing to lunch. Try to organise your home life so that stress is reduced—make sure the family are taking their share of the chores (this is particularly a problem for working women trying to run a job, a home, a husband and a family!). Do not allow yourself to be dragged into too many out-of-work activities—it is very hard to say 'No' but, for your own health and sanity, it is sometimes essential. Console yourself with the thought that it will probably be beneficial for others to learn to do what they have relied on you for in the past.

■ Career management

In Chapter 13 we looked at the responsibilities of a good employer towards the career development of employees. There are also a variety of steps which the ambitious employee can take to improve his or her chances of promotion.

(a) Identify your goals—how far do you really want to go? It is unrealistic to aspire to being chief executive of your bank if you are not willing to commit the time and effort which will be needed. On the other hand, there is no reason to feel obliged to aim for the very top—a more realistic aim will be less stressful and easier to plan for and achieve.

(b) Analyse your personal strengths and weaknesses; make sure that your goals are realistic in relation to these, or else plan to improve them.

(c) Re-examine and redefine your goals at frequent intervals, as you progress and as circumstances change, to ensure they stay realistic.

(d) Find out what your organisation requires of senior personnel. Acquire the knowledge, skills and behaviour patterns which will enable you to achieve these requirements.

(e) Watch out for opportunities to develop and take advantage of them. For example, if staff are required for a special project which may involve hard work but which will give good experience and recognition, be quick to volunteer.

(f) Produce high-quality work and be willing to put in that little extra effort which will mark you out from your colleagues who only do the minimum required.

(g) Make sure that your achievements are noted by those in authority or positions of power.

(h) Make sure that the organisation and your line manager are aware of your ambitions. When discussing progress with your manager, make sure that you are offered the chance to take appropriate training and development courses if these are not automatic.

(i) Study for, and pass, the Chartered Institute of Bankers' examinations—both to improve your knowledge and skills and to demonstrate your commitment to a banking career.

■ Action points

(a) Next time you have a decision to make (at work or at home), examine the steps you go through—do they fit with the description above? Are there steps which you are missing out? If so, do you think the decision would be a better one if you followed them all?

(b) What projects are under way in your branch or office? Who is in charge and how are they managed? How would you have managed them better?

(c) Try out the time management steps suggested above and see if they improve the way you manage your day.

(d) Draw up your own action plan to promote your career. Plan to revise it at least every year.

Questions and answers

Question 1

What is the difference between a programmed and an unprogrammed decision? Give examples of each. Which do you think is easier to make and why? [9]

Should managers make a decision on every problem they face? Justify and explain your answer with reference to different types of management problems. [16]

[Total marks for question—25]

Question 2

(a) What are the common faults of decision-makers? [6]

(b) How is it possible to help a manager to become a better decision-maker? [10]

(c) When should a manager delegate matters for decision and when should he refer them to his superior? [9]

[Total marks for question—25]

Question 3

You have been asked by your manager to convey to the sixth-formers of local schools the advantages of a career in banking. How would you organise this project? Which media would you use and why? (Candidates are not required to discuss the advantages of a banking career).

[Marks for this question—10]

(N.B. This formed part of a longer question)

Question 4

'The most precious managerial resource is time.' What advice would you give to a newly appointed supervisor to help him to use his time effectively?

[Total marks for question—25]

Question 5

About nine months ago, Andrew Barrett was appointed an assistant manager in the large branch where you also are an assistant manager. Recently he approached you informally for some guidance because he feels he is not performing as well as he should.

He says that his boss has criticised him because of the amount of work which he takes home. He is, however, happy with the relationships he has built up with the team who work for him.

You have done some preliminary investigation which reveals that:

(a) Andrew apparently delegates well and there is little scope for the delegation of further aspects of his job.

(b) He has built up his good relationship with his team by encouraging them to bring him their work problems as they arise. He is often willing to devote considerable time to the solution of these problems.
(c) His job description states only that he is required 'to manage the work and people of his section'.
(d) He is quite heavily involved in representing his section at meetings and on working parties.
(e) His boss sets him performance standards which concentrate on the qualitative aspects of tasks. In these standards his boss asks Andrew to produce 'excellent' work.

What suggestions would you make to Andrew to help him to improve his time management and his job performance? Give reasons for your suggestions.

[Total marks for question—25]

Question 6

What steps can the individual take to advance his or her career?

[Total marks for question—25]

Answer 1

Programmed decisions are those made according to some custom, rules or procedures. Most organisations have written or unwritten policies which deal with recurrent issues. For example, there is usually a well established system for the recruitment and placement of personnel, or the allocation of a person to a salary grade, the handling of grievances, etc. Establishing routines of this sort frees managers from the need to seek new solutions to routine problems.

Nonprogrammed decisions are unusual and arise from complex or exceptional circumstances, e.g. how to deal with a very difficult customer; handling a service which is deteriorating sharply; how to improve the image of the branch in the community, etc.

Programmed decisions are easier to make because it is only necessary to follow an established rule or procedure. Nonprogrammed decisions are much more difficult. They call for creativity, problem-solving ability and judgement, and help to distinguish between the effective and ineffective manager.

A manager should not make a decision about every problem because there will be some situations in which:

(a) The problem is best left to solve itself.
(b) The manager is not empowered to make the decision and he should refer it to his boss.
(c) The decision should be taken by subordinates because they are closer to the problem.
(d) The decision requires the expert advice of a specialist so the problem must be shared.
(e) He should share the decision because it will motivate others to be involved in the process and their commitment is important.
(f) The decision might affect other departments who should be involved in the decision.
(g) The decision might have a major impact on his superior's area of responsibility.
(h) He might not possess the information required to make the decision.
(i) It might involve a serious overspend of the department budget.

Answer 2

See the text of this chapter.

Answer 3 (outline)

(a) Letter to each headmaster, explaining your campaign and requesting help from careers masters.
(b) Telephone careers masters and arrange face-to-face meetings to discuss how best to communicate with sixth-formers.
(c) Contact (letter, telephone and face-to-face meeting) with local careers advisory service to seek advice.
(d) Attendance at career conventions to speak, give out brochures, show film, etc.
(e) Go to local schools—communicate time and place through noticeboards, etc.
(f) Follow up with interested parties individually face-to-face. Get them to visit the bank.
(g) Encourage completion of application forms if appropriate.
(h) Afterwards, review success and identify areas for improvement if a similar project is undertaken in the future.

Answer 4

See the text of this chapter.

Answer 5

Delegation and the work of his subordinates

Although it appears that Andrew understands the principles and practice of delegation as it applies to his job, he fails to apply the same ideas to the jobs of his subordinates.

Subordinates may be delegating work upwards. It is important that this should not happen because:

(a) it leads to the boss having time management problems;
(b) it restricts opportunities for the development of the subordinate;
(c) it is important that decisions should be taken at the lowest appropriate level to facilitate the implementation of those decisions.

Andrew will need to ensure that his subordinates are either capable of doing their work, making appropriate decisions and solving work problems by themselves, or supply them with necessary—and planned—training.

Andrew should abandon his 'open door' management policy and institute instead a policy of defined periods when he is available for consultation. He should couple this with a policy of 'management by walking around'.

Prioritisation

Andrew should discuss his job with his boss with the objective of expanding his job description so that it enables him to be clear about what he is supposed to do.

He should aim to establish what his key results areas (or key tasks) are.

Andrew should relate these to the way he actually spends his time—which he can find by, for example, keeping a diary or weekly log. He should then plan to ensure that he devotes appropriate amounts of his time to his key results areas.

Andrew should develop the habit of assessing work tasks according to:

(a) their importance—by reference to his key results areas;
(b) their urgency—by reference to deadlines.

This approach will enable him to assess the priority of tasks confronting him.

Figurehead/liaison role

Andrew should ask himself whether attendance at meetings and working parties is necessary—again referring to his key results areas. He should also consider whether another member of his team could or should represent the section.

If his attendance is necessary, Andrew should question:
(a) whether the meeting has clear objectives;
(b) whether these are best achieved by a meeting;
(c) whether meetings are scheduled at appropriate times;
(d) whether they are run effectively;
(e) whether he is contributing to their effectiveness.

Performance standards

Andrew has been criticised for his performance, but no helpful standards have been set.

Performance standards should be:
— specific,
— measurable,
— attainable,
— relevant,
— time-orientated.

They should focus primarily on:
— cost,
— quantity,
— quality,
— time.

Andrew's boss appears to set only qualitative standards which are vague rather than specific and measurable. 'Excellent' is a subjective standard.

Andrew should negotiate standards with his boss to encourage a clearer, more objective definition of what is expected of him.

Answer 6

In order to advance his own career, the individual should:
— Clarify and reclarify, as his career develops, what his ultimate goals are.
— Recognise that some conflict between himself and the organisation is inevitable and therefore a degree of self-interest is important. No-one will make more effort than he makes himself to advance his career.
— Analyse personal strengths and weaknesses and set realistic goals which will maximise the one and minimise the other.
— Analyse opportunities and work out ways in which they can be exploited.
— Understand company politics, e.g. the unwritten rules, where power lies, who exercises it, etc., and develop political skill.
— Have at least a rudimentary plan, giving a sense of direction.

- Do high-quality work.
- Take training and development opportunities.
- Become visible, but don't make claims which cannot be justified.
- Present the right impression—in terms of ability, hard work, willingness to cooperate, etc.
- Avoid working with incompetent managers—move to another job, where there is a skilful manager, as soon as possible.
- Develop good personal relationships.
- Be prepared to move to get a better job or development opportunity.
- Help the boss to succeed. He is the best possible sponsor.
- Find good mentors and be prepared to learn from them.

(These are the major factors, but there are many others.)

CHAPTER 15

How to fail / how to pass!

- About the examination • How the paper is marked • How to tackle the examination • Answering the questions • How to fail / how to pass

■ About the examination

The Chief Examiner (who at the time of writing is Ian Whyte of Barclays Bank Management Training Centre, Ashdown Park) sets the paper several months before you take it. The paper has to be approved by the Moderator—an independent expert who ensures that the questions are of the right degree of difficulty, cover the syllabus, and are unambiguous and fair—and by the Secretariat and the Education Panel of the Chartered Institute of Bankers itself.

Bear in mind there is a considerable time lag between setting and sitting the paper. This means that you will not be asked about events which happen very close to the date of the exam, but you should be aware of developments up to, say, six months beforehand.

When setting the paper, the Chief Examiner compares the syllabus with previous questions which have been asked, to select topics of current concern or which have not been recently covered, as well as those which form the core of the syllabus. Remember that he needs to be able to allocate 25 marks to each question, so he may well combine more than one topic in a question to broaden the scope.

Management in Banking differs from its predecessor, Nature of Management, in the way the question paper is set out. In Management in Banking the paper is divided into three sections: A, B, and C. Students are required to answer a total of four questions, at least one from each section.

Section A will comprise three questions which relate to topics of current interest (in management in general or in the financial services industry). They may refer to articles in *Banking World* and may include a 'scenario' or case study type question.

Section B will comprise two questions relating to the processes, skills, techniques, theories, models etc. of management. The questions are likely to be in two parts, each addressing a different area of the syllabus, and may relate to the management of organisations, systems, people or yourself.

Section C will contain three scenario questions which ask you to apply theories and models to practical situations.

All questions will carry equal marks (25 per question) and there is no particular division of the syllabus between the sections—questions in each section may address any part (or parts) of the syllabus. Remember, you will need to answer two questions from one of the sections, and one from each of the others, to make up your total of four answers altogether.

How the paper is marked

On average, well over 4,000 students will take the Management in Banking paper at each sitting. The papers are marked by a team of around 20 Assistant Examiners plus the Chief Examiner.

Many students have the idea that Examiners are some curious breed of people who do nothing but mark exam papers all day. In fact this is far from the truth. Most of the Assistant Examiners for Management in Banking are working bankers who mark papers in their spare time. They have only a few weeks of evenings and weekends in which to mark their quota of around 200 papers. It is all the more important, therefore, that you should write clearly and set out your answers in a logical way so that the examiner can easily pick out the points needed to give you your marks.

Immediately after the examination has taken place, the Chief Examiner distributes a marking schedule to each of the team of Assistant Examiners. This sets out the points for which the Chief Examiner is looking and for which marks are to be allocated. About two weeks after the exam, when each Assistant Examiner has had the chance to mark a batch of papers, all the examiners meet to discuss the paper, iron out any remaining ambiguities and ensure consistency of marking. This is confirmed by each Assistant Examiner sending a sample of his or her marked papers to the Chief Examiner for scrutiny.

All marginal scripts are in fact marked by at least two examiners, with the Chief Examiner adjudicating if necessary, so there can be no question of individual bias by an Assistant Examiner. The pass mark is 51 with Distinction for 81 marks or more. Marked script covers are finally returned to the Institute in time for the results to be sent out to candidates about 10 weeks after the examination. This may seem a long time if you are waiting on tenterhooks, but when you multiply the number of different subject papers by the number of candidates, Examiners and indeed countries involved, you will see that it is in fact a mammoth administrative undertaking—something like 35,000 scripts in all in fact!

If you are unlucky enough to fail on three occasions, with a Fail A (46 to 50 marks) on the last two attempts, you may request a Special Examiner's Report on the two Fail A scripts. The cost at the time of writing is around £20, but may well be worthwhile if the report gives you the pointers you need to overcome that last hurdle. The Examiner's Reports on each examination are published as soon as possible after the exam; they are written by the Chief Examiner while the answers are still fresh in his mind, so they are a very valuable source of information to students on the way the Chief Examiner is thinking and what he is looking for in an answer. Make sure you invest in a copy after each exam to give yourself a head start for the next one.

Tackling the examination

- Read the paper
- Read the question
- Watch the time
- Be prepared
- Be aware
- Think!

Read the paper

It may have been said many times before but it is still ignored by some candidates every year—**read the instructions!**

Make sure you check the instructions on the cover of the question paper and the answer paper. You **must** answer the right number of questions from the correct sections to have a good chance of passing. If, for example, you answer too many from one section, only the first ones will be marked, and you will have thrown away 25 marks or more. It is virtually impossible to pass the paper on only three questions (see Fig. 15.1).

The question paper itself confirms that **'answers listed in note-form are acceptable'**. This means that the use of subheadings, numbered points, lists of ideas, etc., (provided that they are logical and sufficiently detailed) makes the examiner's task much simpler as he can spot the main points easily and quickly. Wading through a lengthy essay, however beautifully written, is tedious and irritating for a tired examiner! By the use of a tabulated answer you will also make life easier for yourself as it will help you to organise your thoughts in a logical way—neither leaving out any important points nor covering the same ground twice.

Do remember, too, to complete the boxes on the answer book which ask for your membership number (on the cover and on the book itself) and for the numbers of the questions you have attempted. Once your paper has been marked and the cover sent off to the Institute, your membership number on the answer book is the only way to identify it in the event of any query (see Fig. 15.2).

Read the question

It cannot be repeated often enough that, in the heat of the moment, many candidates fail by not reading the question carefully enough.

Either they answer the question they **hoped** would be set, or they answer the first part and **forget** that there is a second or third part to the question.

Now that the mark allocation within each question is clearly stated on the question paper, you should be able to relate the effort you put in and the amount you write on each part to the number of marks available. There is no point in writing two sides where only three marks are on offer, nor in expecting to pass if you write less than half a page on a part of the question which carries 16 marks. The marks on the question paper are the **maximum** marks which the examiner can allocate for an absolutely complete answer to that part. They cannot be reallocated to other parts of the question by the examiner.

Remember that you need an average of 13 marks out of 25 per question to gain an overall pass mark.

Watch the time

You will need reasonable marks on all four of your answers to be sure of a pass, so don't spend so long on the first couple of questions that you only have 10 minutes left for the last. It is always easier to get the first 12 or 15 marks for a question than to squeeze out the final few marks, so it is usually better to make a reasonable attempt at four questions than try for full marks on one and give very sketchy answers to the rest.

ASSOCIATESHIP EXAMINATIONS

MANAGEMENT IN BANKING

May 19XX

SPECIMEN

1. Read the instructions on the cover of the answer book.

2. **Answer FOUR questions only. At least ONE from each section.**

3. All questions carry 25 marks. Where questions are subdivided, the marks for each subdivision are shown in brackets.

4. Answers in listed note form are acceptable, provided they are clearly and logically presented and the points made are adequately developed.

5. No aids such as calculators, books, dictionaries, papers, mathematical tables or slide-rules, are permitted in this examination.

6. Time allowed: **three hours**.

The total number of questions in this paper is eight.

[P.T.O.

page one

Fig. 15.1 The question-paper cover

The Chartered Institute of Bankers

Emmanuel House 4-9 Burgate Lane Canterbury Kent CT1 2XJ
Tel: 0227-762600

ANSWER BOOK

FOR OFFICE USE ONLY

Membership Number

PLEASE WRITE CLEARLY IN BLOCK CAPITAL LETTERS, ONE CHARACTER PER BOX, WHEN COMPLETING THIS FORM

Surname or Final Name

First Name(s)

SEAL BOOK HERE

Bank

Branch Sort Code

Branch Address

Post Code

SPECIMEN

EXAMINATIONS ....

SUBJECT
(As on question paper) ....

NUMBER OF ADDITIONAL SHEETS USED ....

CALCULATOR DETAILS: ....

SIGNATURE .... DATE ....

INSTRUCTIONS

1. All papers and books including dictionaries must be left with the invigilator. Calculators are not permitted in some examinations, see front of question paper for details. Write the make and model of any calculator used in the space provided.
2. Complete all sections above as requested.
3. Begin each answer on a fresh page, except where the question is sub-divided.
4. Use BOTH sides of the paper.
5. All work must be shown; rough work should be ruled through.
6. If supplementary sheets are used, fasten them securely at the END of this book (within the covers).
7. Seal book by means of gummed slip provided.

PLEASE ADVISE US UNDER SEPARATE COVER IF YOUR BRANCH ADDRESS IS DIFFERENT FROM THE ONE SHOWN ON YOUR ATTENDANCE NOTICE. UK MEMBERS SHOULD ALSO QUOTE NATIONAL SORT CODE NUMBER.

INDICATE WITH AN X IN COLUMN A EACH QUESTION ATTEMPTED →

A	For Examiner's use only	
	Q. No.	Marks
	1	
	2	
	3	
	4	
	5	
	6	
	7	
	8	
	9	
	10	

Fig. 15.2 The answer-book cover

A good rule of thumb is:

— 5 minutes to read the question,
— 10 minutes to plan your answer,
— 20 minutes writing time.

This allows a margin for over-running (it is human nature to choose your best question first and want to write most on this—but don't overdo it!) and a few minutes at the end to re-read your answers and correct any mistakes or add points you remember at the last moment.

It is a good idea to leave a **blank page** between answers if you think you might want to go back and add a few more points at the end. (Remember, you should always start each answer on a fresh page anyway, so just leave one more blank.)

Be prepared

As well as being a good motto for Boy Scouts and Girl Guides, this is excellent advice for those tackling any exam.

Revise all the syllabus, not placing too much reliance on 'question spotting'. In any case, with Management in Banking only starting in its new form in 1991, you will have to wait a few years to have a number of previous papers on which to base any trend assumptions.

When you choose the questions you are going to answer, make sure that you understand what the Chief Examiner is looking for. If the answer to 2 questions seems to be the same, **be careful—you have probably misunderstood one of them!**

Remember these points:

(a) Questions may examine more than one area of the syllabus.
(b) Syllabus topics may be examined in any of the three sections of the paper.
(c) Some areas of the syllabus are core to the subject and will probably be tested in most years, e.g. the business environment, motivation, leadership, etc.
(d) Students with a wide knowledge often have difficulty in limiting their answers to the requirements of the question.

This last point is often overlooked. If you adopt a 'shotgun' technique, peppering your answer with everything you know about a topic, you will waste your time and the Examiner's and probably lose marks rather than gain them. Far better to focus your answer and aim straight at the target—using a 'rifle', to extend the analogy—so that your answer is perhaps briefer but definitely to the point, making clear to the Examiner that you not only know your subject but can apply it to the question posed.

Be aware

Students are always recommended to read widely to keep abreast of new developments. This is not as daunting as it may sound. You should already be familiar with the following:

(a) Examiner's Reports on past papers. These are available from the Chartered Institute of Bankers soon after each exam session at a modest charge, and cover all the Diploma subjects in one volume.

(b) Newspaper reports on financial matters. There is no harm in reading *The Sun* for entertainment, but for information you should be looking at *The Financial Times*, *The Independent* or one of the other 'quality' dailies. Your manager probably has a copy of the *FT* delivered to the office—ask if you may borrow it, and be sure to read the Management page. *The Economist, Financial Weekly,* etc. may be available in your office or you may want to take out a student subscription.

(c) Updating Notes, published annually by the Chartered Institute of Bankers. Each issue covers all the Diploma subjects.

(d) Training manuals. Your own bank will undoubtedly issue manuals for in-house training. See if you can borrow copies, or rummage in the wardrobe and dig out those notes you took on courses you have attended yourself—this is the rainy day for which you put them away!

(e) Product literature. Obtain copies of the leaflets your bank hands out to customers, and its internal circulars to staff, to keep up-to-date with new services, organisational changes, etc.

(f) Standard textbooks as listed in the syllabus.

(g) Hand-outs from your tutors. Don't just file these away—read them!

If you remember to revise from all these sources as well as from your notes you will give yourself a distinct advantage over most of your colleagues, who will ignore many of these obvious sources of help.

Think!

In your answers, don't use words or phrases that you don't understand; explain enough to prove to the examiner that you **do** understand.

Many poor case study answers, in particular, churn out the same cliches time after time without any thought as to whether they apply in that particular case. Regardless of the details of the question, they will advise:

- **Send him on a course**
- **Read his personnel file**
- **Talk to his staff about him**
- **Talk to his colleagues about him**
- **He was wrongly selected**
- **Transfer him**
- **Tell him to shape up or else. . . .**
- **Sack him!**

Many of these options are inappropriate in most situations and need explanation even where they are viable choices:

(a) Send him on a course—courses may be appropriate, but explain why, what kind of course, what will it achieve?
(b) Read his personnel file—Why? What are you hoping to find? What will you do with the information? If a problem is a recent one there is unlikely to be much of help in the file anyway.
(c) Talk to his staff about him; talk to his colleagues about him—Remember that personnel issues are sensitive ones and that confidentiality **must** be respected. Talking to colleagues or subordinates about a member of staff must be handled very carefully. You might easily undermine their authority and make matters worse.
(d) He was wrongly selected; transfer him to another department; tell him to shape up or else. . .; sack him! The examiner is looking for positive suggestions for improving a situation, not just 'give up and sack him'! Transferring someone usually just moves the problem elsewhere and sacking is only a last resort. Training, counselling, delegation and motivation are the sort of options to be explored first.

Remember from whose point of view you are writing. If the question talks about helping a colleague, would you really 'set him objectives' and 'monitor to see he achieves them'? That is what some candidates put in the exam.

∎ Answering the questions

There are two main types of questions set on this subject—descriptive questions and case studies.

Descriptive questions

These test your knowledge of the theory. They normally require a straightforward 'textbook' answer although they can require a discussion of current affairs, or require you to put a particular slant on what you have learnt.

The great danger is to assume that the examiner has asked you to 'write all you know about . . .' when in fact he has asked a much more specific question about a particular portion of the subject. If you just ramble on at great length, much of what you write will be superfluous and you will gain no marks for it.

A good pattern to follow for descriptive questions is as follows:

- **Define** what the answer is to be about (obviously taking your clues from the question).
- **Explain** the subject in some detail.
- **Apply** the theory to answer the specific points in the question.
- **Conclude** your answer by pulling the threads of your argument together and ensuring that you have answered what was asked.

This sort of question will often ask you to list the advantages and disadvantages of something (e.g. a management style). It is perfectly acceptable to do so in the form of two columns of notes, provided that they are sufficiently detailed to show you fully understand what you are writing about. If your notes are too brief you will not get full marks, even if you touch on all the points needed in the answer.

Case studies

Case study questions often worry candidates, but the first rule is: **Don't panic**!

Spend plenty of time reading through the question first of all (read it at least twice) to make certain that you can identify what the examiner is getting at. Make notes of the important points, then make a plan for your answer, and **only then** start to write.

A long question should not put you off—it probably means that half the answer is there already if you look carefully. However, don't waste time just rewriting chunks of the question itself; you will gain no marks for that.

A good pattern to adopt with case studies is as follows:

- **Symptoms.** If you read the question carefully, it will usually be describing things which have gone wrong, or people who are behaving poorly—in other words, the symptoms of a problem. Identify these at the start of your answer and it will help to keep you on track.
- **Causes.** The next thing to do is to suggest what the causes of these symptoms might be.
- **Solutions.** Most case studies ask you to suggest ways in which the problems might be solved. You should not need to make too many assumptions, beyond what you are given in the question. Remember, the examiner must have had a clear answer in his mind when he set the question; your job is to make sure you find the right one(s).
- **Future?** A neat way to end the answer, and possibly pick up a few extra marks, is to consider what is likely to happen in the future. It will often be a good idea to suggest that the situation is reviewed in a few months, to ensure that whatever corrective action was taken has been effective, or that the person concerned is making good progress.

▎How to fail / how to pass

To summarise, I would suggest the following recipes for disaster or success:

> **HOW TO FAIL**
> - **Misread the question**
> - **Do not fit your knowledge to the question. (i.e. answer the question you wish had been asked!)**
> - **Quote every theorist whose name you can remember**
> - **Do not plan your answer but launch into it straight away**
> - **Write ten pages of unbroken text on every question (the shotgun technique)**
> - **Never read a textbook**

Management in banking

HOW TO PASS:

- **Read the question—all of it—several times**
- **Make your answer relevant to the question**
- **Spare a thought for the examiner—write clearly, and make sure your answer is well laid out**
- **Answer the easiest question first to gain confidence but plan your answer well and keep an eye on the time**
- **Use tabulation and note-form to focus your answers**
- **Use your own experience (as manager or managed) to illustrate theory (but don't be too parochial; don't just pour out all your gripes and moans about your bank or manager—he or she might be marking the paper!)**

CHAPTER 16

Hints and tips

- How to revise
- Approaching the exam itself

How to revise

Everyone has their own way of building up to an examination. By this stage in your life you have probably sat more exams than you care to remember and feel that, if you don't know what 'exam technique' is by now, you never will!

If so, fine—but if you feel you would like a few ideas, here is my personal scheme:

(a) Take your full set of notes and a clean pad of paper. Read all through the notes carefully and, picking out the main points, rewrite them in a very abbreviated form.
(b) You will then have perhaps six or a dozen sheets of abbreviated notes. Now put the full set away, and repeat the process with the abbreviated notes and some more blank sheets of paper.
(c) Keep doing this once or twice more, reducing the total each time, until you have just a list of headings and memory joggers which will fit on no more than two sides of paper.
(d) Now learn these pointers off by heart. You will find that once you can recall the 'headings', the rest of what you have learned can be dredged up from the depths of your memory quite easily (provided that you have studied thoroughly in the first place!).
(e) When you get into the exam room, once the invigilator says 'Begin', there is no reason why you should not write out the memory joggers on the inside of the answer book, or a sheet of scrap paper, before you even look at the questions, so you have the confidence of seeing the pointers in front of you if your mind goes blank during the exam.

Approaching the exam itself

You will often be advised not to revise at the last minute, on the basis that if you haven't already learned a subject well, cramming at the last moment will not help. That is probably very good advice for the perfect student—personally I prefer to immerse myself in the exam subject before the exam to make sure my mind is on nothing else!

These days, most banks allow you at least a few hours off before each paper. Do take advantage of this to have an hour or so of peace and quiet just before the exam to get yourself in the right frame of mind—work problems really **can** wait until tomorrow.

There are two mottos suitable to the occasion:

Luck = Prepation meeting Opportunity

and

Fail to prepare—Prepare to fail

If you have genuinely concentrated on your studies and taken advantage of the hints and tips in this book, you have certainly prepared well. The exam itself is your opportunity, so it only remains for me to say:

Good luck!

CHAPTER 17
Topical issues

- Communication in the European market ● Business and the community ● EC Charter ● Demographic timebomb ● Women at the top—a sex war?

Introduction

The Chief Examiner has said that the first section of the Management in Banking examination paper will consist of questions relating to topics of current interest, either within the management field or within the financial services industry.

Any textbook which attempts to address topical issues runs the risk of being out-of-date as soon as it is written, but in this chapter I will point you in the direction of several issues which are in the news at the moment. You should make sure that you continue to read *The Financial Times* (particularly the management column), *Bankers' World* and other quality financial newspapers and journals to keep yourself abreast of developments. There are frequently articles of specific interest to management students in such publications.

Communication in the European market

A great deal has already been written about the changes likely to take place when Europe becomes a single market in 1992. One specific aspect of interest to management students is the problems of communication across cultural barriers—not just in terms of language but in terms of customs and expectations.

The attitude towards 'the boss', for example, varies greatly from country to country in Europe. In France, a manager is expected to give a much more authoritarian and authoritative lead, with all the answers at his finger tips, than his British counterpart. A survey of European managers, reported in *The Daily Telegraph* in October 1989, showed that the further south you go in Europe, the more hierarchical the organisation is likely to be and the more the boss is expected maintain a proper distance from his staff.

You may well have seen the marvellously funny training videos that John Cleese has produced. These sell well in Britain, and in Holland, but very badly in Germany, where every aspect of work is taken very seriously.

Clothes is another minefield—an Italian manager may dress in immaculate sports jacket and flannels, seeming rather too relaxed to us, but he in turn would frown on a British manager who took his jacket off and sat in shirtsleeves in a meeting.

Many Britons find the American habit of using your first name every few sentences rather offputting. The Germans stick to titles and very rarely use first names; the French use Monsieur X; the Greeks use Kyrie Y (as we might refer to the owner's/boss's son as, say, Mister Robert) and so on.

Perhaps more important for businesses hoping to form joint ventures with their European counterparts are the differences in values. A British committee would happily accept a 'majority' decision where 49 per cent of members in fact disagreed; in Spain and other Latin countries, a more genuinely collective agreement would be sought.

Understanding the different attitudes and values of fellow Europeans and resisting the temptation to make snap judgements based on prejudice will be a necessary skill for a growing number of British businessmen and women. Numerous *How to do Business in* . . . books have already been published to help in this quest.

■ Business and the community

For an up-to-date summary of modern business attitudes to the community, get hold of a copy of the *Financial Times* survey: 'Business—The Community Challenge', which was published in the 12 February 1990 issue. It covers businesses both in Britain and overseas and explains that corporations are increasingly aware that the community outside the boundaries of their plants and offices can no longer be disregarded.

Corporate responsibility has become a buzz-word, with consultants available to advise companies on charitable work—to help them give both wisely and well. Clearly this is not pure altruism; the company expects to benefit by good publicity, improved relations with the community, etc.

In the past, many companies have given to charity and helped the community, but have done so in a very uncoordinated way. The job of the consultant is to make this a planned and organised process, fitting in with the organisation's own image (e.g. a company selling to the teenage market should make sure its activities are visible to teenagers). The company can also benefit staff/management relations by combining its own activities with those of the workforce. Midland Bank, for example, has been running a '£ for £' scheme for a couple of years, whereby the bank will match money raised for charity by staff members, pound for pound, up to a certain limit.

■ EC Charter

The EC Commission has recently published its Charter of Fundamental Social Rights. If adopted, this would introduce some entirely new concepts into the UK and European job markets.

The aim is to establish uniformity of employment conditions within the EC so that employers and employees can compete on equal terms and so that discrimination of any kind will become illegal. The new provisions would, for example, remove obstacles to the recognition of job qualifications between professional bodies in different EC countries.

More controversial from a UK perspective are proposals on flexible working and limits on hours, including part-time, seasonal and casual workers, with provisions for annual paid leave and weekly rest periods laid down in a contract of employment. In addition the Charter addresses the provision of amenities such as crèche facilities and nursery arrangements, to enable occupational and family obligations to be more easily reconciled. These issues have barely been touched on yet in UK industry.

Employee participation is also an issue which will cause a major impact, since the recommendations are that information, consultation and participation systems should take into account practices in other EC states—generally far in advance of our own.

Whereas UK legislation on industrial action is being tightened, the EC Charter restricts further limitations on the right to strike and makes provision for European-level bargaining.

All in all, the UK is presently against the adoption of the Charter, mainly because of the huge cost implications for employers of adopting the measures. However we have already been outvoted 11:1, so it seems probable that the Charter will, ultimately be adopted, even if a changeover period is permitted. From the employee's point of view, the measures should be beneficial as they would generally increase workers' rights and expand the channels through which they could be pursued.

▎The demographic timebomb

This rather emotive name has been coined by the press for the situation which is about to hit employers throughout the UK in the next few years. As the birthrate fell sharply during the 1970s, the number of school leavers coming into the jobs market in the 1990s will be much lower than in previous years. There will be a million fewer 16–19-year-olds in 1993 than there were in 1983.

There will simply not be enough new young people to go around. Articles quote examples such as that nursing could take every single suitable young girl leaving school in a couple of years, or that Norwich Union is planning to try to attract all the school leavers in East Anglia. Obviously something must be done to overcome this problem, and many firms are taking a second look at the people who leave their employ every year.

Many of these are women who leave to have a family, and who have traditionally found it hard to rejoin the world of work, having been out of the ratrace for a few years. Now, however, it is fashionable for employers to make special arrangements to attract 'returners', to offer career breaks with a guaranteed job at the end of it, and to offer facilities such as workplace nurseries to make it easier for mothers to come back to work. In doing so, the company is able to make better use of the talent already at its disposal and economise on training, since many of these women will only need a refresher course to bring them 'up to speed'.

A scheme just started by Midland Bank (Campus) offers employees who did not have the benefit of further education before they started work the opportunity to spend a year at a UK university to study management subjects, combined with project work in the bank. This is particularly aimed at helping women and members of ethnic minority groups to fulfil their potential.

Flexible hours

Companies also need to take a flexible approach to working hours, looking at part-time working and job sharing, for example. Boots the Chemists are developing a nationwide scheme for termtime contracts, with mothers working during termtime and students filling the jobs during vacations.

Other companies are offering career breaks, not just to female high-flyers, but on a wider basis. Royal Bank of Scotland, for example, has introduced a scheme enabling employees (male or female) to leave for up to five years to look after a child of any age—whether their own, adopted or fostered—or a sick spouse or elderly relative. When they return they can choose whether to work part- or full-time.

Find out what schemes your own bank is running to offer career breaks.

Older workers

It is not just young mothers whom employers need to attract to fill the vacancies left by reduced numbers of school leavers; this situation has thrown into sharp focus the stupidity of many firms in refusing to employ people past a certain age (in some cases as low as 50, or even 40).

It is now being realised that older workers are among the most reliable and hard-working of employees. Tesco supermarkets are advertising for check-out cashiers in their 50s, for example, and have found that they are less prone to absenteeism and are better able to cope with awkward customers than are teenagers.

The preconception that intellectual ability or physical capabilities must decline with age is not supported by the evidence. Perhaps it is more true to say that differences widen as people get older—the good get better and the bad get worse. The best older managers are often better than their younger counterparts: witness the success of the Hanson Group and the turnaround of British Airways (run respectively by Lord Hanson and Lord King, both well over 50), not to mention Sir Ian MacGregor, who was already in his 70s when he took over the running of the National Coal Board, after sorting out British Steel.

Whilst the long-term unemployed older workers may be grateful for the chance of any job, employers must not assume that this will apply to all older workers. In households where the mortgage has been paid off, the children have left home, and many older people have inherited houses from their parents, the real level of household incomes is comparatively high. Such potential employees can afford to be choosy when picking what work they are prepared to do, and on what terms—such as good health cover, a more relaxed working environment, and strong social aspects of work.

Disability or ability?

Similarly, people with disabilities are often amongst the most highly motivated employees—perhaps because they have to fight so hard to be given the chance of a job in the first place, by a society which tends to assume that anyone with a handicap is stupid.

Technical aids, such as specially adapted computers for the deaf or blind, are opening up job prospects, but old prejudices remain. Nearly 80 per cent of all disabled people of working age are unemployed, compared with 6 per cent of the general population. Many firms ignore the quota system, which requires them to employ 3 per cent of registered disabled workers in a workforce of 20 or more. However, one manufacturer in Rotherham employs 17 disabled people out of a workforce of 65 and finds that they work better than the able-bodied because they are eager to prove that they can do the job.

▌ Women at the top — a sex war?

Despite the initiatives mentioned above, there is still a very small percentage of women in the most senior posts in companies. By the year 2000, it is predicted that 44 per cent of Britain's workforce will be female, yet in 1988 only 20 per cent of all managers in Britain were women (although this was better than the 11 per cent in 1975). A recent survey of women on the boards of top UK industrial companies found that among the largest 200 companies, only 11 per cent had women on their boards; of the 24 women concerned, only six held executive board status (in other words, to be blunt, the remainder were probably there because the company felt the need for a 'token woman' on the board). There are many possible reasons why this situation exists—traditionally male-dominated companies, women's own reluctance to push themselves forward, the difficulty of maintaining a successful career path as well as raising a family, etc.—but the result is that many companies are failing to make full use of their pool of experienced staff.

Research has consistently shown that whilst men and women make equally **good** managers, they do so in **different ways**. Work, success and ambition mean different things to the two sexes. When asked what made them happiest at work, the majority of men cited simply achievement; women tended combine this with the idea of making other people happy too.

No generalisations can hold good for all individuals, but it does seem that men, in general, tend to be competitive, single-minded, risk-taking, aggressive, preoccupied with dominance, hierarchy and the politics of power. The average women is rather less concerned with these things, but has wider conceptual horizons where the nature of the occupation is much more important than formal achievement and financial success. In decision-making, a woman's strength is her ability to perceive the human dimension of a problem and to be more sensitive to the personal and moral aspects. Those successful women who, rather than try to play men at their own game, have chosen to set up their own businesses have often done so on rather different lines. They make relationships rather than play games (men tend to see work largely as a game, and a very serious one at that, like all masculine games). Women run their businesses more on a basis of trust than of fear, of cooperation rather than rivalry, making best use of their own natural skills.

Gradually, some companies are coming to realise that the feminine virtues can be good for business; that it is not necessary for a woman to act as an honorary man to be a successful manager; and that, perhaps, the male manager who neglects his wife and his health for the sake of the company is not necessarily doing the job the best or the only way.

If you would like to read more about the differences between men and women in the way they tackle work, read *BrainSex* by Anne Moir and David Jessel, published by Michael Joseph Ltd.

▌ Conclusion

As I said at the start, this chapter can only give you a few pointers as to the type of subjects currently forming live issues in the management field. When you read the papers and discover new issues, think of two things—what is the issue about, and what will its implications be for managers? Those two sides of each story should enable you to tackle any question set on topical issues in the examination.

Index

Action-centred leadership, 129
Adhocracy, 41, Fig. 4.7
Advertisements (for staff), 191
Adair, John, 129
Application forms, 191
Appraisal, 151
Appraisal interviews, 83, 163
Appraisal systems, 83
Ashridge model, 128

Bank manager, new image, 27
Bank manager, traditional stereotype, 26
Barriers to communications, 172
Barriers to delegation, 134
Belbin, 176
'Big Bang', 15
Blake Mouton grid, 126
Bosses, relations with, 133
Budgetary control, problems of, 70
Budgets, 66
Budgetary control systems, 66
Bureaucracies, 45

Career development, 193, 196
Career management, self, 211
Case studies, 225
Change, 178
Classical School, 94
Coaching, 151
Communication, 9, 172
Communication in Europe, 229
Communication in organisations, 47
Communication rules, 173
Committees, 181
Competition, 10, 15
Computerised information, 60
Computers, development of, 64

Computers, use in banks, 61
Contingency theory, 99, 130
Centralisation vs. decentralisation, 50
Controlling, 118
Co-operation between departments, 52
Counselling, 152
Counselling interviews, 165
Credit scoring, 72
Culture in organisations, 41
Curriculum vitae (c.v.), 192
Customer interviews, 162
Customers, relations with, 132
Cybernetics, 98

Decision-making, 205
Decision-making, computers as aids, 65
Decision-making, faults, 206
Decision-making, referring down, 206
Decision-making, referring up, 207
Decisions, programmed, 205
Decisions, unprogrammed, 206
Delegation, 134
Demographic change, 8
Demographic time bomb, 231
Descriptive questions, 224
Development, 151
Disabled employees, 197, 232
Discrimination, direct, 196
Discrimination, indirect, 197
Disciplinary interviews, 164
Disciplinary procedures, 86
Divisionalised structure, 39, Fig. 4.5
Drucker, Peter, 126

Economic factors, 6
Education (as environmental factor), 8
EC Charter, 230
Employee relations, 29
Equal opportunities, 196
Europe 1992, 229
Examination itself, 217
Exit interviews, 165
Expectancy theory, 146
Expert systems, 66

Fayol, Henri, 96, 111
Feedback, 151
Fifth Generation Computer Languages, 66
Financial Services Act (1986), 17
Flexible hours, 231
Forecasting, 114
Formal and informal groups, 175

Genuine occupational qualification, 197
Grievance interviews, 164
Grievance procedures, 85
Grievances, external agencies, 85
Group dynamics, 174
Group roles, 176
Groups, 172

Handy, Charles, 44
Hawthorne experiments, 97
Helicopter view, 209
Hertzberg, Fred, 80, 145
Hierarchy of needs, 144
How to fail/pass, 225
Human Relations School, 96
Human resource management, 26
Hygiene factors, 145

Increasing power, 199
Increments, 83
Individuals, differences between, 142
Induction, 149
Industrial relations, 29
Inflation, 7
Information, computerised, 60
Information, importance of, 59
Information Technology, 63
Intelligence, 142
Internal customer, 52
Inter-personal relationships, 131
Interviewing, 158
Interviews, selection, 193
IT, 63

Job analysis, 78, 191
Job description, 79, 191
Job enlargement, 80

Job enrichment, 80
Job evaluation, 81
Job rotation, 80

Leadership style, 125
Learning, 150
Legal factors, 6
Listening, 161
Local community, 11, 230
Luthans, Fred, 44

Management by exception, 118
Management functions, 100
Machine bureaucracy, 38, Fig. 4.4
Management information systems, 59, 65
Management information, in banks, 60
Management job, characteristics, 111
Management processes, 100
Management roles, 101
Management styles, 125
Management theories, 94
Managers, female, 233
Managers, male, 233
Managing change, 178
Manpower planning, 27
Marking the paper, 218
Maslow, A H, 144
Mayo, Elton, 96
McGregor, Douglas, 143
Meetings, 181
Mintzberg, Henry, 101, 116
Mintzberg's *Structure in 5's*, 35
MI, 59
MIS, 59, 65
Misconduct, 86
Monitoring, 117
Motivation, 143

Need to know/nice to know, 48, 59
Non-quantitative job evaluation systems, 82
Note-taking, 161

Older workers, 232
Off-the-job training, 195
On-the-job training, 195

Open questions, 160
Organisational culture, 41
Organisational design and development, 35
Organisational structure, 35
Organisation and Method (O&M), 95
Organising, 116

Paperless office, 63
Peers, relations with, 133
People-based organisations, 47
Personality, 143
Personnel specification, 147, 191
Personnel systems, 78
PEST factors, 4
Physique, 142
Planning, 114
Political factors, 5
Positive action, 198
Power, in organisations, 44
Power, personal, 198
Problem-solving, 205
Professional bureaucracy, 39, Fig. 4.6
Profit-sharing, 84
Programmed decisions, 205
Project-based organisations, 46
Project planning, 207
Project management, 207

Qualitative job evaluation systems, 82
Questioning, 160

Race Relations Act 1976, 196
Recruitment, 190
Recruitment policies, 26
Resistance to change, 179
Revision, 227
Reward policy, 84
Risk management, 70
Risks, in banking, 71

Salary increments, 84
School leavers, shortage of, 27, 28
Scientific management, 95
Selection, 147, 190
Selection interviews, 162

Seven-point plan, 147
Sex Discrimination Act 1975, 196
Sex war?, 233
Short-listing, 192
Significant variances, 117
Social accountability, 11
Social factors, 7
Social values, 8
Stakeholders, 18
Strengths and weaknesses, 16
Stress management, 210
Subordinates, relations with, 133
Successful groups, 177
Systems approach, 98
Systems analysis, 98

Tackling the exam, 218
Targets, 115
Taylor, F W, 95
Team formation, 176
Technological factors, 9
Technology, importance of, 60
Tests (selection), 192
Theory X/Theory Y, 143
Time management, 208
Time and motion study, 95
Timewasters, 209
Topical issues, 229
Trade Unions in banks, 30
Traditional stereotype, 26
Training, 193
Training, impact of environmental changes, 28
Training, impact of technology, 29
Training gap, 194
Training, needs, 150
Training plan, 194
Trait theory, 130
Transition from worker to manager, 104
Transactional analysis, 132

Unprogrammed decisions, 206

Variances, in budgets, 68
Volvo experiment, 81, 178

Weiner, Herbert, 98
What-if analysis, 114
Woodward, Prof. Joan, 99
Work, design of, 78
Work measurement, 78, 95
Work study, 78
Worker to manager, transition, 104

Zero-based budgeting, 69